SURVIVE IN GERMAN

L.G. Alexander Ingeborg Bauer Antony Peck

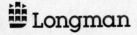
Longman

LONGMAN GROUP LIMITED
London

Associated companies, branches and representatives throughout the world

© Longman Group Ltd 1980

First published 1980

ISBN 0 582 74712 0
LG 74714 7

Printed in Great Britain at The Pitman Press, Bath

Drawings by Ed McLachlan

Contents

Survive in German

A few sounds

PART A: *Study Section*

Survive in German

Who is 'Survive in German' for?
Anyone going to a German-speaking country.
Anyone whose work brings them in touch with German speakers.

Why 'Survive'?
To survive in a foreign country, you have to be able to cope with everyday situations – finding your way around, asking for information, understanding when you take part in a simple conversation. 'Survive in German' is designed to enable you to do just that.

What is in 'Survive in German'?
1 The most commonly used German expressions and sentences – printed in the book and recorded on the cassette.
2 A 'Mini Dictionary' of about 5000 words to suit your needs, whether you are travelling for business or pleasure.
3 A pronunciation key specially designed for English speakers beginning to learn German.
4 Useful information which you may need when travelling in Germany.

What does this book consist of?
PART A: *Study Section*
This contains sets of key sentence 'patterns' which *you* can adapt to the situation you find yourself in, by inserting in the gaps the words you need from the Mini Dictionary.

There are eleven small sections of key sentences.

Sections 1–9 cover *general* areas of language useful in more than one situation eg getting about, expressing wishes, giving information about yourself, talking about time etc as well as useful basic expressions.

Section 10 contains simple conversations showing you how to use the key sentences from Sections 1–9 in a variety of *particular* situations.

Section 11 deals with telephoning and emergencies.

The Mini Dictionary is the main feature of this section. It is an alphabetical list of words which will fit into the key sentences in Part A. Each word is followed by the German translation and the pronunciation.

The reference section also includes information sections about:

1 Eating out – list of typical items you will find in German menus.

2 Signs you may see – on the roads, in shops and public places.

3 Countries – their currencies, nationalities and languages.

4 Motoring – parts of the car and useful expressions.

5 Equivalents – weights, measures and sizes.

6 Writing letters – three model letters you may need to write.

There is also a 'Mini Grammar' – a summary of basic points about German which you may want to refer to. This, in addition to the footnotes accompanying the key sentences, gives an idea of how German 'works' in comparison with English.

What does the cassette consist of?
All the key sentences and simple conversations in the book (Part A: Study Section) are recorded on the C90 cassette. This gives you the chance to get used to both speaking and listening to real German. You can use the cassette with the book or just by itself – at home or in your car cassette recorder, before you travel or while you're travelling.

Key sentences: you will hear first the English expression, then its German equivalent, followed by a pause for you to repeat.

Simple conversations: just listen to these a few times to help you to understand what you hear.

How do you find what you want to say?
Suppose that you want a ticket, some coffee, a toothbrush or a room.

1 Turn to 'Wants and needs' (Part A: Study Section 7).

2 You want to say 'I'd like /...../ please'.

3 Find this key sentence pattern and its German equivalent – '*Ich möchte* /...../, *bitte*'.

4 Look up the word you want in the Mini Dictionary eg ticket.

5 You are now ready to say:
  Ich möchte /eine Karte/, bitte (I'd like a ticket please).

How do you make yourself understood?

'Survive in German' uses a simple but effective pronunciation system to help you say correctly all the words you need. The pronunciation system has special symbols for a few sounds in German which don't exist in English – you'll find it well worth your while to learn them.

The cassette gives you further help in pronouncing the kind of German that will be understood. Copy the key sentences as accurately as you can.

How to get the most out of 'Survive in German'

Before you begin to use 'Survive in German':
  – look at the contents list to see how the sections are organised.
  – leaf through the whole book to see what is in each section.
  – play through some of the cassette to get the feel of the language.

Any time you spend familiarising yourself with the kit and mastering some of the key sentences, will be time well spent.

If you're prepared to spend up to five hours try to master some or all of the introductory section 'Very Basic Survival'. This section, with the help of the cassette and the Mini Dictionary, will take you a long way.

If you're prepared to spend up to twenty hours try to master Part A completely with the aid of the cassette, before setting out on your travels.

This will give you a very good start and will help you survive in a wide variety of situations and begin to communicate with the Germans. Furthermore 'Survive in German' provides a sound and accurate basis for further study. The more you put into 'Survive in German' the more you'll get out of it.

A FEW HINTS

1 Masculine, feminine or neuter?

In German, names of things are either masculine, feminine or neuter. In the Mini Dictionary names of things are given with the article, '*der*' (masculine), '*die*' (feminine) or '*das*' (neuter). Here is a table to help you:

Masculine		Feminine		Neuter	
der Brief	the letter	die Karte	the ticket	das Bier	the beer
ein Brief	a letter	eine Karte	a ticket	ein Bier	a beer

In German, the ending of some words may change according to whether they are, for example, the subject or the object of a sentence. Eg '*ein Koffer*' (a suitcase, masculine) becomes '*einen Koffer*' when it is the object of a sentence:

Haben Sie einen Koffer? (Have you got a suitcase?)

This only affects masculine words. Feminine and neuter words do not change:

Haben Sie eine Karte? (Have you got a ticket?)
Ich sehe das Haus (I see the house)

Masculine		Feminine		Neuter	
Subject	Object	Subject	Object	Subject	Object
der Zug	**den** Zug	die Karte	**die** Karte	das Haus	**das** Haus
ein Zug	**einen** Zug	eine Karte	**eine** Karte	ein Haus	**ein** Haus

Confusing the gender of words and their endings will not stop you from surviving in German!

When describing something, you can avoid the masculine/feminine/neuter dilemma by using: '*Das ist*' (That is) + adjective to describe things of any gender:

Das ist gut (That's fine)
Das ist zu teuer (That's too expensive)

However, if you want to use pronouns (he, she, it etc) these should be of the same gender as the noun. So, for example, you would use '*er*' when referring to '*der Brief*' (the letter), '*sie*' for '*die Karte*' (the ticket), and '*es*' for '*das Bier*' (the beer). This may seem rather odd at first but it's simply a matter of getting used to it.

2 You: 'Sie' or 'du'?

In German, there are two ways of saying 'you' (*Sie* or *du*) when talking to one person:

'*Sie*': the form you will use and hear most. To be on the safe side, always start by using '*Sie*' unless the person to whom you are talking has already used the '*du*' form.

'_Du_' is usually reserved for people you know well. The younger generation use it a lot. The '_du_' form of a few common expressions you may hear or want to use is given in the Study Section and are followed by (informal).Otherwise, the '_Sie_' form has been used throughout.

When talking to more than one person, '_Sie_' is most used. However, you may also hear '_ihr_', which is the plural form of '_du_'. This, like '_du_', is only used for people you know well. For more information, see the Mini Grammar.

3 Points to remember

Watch out for word order. Although in general the verb comes second:
Eg *Ich spreche ein bißchen Deutsch* (I speak a little German)
you may hear more complicated sentences where you have to wait right until the end of the sentence for the verb!
Eg *Gut, daß Sie Deutsch sprechen* (I'm glad you speak German)
Note that all nouns in German are written with a capital letter eg '_der Zug_' (the train). The symbol 'ß' is frequently used in German. It represents double 's' and is pronounced like 'ss'.

One last word

You don't learn a language by learning lists of words and grammatical rules off by heart. Just as you learn to drive by driving not from a car manual, you learn a language by hearing it, speaking it and, above all, by enjoying it.

A few sounds

You will hear on the cassette a few sounds which are particularly difficult for English speakers. Listen and repeat:

[ey]	spät (late), Käse (cheese)
[kh] – as in Scottish 'loch'	acht (eight), noch (still)
[h]	ich (I), hungrig (hungry)
[œ]	wöchentlich (weekly)
[œ]	schön (beautiful)
[ü]	fünf (five), hübsch (pretty)
[üh]	Tür (door), für (for)

You will find a complete pronunciation key before the Mini Dictionary.

PART A
STUDY SECTION

NB

/　　/　　means that the word or expression can be replaced by other words or expressions from Part B: The Reference Section or by other numbers from Part A: Section 1.26.

▭　　means that the text is recorded on the cassette. * indicates that these words or expressions are recorded within 'Very basic survival' and not repeated on the cassette in later sections.

Stress within a sentence or an individual word is indicated in **bold** type.

1 Very basic survival

1.1 General expressions

Please	**Bi**tte
Thank you	**Dan**ke
Yes	Ja
No	Nein
Yes please	Ja, **bi**tte
No thank you	Nein, **dan**ke (or often simply '**Dan**ke')
Sorry?	Wie **bi**tte?
Sorry!	Ent**schul**digung!
Excuse me!	Ent**schul**digung!
I'm sorry	Es tut mir **leid**
That's all right	Das macht nichts
You're welcome	**Bi**tte schön
OK	OK
All right	In **Ord**nung!
Good!	Gut!
Good idea!	**Gu**te **I**dee!
Great!	Toll!
Fine!	Sehr gut!
Of course!	Na**tür**lich!
Look out!	Paß **auf**!
Nothing	Nichts
Everything	Alles
I don't know	Ich **weiß** nicht

What's this?	Was ist **das**?
What's the matter?	Was ist **los**?
I've lost /my passport/	Ich habe /meinen **Paß**/ ver**loren**
Now	Jetzt
Soon	Bald
Later	**Spä**ter
And	Und
But	**Aber**
Or	**O**der

1.2 I've got/I haven't got

I've got /a suitcase/	Ich habe /einen **Kof**fer/
I've got /a reservation/	Ich habe /eine Reser**vier**ung/
I've got /a car/	Ich habe /ein **Au**to/
I've got some /tickets/	Ich habe /**Kar**ten/
I haven't got /a suitcase/	Ich habe /keinen **Kof**fer/
I haven't got /a reservation/	Ich habe /keine Reser**vier**ung/
I haven't got /a car/	Ich habe /kein **Au**to/
I haven't got /any change/	Ich habe /kein **Klein**geld/
I haven't got any /warm clothes/	Ich habe keine /warmen **Kleid**er/
I haven't got enough /money/	Ich habe nicht ge**nug** /**Geld**/

1.3 Have you got?

Have you got /the key/?	Haben Sie /den **Schlüs**sel/?
Have you got /the ticket/?	Haben Sie /die **Kar**te/?
Have you got /the form/?	Haben Sie /das Formu**lar**/?
Have you got /a key/?	Haben Sie /einen **Schlüs**sel/?
Have you got /a ticket/?	Haben Sie /eine **Kar**te/?
Have you got /a form/?	Haben Sie /ein Formu**lar**/?

Have you got any /luggage/?	Haben Sie /Gepäck/?
Have you got the /keys/?	Haben Sie die /Schlüssel/?
Have you got the /tickets/?	Haben Sie die /Karten/?
Have you got the /forms/?	Haben Sie die /Formulare/?
Have you got any /tickets/?	Haben Sie /Karten/?

1.4 I'd like

I'd like /a ticket/ please	Ich möchte /eine Karte/, bitte
I'd like /a room/ please	Ich möchte /ein Zimmer/, bitte
I'd like /an envelope/ please	Ich möchte /einen Umschlag/, bitte
I'd like some /coffee/ please	Ich möchte /Kaffee/, bitte
I'd like some /tickets/ please	Ich möchte /Karten/, bitte
I'd like something to /drink/ please	Ich möchte etwas zu /trinken/, bitte
I'd like this please	Ich möchte dies, bitte
I'd like that please	Ich möchte das, bitte
I'd like these please	Ich möchte diese, bitte
I'd like those please	Ich möchte diese da, bitte

1.5 Is there?/Are there?

Is there /a letterbox/ near here?	Gibt es hier /einen Briefkasten/?
Is there /a bank/ near here?	Gibt es hier /eine Bank/?
Is there /a hotel/ near here?	Gibt es hier /ein Hotel/?
Is there any /beer/?	Gibt es noch /Bier/?
Are there any /seats/?	Gibt es noch /Plätze/?

3

1.6 There is/There are

There's /a letterbox/ near here	Es gibt hier /einen **Brief**kasten/
There's /a bank/ near here	Es gibt hier /eine **Bank**/
There's /a hotel/ near here	Es gibt hier /ein **Hotel**/
There's some /beer/	Es gibt /**Bier**/
There are some /seats/	Es gibt noch /**Plätze**/

1.7 There isn't/There aren't

There isn't /a letterbox/ near here	Es gibt hier /keinen **Brief**kasten/
There isn't /a bank/ near here	Es gibt hier /keine **Bank**/
There isn't /any beer/	Es gibt /kein **Bier**/
There aren't any /hotels/ near here	Es gibt hier keine /**Hotels**/
There aren't any /seats/	Es gibt keine /**Plätze**/

1.8 Greetings

Hello	Guten **Tag**!
Hi!	Tag!
Goodbye	Auf **Wie**dersehen!
Bye!	Tschüs!
Good morning	Guten **Mor**gen!
Good afternoon	Guten **Tag**!
Good evening	Guten **Abend**!
Good night	Gute **Nacht**!

1.9 Social

Would you like a drink?	Möchten Sie etwas **trin**ken?
Would you like a drink? (informal)	Möchtest du etwas **trin**ken?
Cheers!	Zum **Wohl**!

4

How do you do	Guten **Tag**!
How are you?	Wie **geht** es Ihnen?
How are you? (informal)	Wie **geht** es dir?
Very well thank you	**Dan**ke, gut
And you?	Und **Ih**nen?
And you? (informal)	Und **dir**?
Fine thanks	**Dan**ke, gut
Nice to meet you	Nett, Sie **ke**nnenzulernen
Nice to meet you (informal)	Nett, dich **ke**nnenzulernen

1.10 Indicating

Look!	**Schau**en Sie!
This ... Not this	**Die**ses ... Nicht **die**ses
That ... Not that	Das ... Nicht das
These ... Not these	Die ... Nicht die
Those ... Not those	Die da ... Nicht die da

For me	Für **mich**
For you	Für **Sie**
For you (informal)	Für **dich**
For him	Für **ihn**
For her	Für **sie**
For us	Für **uns**
For you (plural, informal)	Für **euch**
For them	Für **sie**
Not for me	**Nicht** für mich
(Just add 'nicht' for 'not')	

1.11 Directions – going places

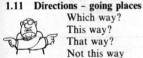

Which way?	Welche **Rich**tung?
This way?	**Hier** entlang?
That way?	**Dort** entlang?
Not this way	Nicht **hier** entlang
Not that way	Nicht **dort** entlang
Left	Links
Right	Rechts
Straight on	Gerade**aus**
Here	Hier
There	Dort
The station please	Zum **Bahn**hof, bitte

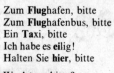

The airport please	Zum **Flug**hafen, bitte
The airport bus please	Zum **Flug**hafenbus, bitte
A taxi please	Ein **Ta**xi, bitte
I'm in a hurry	Ich habe es **ei**lig!
Stop here please	Halten Sie **hier**, bitte

Where is it please?	Wo **ist** es, bitte?
Is there /a bank/ near here?	Gibt es hier /eine **Bank**/, bitte?
Is there /a hotel/ near here?	Gibt es hier /ein **Hotel**/, bitte?
Where can I get /a bus to the airport/ please?	Wo hält /ein **Bus** zum **Flug**hafen/, bitte?
Where can I buy some /postcards/ please?	Wo kann ich /**Post**karten/ kaufen, bitte?
/Which platform/ please?	/Welcher **Bahn**steig/, bitte?

| A first class single to /Munich/ please | /**München**/ **ein**fach **er**ster Klasse, bitte |
| A second class return to /Hamburg/ please | /**Hamburg**/ **hin** und **zurück zwei**ter Klasse, bitte |

1.12 Suggestions

Let's go	**Gehen** wir!
Let's go and /have a drink/	**Gehen** wir /etwas **trinken**/
Let's meet /at 9/	**Treffen** wir uns /um **neun** Uhr/

Now take a part

You meet a friend in a bar one evening.

Guten Abend!
Guten Abend, Paul!
Wie geht es dir?
Danke gut, und dir?
Danke gut.

You want to know which platform your train leaves from.

Nach Bonn, welcher Bahnsteig, bitte?
Bahnsteig eins.
Wo ist es, bitte?
Geradeaus.
Danke.

1.13 When?

Today	**Heu**te
This morning	Heute **mor**gen
This afternoon	Heute **nach**mittag
This evening	Heute **a**bend
Tonight	Heute **a**bend
Tomorrow	**Mor**gen
Yesterday	**Ge**stern
Not today	**Heu**te nicht
(Just add 'nicht' for 'not')	

When does /the train/ leave?	Wann fährt /der **Zug**/ ab?
When does /the bus/ arrive?	Wann kommt /der **Bus**/ an?
When do the /shops/ open?	Wann machen die /**Geschäf**te/ auf?
When do the /banks/ close?	Wann machen die /**Bank**en/ zu?
When does it begin?	Wann be**ginnt** es?
When does it end?	Wann **end**et es?

1.14 Questions

What?	Was?
When?	Wann?
Where?	Wo?
Who?	Wer?
Which?	**Wel**ches?

How?	Wie?
How much? /A kilo/ please?	**Wieviel**? /Ein **Kilo**/, bitte
How many? /Three/ please	**Wieviele**? /**Drei**/, bitte
Why?	**Warum**?
Because	Weil
Why not?	Warum **nicht**?
Anything else?	**Noch** etwas?

1.15 Shopping

Can I help you?	Bitte schön?
I'm just looking	Ich **schaue** mich nur um
I'd like to /try this on/	Ich möchte /das **an**probieren/
It's in the window	Es ist im **Schau**fenster
I'll take it	Ich **nehm**e das
I'll leave it	Ich **nehm**e das nicht

1.16 Money

How much is it please?	**Wieviel ko**stet **das**, bitte?
How much are they please?	**Wieviel ko**sten **sie**, bitte?
What's the exchange rate for /the pound/ please?	Was ist der **Kurs** für /das **Pfund**/, bitte?
Do you take /traveller's cheques/?	Nehmen Sie / **Rei**seschecks/?
In /tens/ please	In /**Zehnmark**scheinen/, bitte

The bill please	**Zah**len, bitte!
Is service included?	Ist das mit **Bedi**enung?
Is VAT included?	Ist das mit **Mehr**wertsteuer?

1.17 The restaurant

| For /4/ please | Für /**vier**/ Personen, bitte |
| What would you like to drink? | Was möchten Sie **trink**en? |

8

The menu please	Die **Spei**sekarte, bitte
What do you recommend?	Was emp**feh**len Sie?
With /chips/	Mit /Pommes **frites**/
Without /cream/	**Ohne** /**Sahne**/
What is it (exactly) please?	Was ist das (ge**nau**), bitte?

1.18 Quantity

Another (masculine and neuter)	Noch ein
Another (feminine)	Noch eine
A little	Ein **we**nig
More	Mehr
Less	**We**niger
Some more /coffee/ please	Etwas mehr /**Kaf**fee/, bitte
Enough thank you	Es **reicht**, danke

1.19 Accommodation

Have you got /a double room/ please?	Haben Sie /ein **Dop**pelzimmer/, bitte?
With /bath/	Mit /**Bad**/
Without /bath/	**Ohne** /**Bad**/
For /2/ nights please	Für /**zwei**/ Nächte, bitte
Is /breakfast/ included?	Mit /**Früh**stück/?
Please call me at 7 o'clock	Bitte **ru**fen Sie mich um **sie**ben Uhr

---

Now take a part

In a restaurant – you want to order a steak and chips and some beer.

Guten Abend!
Guten Abend! Ich möchte ein Steak, bitte.
Ein Steak. Ja. Mit Pommes Frites?
Ja, bitte.
Mit Pommes Frites. Noch etwas?

Ja. Ein Bier, bitte.
Ein Bier. Sehr gut. Danke.

At a hotel – you want a room.

Guten Abend! Bitte schön?
Hm – ja. Haben Sie ein Doppelzimmer, bitte?
Hm – für wieviele Nächte?
Für zwei Nächte, bitte.
Mit oder ohne Bad?
Mit Bad.
Ja, sehr gut.
Wieviel kostet das, bitte?
Das kostet 80 Mark pro Nacht.
Ich nehme das, bitte.

1.20 Asking a favour

Could you /mind my bag/ please?	Könnten Sie /auf meine **Ta**sche aufpassen/, bitte?
Could you /keep my seat/ please?	Könnten Sie /auf meinen **Platz** aufpassen/, bitte?

1.21 Information

I'd like some information about /hotels/ please — Ich möchte eine **Aus**kunft über /**Ho**tels/, bitte

1.22 The petrol station

Fill it up please — **Voll**, bitte
/15/ litres please — /**Fünf**zehn/ Liter, bitte
/40/ marks' worth please — Für /**vier**zig/ Mark, bitte
(Equivalents see p299)

1.23 The Post Office

How much is /a letter/ to /England/ please? — Was kostet /ein **Brief**/ nach /**Eng**land/, bitte?
1 /70 pfennig/ stamp please — Eine **Brief**marke zu /**sieb**zig Pfennig/, bitte

2 /50 pfennig/ stamps please	**Zwei** Briefmarken zu /**fünf**zig Pfennig/, bitte
Airmail please	**Luft**post, bitte
Express please	**Eil**boten, bitte
(Money see p296)	

1.24 Language

Could you repeat that please	Bitte **noch** einmal
I don't understand	Ich ver**steh**e nicht
Slower please	**Lang**samer, bitte
I don't speak /German/	Ich spreche kein /**Deutsch**/
Do you speak /English/?	**Sprech**en Sie /**Eng**lisch/?
Would you write it please	**Schreib**en Sie das bitte auf

1.25 The telephone

(In German you simply say your name when you answer the phone.)

Goodbye	Auf **Wieder**hören
May I speak to /Mr Schmidt/ please?	Kann ich bitte /Herrn **Schmidt**/ sprechen?
I'll call back later	Ich rufe **noch** mal an
(See how to cope with the telephone p55)	

1.26 Numbers

0 null	14 **vier**zehn
1 eins	15 **fünf**zehn
2 zwei	16 **sech**zehn
3 drei	17 **sieb**zehn
4 vier	18 **acht**zehn
5 fünf	19 **neun**zehn
6 sechs	20 **zwan**zig
7 **sieb**en	21 **ein**und**zwan**zig
8 acht	32 **zwei**und**dreiß**ig
9 neun	43 **drei**und**vier**zig
10 zehn	54 **vier**und**fünf**zig
11 elf	65 **fünf**und**sech**zig
12 zwölf	76 **sechs**und**sieb**zig
13 **drei**zehn	87 **sieben**und**acht**zig

11

98 acht**und**neu**nzig**	877 acht**hundert**sieben-
100 **hund**ert	**und**siebzig
101 **hund**ert**eins**	988 **neun**hundertacht-
211 **zwei**hundert**elf**	und**acht**zig
322 **drei**hundertzwei-	1000 **tau**send
undzwanzig	1001 tausend**eins**
433 **vier**hundertdrei-	2112 **zwei**tausend**ein-**
und**drei**ßig	hundert**zwölf**
544 **fünf**hundertvier-	3223 **drei**tausend**zwei-**
und**vier**zig	hundertdrei -
655 **sechs**hundertfünf-	und**zwan**zig
und**fünf**zig	4334 **vier**tausend**drei-**
766 **sieben**hundertsechs-	hundertvier -
und**sech**zig	und**drei**ßig
	10,000 **zehn**tausend

0.1 = 0,1 null komma eins (literally 'nought comma one')

1.27 The days of the week

Monday	**Mon**tag
Tuesday	**Diens**tag
Wednesday	**Mitt**woch
Thursday	**Donners**tag
Friday	**Frei**tag
Saturday	**Sonn**abend (in North Germany) **Sams**tag (in South Germany)
Sunday	**Sonn**tag

1.28 The months of the year

January	**Jan**uar
February	**Feb**ruar
March	März
April	**Ap**ril
May	Mai
June	**Jun**i
July	**Jul**i
August	Au**gust**
September	Sep**tem**ber
October	Ok**tob**er
November	No**vem**ber
December	De**zem**ber

12

1.29 The alphabet

For pronunciation, listen to the cassette. See also 3.2.

A *a*	B *be*	C *ce*	D *de*	E *e*	F *ef*
G *ge*	H *ha*	I *i*	J *jot*	K *ka*	L *el*
M *em*	N *en*	O *o*	P *pe*	Q *ku*	R *er*
S *es*	T *te*	U *u*	V *vau*	W *we*	X *ix*
Y *ipsilon*		Z *zet*			

NB The symbol 'ß' is used frequently in German. It represents double 's' and is pronounced like 'ss'.

Now take a part

You want to buy some stamps.

Entschuldigung, wo kann ich Briefmarken kaufen, bitte?
Geradeaus, dann rechts.
Danke.

Guten Tag! Bitte schön!
Guten Tag! Ja. Was kostet ein Brief nach England, bitte?
Luftpost, bitte.
70 Pfennig.
Drei Briefmarken zu 70 Pfennig, bitte.
Noch etwas?
Nein, danke.
2,10 Mark.
Danke.
Bitte schön.

---

2 More expressions

*Thanks	**Dan**ke
Thank you very much	**Dan**ke schön
It's very kind of you	Das ist sehr **freund**lich
I'm very sorry	Es tut mir sehr **leid**
I'm sorry I'm late	Ent**schul**digen Sie die Ver**spä**tung
I'm sorry I don't know	Es tut mir **leid**. Ich **weiß** es nicht
I don't mind	Das ist mir e**gal**
That's right	Das **stimmt**
Excellent!	Sehr **gut**!
I don't like it	Das **mag** ich nicht
Perhaps	Viel**leicht**
It depends	Es **kommt** darauf an
If possible	Wenn **mög**lich
Give my regards to /Mrs Schmidt/	Viele **Grü**ße an /Frau **Schmidt**/
See you soon	Bis **bald**!
Have a good time!	Viel **Spaß**!
Have a good trip!	Gute **Rei**se!
Sleep well!	Schlafen Sie **gut**!
Sleep well! (informal)	Schlaf **gut**!
Is this seat free please?	Ist dieser Platz **frei**, bitte?

| Do you smoke? | Rauchen Sie? |
| What's this called please? | Wie **heißt** dies, bitte? |

Ready?	**Fer**tig?
Not yet	Noch **nicht**
Just a minute!	**Mo**ment!
Can I come in?	Darf ich **rein**kommen?
Come in!	Her**ein**!

How does it work?	Wie funktion**iert** das?
It doesn't work	Es funktion**iert** nicht
What's the weather like?	Wie ist das **Wet**ter?
It's /hot/	Es ist /**heiß**/

Now take a part

Saying goodbye to someone you have met.

Auf Wiedersehen!
Auf Wiedersehen!
Gute Reise und viele Grüße an Barbara.
Auf Wiedersehen! Bis bald.

---

3 Personal information

3.1 Name

What's your name please?	Wie ist Ihr **Name**, bitte?
My name's /John Harrison/	Mein **Name** ist /John Harrison/

3.2 Name (spelling)

How do you spell it?	Wie **schreibt** man das?
J-O-H-N H-A-R-R-I-S-O-N	John J-O-H-N Harrison H-A-R-R-I-S-O-N

(Alphabet see 1.29)

3.1   Use '*Ihr*' (your) when referring to masculine or neuter things eg '*der Name*' (the name), '*das Auto*' (the car).
Use '*Ihre*' (your) when referring to feminine things eg '*die Adresse*' (the address). See also 3.4/3.8.
In more informal situations you may hear:
　　Wie heißen Sie? (What's your name?)
or, amongst family, very good friends, students and with children:
　　Wie heißt du? (What's your name?)

3.2   Practise spelling your name.

3.3 Telephone number

What's your telephone number please?

(01) 235 1278

(Numbers see 1.26)

Wie ist Ihre Telefonnummer, bitte?

(Null eins), zwei, drei fünf, eins zwei, **sieben** acht

3.4 Home address

What's your address?

5, Wood Street, London N8 4PS

Wie ist Ihre **Adre**sse?

Wood Street, fünf, London N acht vier PS

3.5 Date of birth

What's your date of birth?

9th October 1958

(Dates, see 5.5)

Wann sind Sie ge**bor**en?

Am **neun**ten Oktober **neun**zehnhundert**acht**undfünfzig

3.6 Home town

Where do you live?

I live in /London/

Wo **woh**nen Sie?

Ich wohne in /**Lon**don/

3.7 Country of origin

Where do you come from?

I come from /England/

Wo**her** kommen Sie?

Ich komme aus /**Eng**land/

3.3   Practise giving your phone number. Note that German phone numbers are given in pairs.

Note that on the telephone '*zwei*' is often pronounced '*zwo*' to distinguish it from '*drei*'.

3.4   Practise giving your own address.

3.5   With years, say '*neunzehnhundert ...*' (nineteen hundred ...) and add the appropriate number up to 100 (see Numbers 1.26):

1984 *neunzehnhundertvierundachtzig*
1995 *neunzehnhundertfünfundneunzig*

3.6   The polite word for 'you' is '*Sie*'. When it is the subject of a verb, the verb stem ends in '*-en*'. For other ways of saying 'you' in German, see 'A few hints'.

3.8 Nationality

What nationality are you?	Was ist Ihre **Staats**angehörigkeit?
I'm /English/ (male)	Ich bin /**Eng**länder/
I'm /English/ (female)	Ich bin /**Eng**länderin/

3.9 Place of work

Where do you work?	Wo **ar**beiten Sie?
I work in /London/	Ich **ar**beite in /**Lon**don/
I work for /Brown and Webster/	Ich bin bei /**Brown** und **Web**ster/
I haven't got a job	Ich habe **kei**ne Stelle

3.10 Occupation

What do you do?	Was sind Sie von **Be**ruf?
I'm an /architect/	Ich bin /Archi**tekt**/
I'm a /student/ (male)	Ich bin /**Stu**dent/
I'm a /student/ (female)	Ich bin /**Stu**dentin/

3.8   Nouns of nationality have a special feminine form in German. This is usually made by adding '*-in*' to the masculine form:

        Engländer   *Engländerin*
          (Englishman)   (Englishwoman)
         Italiener (Italian)   *Italienerin* (Italian woman)

But the feminine form of '*Deutscher*' (German) is *Deutsche* (German woman). See p252 for a full list of nationalities.

3.10   Practise saying what you do. Note that in German you do not say 'a/an' with jobs or professions. More jobs and professions are given in the Mini Dictionary but if yours isn't listed, consult a bilingual dictionary.

Many names of jobs and professions have both a masculine and a feminine form. The feminine is usually made by adding *-in* to the masculine form:

    der Arzt (doctor)   *die Ärztin*
    der Lehrer (teacher)   *die Lehrerin*
    der Polizist (policeman) *die Polizistin*
    der Verkäufer (salesman) *die Verkäuferin*

3.11. Temporary occupation

What are you doing in /Cologne/?	Was **m**achen Sie in /**Köln**/?
I'm on holiday	Ich bin auf Urlaub
I'm working	Ich **ar**beite

3.12 Temporary address

Where are you staying?	Wo sind Sie **un**tergebracht?
I'm staying /at the Hotel Bristol/	Ich wohne /im Hotel **Bri**stol/
I'm staying with the /Schmidts/	Ich wohne bei /**Schmidts**/
I'm staying with some /friends/	Ich wohne bei /**Freun**den/

3.13 Health/Mood

*How are you?	Wie **geht** es Ihnen?
*How are you (informal)?	Wie **geht** es dir?
What's the matter?	Was ist **los**?
I'm fine	Es geht mir **gut**
I'm not /tired/	Ich bin **nicht** /müde/
I'm /tired/	Ich bin /**müde**/
I'm /hot/	Mir ist /**heiß**/
I'm not feeling very well	Ich **fühle** mich nicht wohl

3.11   The names of several towns are different in German and in English:

Cologne	*Köln*
Dusseldorf	*Düsseldorf*
Hanover	*Hannover*
Munich	*München*
Coblence	*Koblenz*
Nuremberg	*Nürnberg*

3.13   Remember, the '*du*' form should only be used with people you know very well, or with children. Wait for people to use it first!

You may also hear '*Wie geht's?*' (How are you?)

'Mir ist heiß' = literally 'to me it is warm'. Similarly:

I've got /a cough/	Ich habe /**Hu**sten/
I've got a stomach upset	Ich habe einen ver**dor**benen **Ma**gen
I've got a pain in /my shoulder/	/Meine **Schul**ter/ tut weh
I've got /a headache/	Ich habe /**Kopf**schmerzen/
/My leg/ hurts	/Mein **Bein**/ tut weh
I've got a temperature (Temperature see p299)	Ich habe **Fieber**

3.14 Introductions

This is Mr /Ludwig/	Das ist Herr /**Lud**wig/
This is Mrs /Ludwig/	Das ist Frau /**Lud**wig/
This is Miss /Ludwig/	Das ist **Fräu**lein /**Lud**wig/
This is /my mother/	Das ist /meine **Mu**tter/
*How do you do	Guten **Tag**!
This is /Richard/	Das ist /**Ri**chard/
*Hello	Guten **Tag**!

3.13
(cont.)
'*Mir ist warm*' (I'm warm) '*Mir ist kalt*' (I'm cold)
But '*Mich friert's*' (I'm freezing).
Note that in German one does not always use the indefinite article (a/an) when referring to illness:

 Ich habe Kopfschmerzen (I've got a headache)
 Ich habe Fieber (I've got a temperature)
 Ich habe Husten (I've got a cough)

But:

 Ich habe eine Erkältung (I've got a cold)

Note that 'my / / hurts', and 'I've got a pain in my / /', are both expressed in German by '*mein(e) / / tut weh*':

 Mein Arm tut weh (My arm hurts)
 Mein Bein tut weh (My leg hurts)
 Mein Fuß tut weh (I've got a pain in my foot)
 Meine Schulter tut weh (I've got a pain in my shoulder)

Now take a part

At the immigration desk – giving information about yourself.

Woher kommen Sie?
Ich komme aus England.
Wie ist Ihre Adresse?
Castle Street, 12, Hull HU6 4PJ.
Wie schreibt man das, bitte?
C-A-S-T-L-E S-T-R-E-E-T 12, H-U-L-L H-U-6 4-P-J.
Danke, und wo sind Sie in Bonn untergebracht?
Ich wohne im Sternhotel in der Königsstraße.
OK, danke.

4 Getting about

4.1 General directions (1)

*Which way?	Welche **Rich**tung?
Can you tell me the way /to the station/ please?	Wie komme ich /zum **Bahn**hof/, bitte?
Is this the way /to the centre/?	Geht es hier /zur **Stadt**mitte/?
Are you going /to the airport/?	Fahren Sie /zum **Flug**hafen/?
*Straight on	Gerade**aus**
*On the left	Links
*On the right	Rechts
First right	Die **er**ste Straße **rechts**
Second left	Die **zwei**te Straße **links**
Opposite	Gegenüber
*There	Dort
*Here	Hier
Upstairs	Nach **o**ben
Downstairs	Nach **un**ten

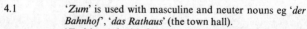

4.1   'Zum' is used with masculine and neuter nouns eg 'der Bahnhof', 'das Rathaus' (the town hall).
'Zur' is used with feminine nouns eg 'die Stadtmitte'.

4.2 General directions (2)

Where can I get /a taxi/?	Wo bekomme ich /ein **Taxi**/?
Where can I buy /a newspaper/?	Wo kann ich /eine **Zeitung**/ kaufen?
*Where can I buy some /postcards/?	Wo kann ich /**Post**karten/ kaufen?
Where can I get something to /eat/?	Wo bekomme ich etwas zu /**e**ssen/ ?

4.3 Exact location (1)

Is there /a letter box/ near here please?	Wo gibt es hier /einen **Brief**kasten/, bitte?
Is there /a bank/ near here please?	Wo gibt es hier /eine **Bank**/, bitte?
Is there /a hotel/ near here please?	Wo gibt es hier /ein **Hotel**/, bitte?

(It's) /opposite/ /the station/	(Er ist) /gegenüber/ /dem **Bahnhof**/
(It's) /opposite/ /the bank/	(Sie ist) /gegenüber/ /der **Bank**/
(It's) /next to/ /the park/	(Es ist) /neben/ /dem **Park**/

4.3   '*Einen*' (a) is used with masculine words eg '*der Briefkasten*'

'*Eine*' (a) is used with feminine words eg '*die Bank*'

'*Ein*' (a) is used with neuter words eg '*das Hotel*'

Prepositions such as '*gegenüber*' (opposite), and '*neben*' (next to), produce changes as follows:

		Summary
(*der Bahnhof*) *gegenüber dem Bahnhof*		
(*der Park*) *neben dem Park*		der → dem
(*die Bank*) *gegenüber der Bank*		die → der
(*das Hotel*) *neben dem Hotel*		das → dem

'It' is translated by '*er*' '*sie*' or '*es*' according to whether the noun is masculine, feminine or neuter.

4.4 Exact location (2)

*/Which platform/ please?	/Welcher **Bahn**steig/, bitte?
/Which station/ please?	/Welcher **Bahn**hof/, bitte?
/Which underground station/ please?	/Welche **Stati**on/, bitte?
/Which bus/ please?	/Welcher **Bus**/, bitte?
/Which bus stop/ please?	/Welche **Bus**haltestelle/, bitte?
/Which train/ please?	/Welcher **Zug**/, bitte?
/Which carriage/ please?	/Welcher **Wa**gen/, bitte?
/Which room/ please?	/Welches **Zim**mer/, bitte?
/Which office/ please?	/Welches **Bü**ro/, bitte?
/Which floor/ please?	/Welcher **Stock**/, bitte?
/Which number/ please?	/Welche **Nu**mmer/, bitte?

4.5 Distance

Is it far?	Ist es **weit**?
How far is it to /Cologne/?	Wie weit ist es nach /**Köln**/?
(About) /50/ kilometres	(Etwa) /**fünf**zig/ Kilometer

(Distances see p297)

4.6 Getting there

How do you get there?	Wie **kommt** man dort**hin**?
By /bus/	Mit /dem **Bus**/
Is there /a train/ to /Munich/ today?	Fährt heute /ein **Zug**/ nach /**Mün**chen/?
Is this /the bus to the airport/?	Ist das /der **Flug**hafenbus/?

4.4   '*Welcher*' is used with masculine words eg *der Bahnsteig*.
'*Welche*' is used with feminine words eg *die Bushaltestelle*.
'*Welches*' is used with neuter words eg *das Zimmer*.

4.6   '*Mit*' ('with', or 'by' for modes of transport) is followed by
'*dem*' with masculine and neuter nouns, and '*der*' with
feminine nouns:

(*der* Bus)	*mit dem Bus* (by bus)
(*der* Zug)	*mit dem Zug* (by train)
(*das* Taxi)	*mit dem Taxi* (by taxi)
(*die* Straßenbahn)	*mit der Straßenbahn* (by tram)

24

Now take a part

You want to find a taxi to take you to the airport.

Entschuldigung.
Ja, bitte schön?
Wo bekomme ich ein Taxi, bitte?
Am Bahnhof. Die erste Straße rechts und die zweite Straße links.
Danke. Das ist sehr freundlich.

Ja?
Zum Flughafen, bitte.
OK, zum Flughafen.
Ist es weit?
Es ist nicht weit. Etwa 3 Kilometer.

5 Time

5.1 General expressions

*Today	**Heu**te
*This morning	Heute **mor**gen
*This afternoon	Heute **nach**mittag
*This evening	Heute **a**bend
*Tonight	Heute **a**bend
*Yesterday	**Ge**stern
Yesterday morning	Gestern **mor**gen
Yesterday afternoon	Gestern **nach**mittag
Yesterday evening	Gestern **a**bend
Last night	Gestern **a**bend
*Tomorrow	**Mor**gen
Tomorrow morning	Morgen **früh**
Tomorrow afternoon	Morgen **nach**mittag
Tomorrow evening	Morgen **a**bend
Tomorrow night	Morgen **a**bend

5.1   '*Abend*' refers to the evening until you go to bed. In German there is no distinction between 'this evening' and 'tonight'.

When '*in*' (in) and '*vor*' (ago) are used with plural words, the letter '*n*' is added to the noun (except when the noun already ends in '-*n*').

     vier Monate (4 months) <u>*in* vier Monate<u>n</u></u> (in 4 months)
     zwei Wochen (2 weeks) <u>*vor* zwei Wochen</u> (2 weeks ago)

26

This week	**Die**se Woche
This month	**Die**sen Monat
This year	**Die**ses Jahr
Last week	**Letz**te Woche
Last month	**Letz**ten Monat
Last year	**Letz**tes Jahr
/2/ weeks ago	Vor /**zwei**/ Wochen
/3/ months ago	Vor /**drei**/ Monaten
/4/ years ago	Vor /**vier**/ Jahren
Next week	**Näch**ste Woche
Next month	**Näch**sten Monat
Next year	**Näch**stes Jahr
In /2/ weeks	In /**zwei**/ Wochen
In /4/ months	In /**vier**/ Monaten

5.2 The time

What's the time please? Wieviel **Uhr** ist es, bitte?

Es ist **sieben** Uhr   Es ist **fünf** (Minuten)   Es ist **zehn** (Minuten)
nach **sieben**   nach **sieben**

Es ist **elf** (Minuten)   Es ist **Vier**tel nach   Es ist **fünfundzwan**zig
nach **sieben**   **sieben**   (Minuten) nach **sieben**

Es ist halb **acht**   Es ist **zwan**zig   Es ist **Vier**tel
(Minuten) vor **acht**   vor **acht**

5.2   'It's half past _seven_' (ie half _past_ the hour, seven, in
English) is translated by '_Es ist halb acht_' (ie half _towards_

27

5.3 The time (24 hour clock)

When does /the (next) train/ arrive?	Wann kommt /der (**näch**ste) **Zug**/ an?
When does /the (last) bus/ leave?	Wann fährt /der (**letz**te) **Bus**/ ab?
When's /the (next) train/ to /Düsseldorf/?	Wann fährt /der (**näch**ste) **Zug**/ nach /**Düs**seldorf/?
At 1.03	Um **ein** Uhr **drei**
At 3.12	Um **drei** Uhr **zwölf**
At 4.15	Um **vier** Uhr **fünfzehn**
At 15.22	Um **fünf**zehn Uhr **zwei**und**zwan**zig
At 16.45	Um **sech**zehn Uhr **fünf**und**vier**zig
At 17.00	Um **sieb**zehn Uhr
At 17.52	Um **sieb**zehn Uhr **zwei**und**fünf**zig
At 24.00	Um **vier**und**zwan**zig Uhr
(Numbers see 1.26)	

5.4 The date

What's the date today?	Der Wie**viel**te ist heute?
(It's) /January/ 1st	(Es ist) der **ers**te /Januar/
(It's) /February/ 2nd	(Es ist) der **zwei**te /Februar/

5.2 (cont.)	the _next_ hour, eight, in German). Don't get confused you don't want to arrive an hour late! *Nach* = past *Vor* = to NB *Mittag* = midday *Mitternacht* = midnight
5.3	'*Ankommen*' (to arrive) and '*abfahren*' (to leave – when using a vehicle) are separable verbs. See the Mini Grammar p288.
5.4	For the 6th and 9th–19th you add '-*te*' to the number. (See Numbers, 1.26.) eg *neun* (9) *neunte* (9th) *achtzehn* (18) *achtzehnte* (18th)

(It's) /March/ 3rd	(Es ist) der **dri**tte /März/
(It's) /April/ 4th	(Es ist) der **vier**te /April/
(It's) /May/ 5th	(Es ist) der **fünf**te /Mai/

5.5 Specific times (1)

When do you close?	Wann **ma**chen Sie zu?
*When do the /shops/ open?	Wann machen die /Ge**schäf**te/ auf?
*When do the /banks/ close?	Wann machen die /**Ban**ken/ zu?
When do you serve /breakfast/?	Wann ser**vie**ren Sie /**Früh**stück/?
*When does it /begin/?	Wann /be**ginnt**/ es?
*When does it /end/?	Wann /**en**det/ es?
At /4/ o'clock	Um /**vier**/ Uhr
At /2.0/ a.m.	Um /**zwei** Uhr/ **mor**gens
At /4.20/ p.m.	Um /**vier** Uhr zwanzig/ **nach**mittags
From /8.0/ to /10.0/	Von /**acht**/ bis /**zehn**/
On /Monday/	Am /**Mon**tag/
On /Mondays/	/**Mon**tags/
In /June/	Im /**Ju**ni/
On /July 6th/	Am /**sechs**ten **Ju**li/
On /Monday, August 7th/	Am /**Mon**tag, dem **sieb**ten **Au**gust/
In /1995/	/**Neun**zehnhundert-**fünf**und**neun**zig/
In /summer/	Im /**Som**mer/

5.4 (cont.)	7th and 8th are irregular:
	     sieben (7) *sieb*te (7th)
	     acht (8) *acht*e (8th)
	 For 20th–31st you add -*ste*:
	     eg *zwanzig* (20) *der zwanzigste* (the 20th)
	     einunddreißig (31) *der einunddreißigste* (the 31st)

5.5	'*Es*' refers to neuter things eg '*das Theater*'. To refer to masculine things use '*er*'. To refer to feminine things use '*sie*'.
5.5	'*Aufmachen*' (to open) and '*zumachen*' (to close) are separable verbs. See the Mini Grammar p288.

5.6 Specific times – future (2)

When will you /leave/?	Wann /**fahren**/ Sie /**ab**/?
When will she /arrive/?	Wann /**kommt**/ sie /**an**/?
When will it be /ready/?	Wann ist es /**fertig**/?
When will it be /finished/?	Wann ist es /**zu Ende**/?

At /2/ o'clock	Um /**zwei**/ Uhr
Next /Tuesday/	**Näch**sten /**Dienstag**/
In /3/ hours	In /**drei**/ Stunden
In /2/ days	In /**zwei**/ Tagen

| I'll be back /in 10 minutes/ | Ich bin /in **zehn** Minuten/ wieder da |

5.7 Specific times – past (3)

| When did you arrive? | Wann sind Sie **an**gekommen? |

At /3/ o'clock	Um /**drei**/ Uhr
Last /Thursday/	**Letz**ten /**Donnerstag**/
/2/ days ago	Vor /**zwei**/ Tagen
/5/ minutes ago	Vor /**fünf**/ Minuten

5.8 Duration

How long will you be /here/?	Wie **lange** bleiben Sie /**hier**/?
How long will you be /away/?	Wie **lange** bleiben Sie /**weg**/?
How long will it /take/?	Wie **lange** /**dauert**/ das?
How long will /the train/ be delayed?	Wieviel Verspätung hat /**der Zug**/?

(About) /an hour and a half/	(Ungefähr) /**ein**einhalb Stunden/
/3/ days	/**Drei**/ Tage
Until /Friday/	Bis /**Frei**tag/

5.6 'sie' (she) can be replaced by 'er' (he) or 'es' (it).

5.8 'Bleiben' means literally 'to stay'.
You may also hear 'anderthalb Stunden' for 'an hour and a half'.

Now take a part

At the station – you want to find out about train times and then buy a ticket.

Wann fährt der nächste Zug nach Köln?
Heute abend. Um 18.15.
Wann kommt der Zug an?
Er kommt um 19.36 an.
Wieviel kostet die Fahrkarte?
Einfach oder hin und zurück?
Einfach, bitte.
13,90 Mark
OK. Köln, einfach, bitte.
Danke.

6 Information about things

6.1 Names of things (singular)

What's this?	Was ist das?
It's /a salad/	Das ist /ein **Salat**/
It's /a dessert/	Das ist /eine **Nach**speise/
It's /a drink/	Das ist /ein **Getränk**/
It's /fish/	Das ist /**Fisch**/
It's /beer/	Das ist /**Bier**/

6.2 Names of things (plural)

What are these?	Was ist das?
They're /noodles/	Das sind /**Nudeln**/
They're /sweets/	Das sind /**Bonbons**/
They're /spices/	Das sind /**Gewürze**/

6.3 Description (singular)

What does it look like?	Wie **sieht** es **aus**?
Is it /heavy/?	Ist es /**schwer**/?
It's like this	Es ist wie **das**

6.1   Remember: '*ein*' for masculine things
      '*eine*' for feminine things
      '*ein*' for neuter things

6.3   Use '*es*' if you're referring to neuter things.
      Use '*er*' if you're referring to masculine things.

It's /big/	Es ist /**groß**/
It's very /big/	Es ist **sehr** /groß/
It's too /big/	Es ist **zu** /groß/
It's not /big/ enough	Es ist **nicht** /groß/ genug
It's a little /small/	Es ist etwas /**klein**/
It's got /a key/	Es hat /einen **Schlüssel**/

6.4 Description (plural)

| What do they look like? | Wie **sehen** sie **aus**? |
| Are they /waterproof/? | Sind sie /**wa**sserdicht/? |

They're /round/	Sie sind /**rund**/
They're /sharp/	Sie sind /**scharf**/
They're very /long/	Sie sind **sehr** /lang/
They've got /filters/	Sie haben /einen **Fi**lter/

6.5 Colour

| What colour is it? | Welche **Far**be hat es? |
| It's /red/ | Es ist /**rot**/ |

6.6 What's it made of?

| What's it made of? | **Wo**raus ist es? |
| It's made of /metal/ and /plastic/ | Es ist aus /**Metall**/ und /**Pla**stik/ |

6.7 Use

| What's it for? | **Wozu** ist das? |
| It's used for /cooking/ | Das **braucht** man zum /**Ko**chen/ |

6.3	Use '*sie*' if you're referring to feminine things.
(cont.)	See 4.3 for an explanation of '*einen*'.
6.4	'*Sie*' means both 'she' and 'they'. You can tell the difference by the verb ending. When '*sie*' means 'they', the verb always ends in '*-en*', when it means 'she' the verb usually ends in '*-t*'.
	'*Sie haben einen Filter*' – literally 'They've got a filter' ie one filter each.
6.7	'*Kochen*' is the infinitive, 'to cook', but it can be used with a capital letter to mean 'cooking'. In the Mini Dictionary, all verbs are given in the infinitive, so you can look up for example, 'clean' (*putzen*) and say:
	It's used for /cleaning/ *Das braucht man zum* /*Putzen*/

6.8 Size (clothing) & weight

What size is it?	Welche **Größe** ist das?
What size do you want?	Welche **Größe** wollen Sie?
Size /7/	Größe /**vier**zig/
(Sizes see p297)	
How much does it weigh?	Wieviel **wiegt** das?
(It weighs) /500/ grams	(Das wiegt) /**fünf**hundert/ Gramm
(Weight see p298)	

6.9 Length & width

How big is it?	Wie **groß** ist es?
It's (about) /15/ cms long	Es ist (ungefähr) /**fünf**zehn/ Zentimeter lang
About /30/ cms wide	Ungefähr /**dreiß**ig/ Zentimeter breit
/30/ cms by /15/ cms	/**Dreiß**ig/ Zentimeter mal /**fünf**zehn/ Zentimeter
(Lengths see p297)	

6.10 Cost

*How much is it please?	Wieviel **ko**stet das bitte?
*How much are they please?	Wieviel **ko**sten sie bitte?
It's /43/ Marks	Das kostet /**drei**und**vier**zig/ Mark
They're /40/ Marks	Sie kosten /**vier**zig/ Mark
(Money see p296)	

6.11 Possession

Whose is it?	**Wem** gehört das?
It's /mine/	Das gehört /**mir**/

6.11   '*Das gehört mir*' literally means 'that belongs to me', just as '*Der Stil gefällt mir*' literally means 'the style is pleasing to me' (see 6.12). If you are talking about several things, '*gehört*' changes to '*gehören*' and '*gefällt*' to '*gefallen*'.

Is this /yours/?	Gehört das /**Ihnen**/?
*Yes, it is	Ja
*No, it isn't	Nein

6.12 Likes/Dislikes

Do you like /the colour/?	**Gefällt** Ihnen /die **Farbe**/?
Do you like /the belts/?	**Gefallen** Ihnen /die **Gürtel**/?
*Yes, I do	Ja
I like /the style/	/Der **Stil**/ gefällt mir
*No, I don't	Nein
I don't like /the shape/	/Die **Form**/ gefällt mir nicht
Do you like it?	**Gefällt** es Ihnen?
Yes, I love it	Ja, sehr
No, I hate it	Nein, **gar** nicht
Did you like /the film/?	Hat Ihnen /der **Film**/ gefallen?
No, not very much	Nein, nicht sehr

Now take a part

You've lost something and you have to describe it.

Guten Morgen! Bitte schön?
Ja. Ich habe meine Tasche verloren.
Wie sieht sie aus?
Sie ist klein und rund.
Welche Farbe hat sie?
Sie ist rot.
Ja. Woraus ist sie?
Sie ist aus Plastik.
In Ordnung. Moment, bitte. Gehört die Ihnen?
Ja, sie gehört mir. Danke schön.
Bitte schön.

35

7 Wants and needs

7.1 Have you got?/I've got/I haven't got (singular)

*Have you got /the ticket/?	Haben Sie /die **Kar**te/?
Have you got /a roadmap/?	Haben Sie /eine **Straße**nkarte/?
Have you got any /beer/?	Haben Sie /**Bier**/?
Have you got /your passport/?	Haben Sie /Ihren **Paß**/?
*Yes, I have	Ja
I've got /a reservation/	Ich habe /eine Reser**vie**rung/
I've got some /coffee/	Ich habe /**Ka**ffee/

7.1   '*Ja/Nein*' are quite enough in German for 'Yes, I have/No, I haven't' and 'Yes, there is/No, there isn't'. Remember that '*ein*' changes to '*einen*' when the masculine noun referred to is the direct object of the sentence. There is no equivalent of 'some' or 'any' in German.
'*Karte*' = general word for ticket.
'*Fahrkarte*' = ticket for a train, plane, bus etc.
'*Eintrittskarte*' = 'entrance' ticket for the cinema, theatre etc.

*No, I haven't	Nein
I haven't got /the ticket/	Ich habe /die **Kar**te/ nicht
I haven't got /a ticket/	Ich habe /keine **Kar**te/
*I haven't got /any change/	Ich habe /kein **Klein**geld/

7.2 Have you got?/I've got/I haven't got (plural)

*Have you got the /keys/?	Haben Sie die /**Schlü**ssel/?
Have you got any /postcards/?	Haben Sie /**Post**karten/?
Have you got your /suitcases/?	Haben Sie Ihre /**Kof**fer/?
*Yes, I have	Ja
I've got some /stamps/	Ich habe /**Brief**marken/
*No, I haven't	Nein
I haven't got any /suitcases/	Ich habe keine /**Kof**fer/
I haven't got any /tickets/	Ich habe keine /**Fahr**karten/
I haven't got the /tickets/	Ich habe die /**Fahr**karten/ nicht

7.3 Is there?/Are there?

*Is there /a hotel/ near here?	Gibt es hier /ein **Hotel**/?
Is there any /tea/?	Gibt es noch /**Tee**/?
Are there any /restaurants/ near here?	Gibt es hier /**Restau**rants/?

7.2	'die' = the (plural)
	'Ihre' = your (plural)
	'keine' = not any (plural)
	There isn't a regular way of forming the plural of nouns in German. In the Mini Dictionary each noun is given with its plural ending in brackets:
	eg *die Postkarte (-n)* (the postcard)
7.3	Here, 'noch' literally means 'left', but usually means 'still', or 'yet' as in 'noch nicht' (not yet). See also 1.5.

7.4 There is/There are

*Yes, there is	Ja
*There's some /beer/	Es gibt /Bier/
There are /2/ /hotels/ in the town	Es gibt /zwei/ /Hotels/ in der Stadt

7.5 There isn't/There aren't

*No, there isn't	Nein
*There isn't /any beer/	Es gibt /kein **Bier**/
*There aren't any /seats/	Es gibt keine /**Plätze**/

7.6 I'd like

I'd like /a cut and blow dry/ please	Ich möchte /einen **Fön**schnitt/, bitte
I'd like /a beer and a sandwich/ please	Ich möchte /ein **Bier** und ein belegtes **Brot**/, bitte
*I'd like some /coffee/ please	Ich möchte /**Kaffee**/, bitte
I'd like some /cigars/ please	Ich möchte /**Zigarren**/, bitte
I'd like /breakfast in my room/ please	Ich möchte /das **Früh**stück auf mein **Zimmer**/, bitte

---

7.5   If the noun used as the direct object is a masculine one, the word '*kein*' takes an '-*en*' ending. For feminine nouns the ending is '-*e*'. There is no ending for neuter nouns. In the plural, you always use '*keine*'.

7.6   When you want to indicate or point to things without referring to them by name, you can use the following expressions.

   Dies for something near: *ich möchte dies, bitte* (I'd like this please)

   Das for something further away: *ich möchte das, bitte* (I'd like that please)

   Diese for more than one thing, near: *ich möchte diese, bitte* (I'd like these please)

   Diese da for more than one thing further away: *ich möchte diese da, bitte* (I'd like those please)

*I'd like this please	Ich möchte **dies**, bitte
*I'd like that please	Ich möchte **das**, bitte
*I'd like these please	Ich möchte **die**se, bitte
*I'd like those please	Ich möchte diese **da**, bitte

7.7 Would you like?

What would you like?	Was **möch**ten Sie?
What would you like? (informal)	Was **möch**test du?
Would you like /a streetmap/?	Möchten Sie /einen **Stadt**plan/?
Would you like some /wine/?	Möchten Sie /**Wein**/?
Would you like some /biscuits/?	Möchten Sie /**Kekse**/?
*Yes please	**Ja**, bitte
*No thank you	**Nein**, danke

7.8 I'd prefer

I'd prefer /an omelette/	Ich hätte lieber /ein **Omelett**/
I'd prefer some /red wine/	Ich hätte lieber /**Rot**wein/

7.9 I need

I need /a towel/	Ich brauche /ein **Hand**tuch/
I need some /soap/	Ich brauche /**Seife**/
Do I need /a visa/?	Brauche ich /ein **Vi**sum/?
What do I need?	Was **brau**che ich?

7.10 Exact quantities

How many would you like?	**Wieviele** möchten Sie?
I'd like /3/	Ich möchte /**drei**/
How much would you like?	**Wieviel** möchten Sie?
I'd like /a slice/ of /ham/	Ich möchte /eine Scheibe/ /**Schin**ken/
(Numbers see 1.26)	

39

7.11 Which one?

Which one do you want?	**Wel**ches wollen Sie?
Which ones do you want?	**Wel**che wollen Sie?
This one please	**Dies**, bitte
That one please	**Das**, bitte
These ones please	**Die**se, bitte
Those ones please	Diese **da**, bitte
I want the big one (masculine)	Ich will den **Groß**en
I want the big one (feminine)	Ich will die **Groß**e
I want the big one (neuter)	Ich will das **Groß**e
I want the big ones	Ich will die **Groß**en

7.12 Quantities

How many?	Wie**vie**le?
How many /apples/ would you like?	Wieviele/**Äp**fel/ möchten Sie?
Not many – /3/ please	Nicht viele – /**drei**/, bitte

7.11   *Welcher* is used with masculine nouns in the singular. *Welche* is used with feminine nouns in the singular. *Welches* is used with neuter nouns in the singular. *Welche* is used with plural nouns.

In German you do not translate the word 'one' in the examples 'I want the big one' etc. However the article 'the' and the adjective after it vary their endings according to the gender of the noun referred to since it is the direct object of the verb:

    with masculine words use *den* and add *-en* to the adjective.

    with feminine words use *die* and add *-e* to the adjective.

    with neuter words use *das* and add *-e* to the adjective.

    with plural words use *die* and add *-en* to the adjective.

'Do you want?/I want' can be translated by '*Wollen Sie?/Ich will*', but it is more polite to use '*Möchten Sie?/Ich möchte*'. See 7.13.

How much?	Wieviel?
How much /cream/ would you like?	Wieviel /**Sah**ne/ möchten Sie?
Not much	Nicht viel

A lot	Viel
*Less	Weniger
*More	Mehr
Enough	Genug
A few /tomatoes/	Ein paar /**Tomaten**/
A little /cream/	Ein wenig /**Sah**ne/

7.13 I want/I don't want

I want some /coffee/	Ich möchte /**Kaff**ee/
I want some /stamps/	Ich möchte /**Brief**marken/
I want some more /coffee/	Ich möchte etwas mehr /**Kaff**ee/

I don't want many	Ich möchte nicht vie**le**
I don't want much	Ich möchte nicht **viel**
I don't want so many	Ich möchte nicht so vie**le**
I don't want so much	Ich möchte nicht so **viel**

7.14 Comparisons

Have you got anything /bigger/?	Haben Sie etwas /**Größ**eres/?
I want something /bigger/	Ich möchte etwas /**Größ**eres/
I want something /more comfortable/	Ich möchte etwas /**Bequem**eres/
I want something /cheaper/	Ich möchte etwas /**Bill**igeres/

7.14   To form the comparative simply add '-*er*' to the adjective exactly as in English eg *klein* – *kleiner* (small – smaller) The examples given here end with an extra '-*es*' which is the ending needed with '*etwas*' ('anything' or 'something') eg '*etwas Größeres*'.

7.15 Anything else?/Anything for ...?

Do you want anything else?	Wollen Sie **noch** etwas?
Do you need anything else?	Brauchen Sie **noch** etwas?
Would you like anything else?	Möchten Sie **noch** etwas?
Have you got anything for /a cough/?	Haben Sie etwas gegen /**Hu**sten/?
Have you got anything for /children/?	Haben Sie etwas für /**Kin**der/?

7.16 Food (style, variety, flavour)

How would you like it?	**Wie** möchten Sie es?
I'd like it /well done/ please	Ich möchte es /**gut durch**gebraten/, bitte
What kind of /sandwich/ would you like?	Was für /ein belegtes **Brot**/ möchten Sie?
I'd like /a ham sandwich/ please	Ich möchte /ein **Schin**kenbrot/, bitte
I'd like /an ice cream/ please	Ich möchte /ein **Eis**/, bitte
What flavour would you like?	Welchen **Ge**schmack möchten Sie?
/Vanilla/ please	/**Va**nille/, bitte

7.15   '*Gegen*' literally means 'against', which is quite logical when you think about it!

42

Now take a part

Buying some groceries

Guten Morgen! Bitte schön?
Guten Morgen! Haben Sie Kaffee?
Ja. Wieviel möchten Sie?
Ich möchte ein Kilo, bitte.
Gut! Noch etwas?
Ja, Ich möchte Äpfel, bitte.
Wieviele?
Nicht viele – genug, Danke.
OK. Das kostet 9,25 Mark, bitte.
Danke.

8 Getting help – getting things done

8.1 General expressions

How does it work?	Wie funktio**niert** es?
Like this	So
It works with /batteries/	Es funktio**niert** mit /Batterien/
It doesn't work	Es funktio**niert** nicht
It's broken	Es ist ka**putt**
It's out of order	Es ist außer **Betrieb**
It makes a /funny/ noise	Es macht ein /**ko**misches/ **Geräusch**
I can't open it	Ich kann es nicht **öffnen**
I can't do it	Ich **scha**ffe es nicht

8.2 (Could you) please

Could you /call/ /a taxi/ for me	Könnten Sie mir /ein **Taxi**/ /rufen/

8.2   When the English word 'me' really means 'for me' or 'to me', the German equivalent is '*mir*'. When you want to express 'me' simply as the direct object of the sentence, use '*mich*'.

Could you tell me when we get there	Könnten Sie es mir sagen, wenn wir dorthin kommen

*Please call me at /7/ o'clock	Bitte rufen Sie mich um /sieben/ Uhr
Please leave me alone	Bitte lassen Sie mich in Ruhe

8.3 Getting things done

I'd like to have /this shirt/ /washed/ please	Ich möchte /dieses Hemd/ /waschen/ lassen, bitte
I'd like to have /this film/ /developed/ please	Ich möchte /diesen Film/ /entwickeln/ lassen, bitte
I'd like to have /this camera/ /repaired/ please	Ich möchte /diesen Fotoapparat/ /reparieren/ lassen, bitte
I'd like to have /this skirt/ /cleaned/ please	Ich möchte /diesen Rock/ /reinigen/ lassen, bitte
I'd like to have /this/ /delivered/ please	Ich möchte /dies/ /schicken/ lassen, bitte

---

8.3   '*Ich möchte*' (I would like to), '*ich muß*' (I must) and '*ich kann*' (I can) and the other 'modal' verbs listed in the Mini Grammar p286 are always followed by the infinitive in German. Here are some examples using '*zahlen*' (to pay):

Ich möchte zahlen	I would like to pay
Möchten Sie zahlen?	Would you like to pay?
Ich muß zahlen	I must pay
Müssen Sie zahlen?	Must you pay?
Ich kann zahlen	I can pay
Können Sie zahlen?	Can you pay?

See also 9.1/9.2/9.3/9.4.

How to express 'this' in German when 'this' is followed by a noun:

Masculine nouns eg <u>der</u> Film – <u>dieser</u> Film
Feminine nouns eg <u>die</u> Uhr – <u>diese</u> Uhr
Neuter nouns eg <u>das</u> Hemd – <u>dieses</u> Hemd

You will notice that with masculine nouns, '*dieser*' becomes '*diesen*' when it is the object of the sentence (just as '*der*' becomes '*den*'). For a fuller explanation, see the Mini Grammar, p276.

Now take a part

You take your camera to a camera shop to be repaired.

Guten Morgen! Bitte schön?
Guten Morgen! Ich möchte diesen Fotoapparat reparieren lassen, bitte.
Was ist damit los?
Ich weiß nicht. Er funktioniert nicht. Ich kann ihn nicht öffnen.
Moment, bitte. Wie ist Ihr Name, bitte?
Mein Name ist Anderson. John Anderson.
Danke.
Wann ist er fertig?
Nächsten Freitag.
Danke. Auf Wiedersehen!
Auf Wiedersehen!

9.1 Wishes

Do you want to /hire/ /a car/?	Möchten Sie /ein **Au**to/ /mieten/?
I want to /hire/ / a car/	Ich möchte /ein **Au**to/ /mieten/
I don't want to /go/ /by bus/	Ich möchte **nicht** /mit dem **Bus**/ /fahren/
What would you like to /do/?	Was möchten Sie /**tun**/?
Would you like to /go/ to /Bonn/?	Möchten Sie nach /**Bonn**/ /fahren/?
Would you like to /do some shopping/?	Möchten Sie /**ein**kaufen gehen/?
I'd love to /go/ to /Bonn/	Ich möchte sehr **gern** nach /**Bonn**/ /fahren/
I'd like to /do some shopping/	Ich möchte /**ein**kaufen gehen/

I'd like to see you again	Ich möchte Sie gern **wie**dersehen
I'd prefer to /go to the cinema/	Ich würde lieber /ins **Ki**no gehen/

9.2 Possibility

Can I /hire/ /a car/?	Kann ich /ein **Au**to/ /mieten/?
Where can I /hire/ /a bicycle/?	Wo kann ich /ein **Fahr**rad/ /mieten/?
I can /meet/ you /tomorrow/	Ich kann Sie /**mor**gen/ /treffen/
I can't /meet/ you /tomorrow/	Ich kann Sie /**mor**gen/ nicht /treffen/

9.3 Permission

May I /borrow/ /your pen/?	Darf ich /Ihren **Fü**ller/ /borgen/?
Yes, of course	Ja, na**tür**lich

9.4 Necessity

Must I /pay/ now?	Muß ich jetzt /be**zah**len/?
Where must I /go/?	Wohin muß ich /**ge**hen/?
I must /leave/ early	Ich muß **früh** /**ab**fahren/
I must /catch/ /the next train/	Ich muß mit /dem nächsten **Zug**/ /fahren/
I needn't /catch/ /the next train/	Ich muß nicht mit /dem nächsten **Zug**/ /fahren/

9.5 Intention

Are you going to /hire/ /a car/?	Werden Sie /ein **Au**to/ /mieten/?
I'm going to /buy/ /a map/	Ich werde /eine **Land**karte/ /kaufen/
I'm going to /see/ /him/ tomorrow	Ich werde /ihn/ **mor**gen /sehen/

9.4 Remember that '*mit dem Zug*' means 'by train' (literally 'with the train').

9.6 Suggestions

*Let's go	**Gehen wir**
Let's go and /eat/	**Gehen wir /essen/**
Let's go /to the cinema/	**Gehen wir /ins Kino/**
Let's go /shopping/	**Gehen wir /einkaufen/**
Let's go /swimming/	**Gehen wir /schwimmen/**
Let's meet /tomorrow/	**Treffen wir uns /morgen/**
Let's meet /next Tuesday/	**Treffen wir uns /nächsten Dienstag/**
Let's meet /at 9/	**Treffen wir uns /um neun/**

Now take a part

Arranging to meet someone again.

Ich möchte Sie gern wiedersehen. Kann ich Sie morgen treffen?
Ja, toll! Wann?
Um sechs Uhr?
Ja. Wo?
In Ihrem Hotel. Was möchten Sie tun?
Ich möchte ins Kino gehen.
Sehr gut. Bis morgen abend!
Auf Wiedersehen!

---

10 A variety of situations

The language you have learned in the Study Section can of course be used in many different situations. This section contains a number of examples of the sorts of conversations you should be able to take part in or understand. Even if you don't understand every word, you will often be able to get the gist of what people are saying depending on the situation you are in. The figures on the right refer, where applicable, to sections you have already studied.

10.1 Meeting someone – Someone you don't know is meeting you at the airport.

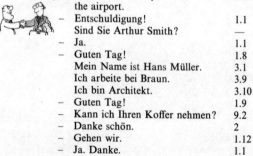

– Entschuldigung!	1.1
Sind Sie Arthur Smith?	—
– Ja.	1.1
– Guten Tag!	1.8
Mein Name ist Hans Müller.	3.1
Ich arbeite bei Braun.	3.9
Ich bin Architekt.	3.10
– Guten Tag!	1.9
– Kann ich Ihren Koffer nehmen?	9.2
– Danke schön.	2
– Gehen wir.	1.12
– Ja. Danke.	1.1

10.2 Introductions – Someone introduces you to a third person.

– Das ist Herr Frisch,	3.14
und das ist Herr Smith.	3.14
– Guten Tag!	3.14
– Guten Tag!	3.14
Wann sind Sie hier angekommen,	5.7
Herr Smith?	
– Gestern abend.	5.1
– Wie lange bleiben Sie hier?	5.8
– Drei Tage.	5.8

10.3 The hotel – Mr and Mrs Smith and their two children have just arrived at a hotel. They previously booked two rooms.

– Guten Morgen!	1.8
– Guten Morgen!	1.8
– Mein Name ist Smith.	3.1
Ich habe eine Reservierung für	1.2
zwei Zimmer.	
– Smith. Wie schreibt man das,	3.2
bitte?	
– S-M-I-T-H.	1.29
– Ach ja. Herr and Frau Smith und	—
zwei Kinder.	
Zwei Doppelzimmer mit Bad.	1.19
– Das stimmt.	2
– *Bitte tragen Sie sich ein!*	—
– Ja.	1.1
– Danke.	1.1
Zimmer 401 und 402. Hier sind	1.26
die Schlüssel.	
– Welcher Stock, bitte?	4.4
– Vierter Stock.	—

Bitte tragen Sie sich ein! (Please sign the register).

10.4 Making reservations ...

10.4.1 ... at the theatre

– Ich möchte zwei Plätze *im ersten*	7.6
Rang, bitte	
– Wann?	1.14
– Samstag abend, bitte.	1.27/5.1

– Ja. Es gibt noch Plätze.	1.6
– Wieviel kosten sie, bitte?	6.10
– 15 Mark.	1.26
– Ich möchte etwas Billigeres, bitte.	7.14
– Ich have zwei Plätze *im Parkett*.	1.2
Zweite Reihe. Sie kosten 10 Mark.	6.10
– *Die nehme ich*.	—
– *Bitte*.	—
– Danke.	1.1

im ersten Rang (in the dress circle). *im Parkett* (in the stalls). *Zweite Reihe* (second row). *Die nehme ich* (I'll take them). *Bitte* (here '*bitte*' means 'thank you').

10.4.2 ... at a restaurant

– Ich möchte einen Tisch für heute abend, bitte.	7.6/5.1
– Für wieviele Personen?	1.14
– Für zwei Personen, bitte.	1.17
– *Um wieviel Uhr, bitte?*	—
– Um acht Uhr dreißig.	5.5
– Ich habe um neun Uhr einen Tisch.	1.2/5.5
Ist das in Ordnung?	1.1
– Sehr gut! Danke.	1.1

Um wieviel Uhr, bitte? (At what time please?)

10.5 The restaurant – You are ordering food.

– Die Speisekarte, bitte.	1.17
– Ja, natürlich.	1.1
Möchten Sie auch die *Weinkarte*?	7.7
– Ja, bitte.	1.1
– Was möchten Sie?	7.7
– Ich möchte *Suppe*, und dann ein Steak.	7.6
	—
– Wie möchten Sie es?	7.16
– Gut durchgebraten, bitte.	7.16
Und ich möchte Pommes frites und Salat, bitte.	7.6/1.17
– Möchten Sie noch etwas?	7.15
– Ja. Ein Bier, bitte.	1.1

Weinkarte (winelist). *Suppe* (soup).

10.6 Travel – At a Tourist Information Office – You want to know
how to get to Hamburg.

– Guten Morgen!	1.8
Ich möchte nach Hamburg fahren.	9.1
Ich möchte eine Auskunft über Züge, bitte.	1.21
– Es gibt *stündlich* einen Zug.	7.4
– Wann fährt der nächste Zug ab?	5.3
– Um 14.20.	1.26/5.3
– Wieviel kostet das hin und zurück?	6.10/1.11
– 51 Mark.	1.26
– Danke.	1.1

stündlich (hourly).

10.7 Shopping ...

10.7.1 ... buying a pair of shoes

– Bitte schön?	1.15
– Ich möchte ein Paar Schuhe.	7.6
Kann ich die anprobieren, bitte?	1.15/9.2
– Ja. Welche Größe bitte?	6.8
– Größe 40.	6.8/1.26
– *Bitte schön.*	—
– Danke.	1.1
– *Geht es*?	—
– Ja. Sie sind sehr *bequem*. Was kosten sie?	6.4/6.10
– 50 Mark.	1.26
– *Die nehme ich.* Danke.	1.1

Bitte schön here means 'Here you are'. *Geht es*? (Are they all right?).
bequem (comfortable). *Die nehme ich* (I'll take them).

10.7.2 ... deciding not to buy

– Ich möchte einen Fotoapparat.	7.6
Wieviel kostet *der hier*?	6.10
– 200 Mark.	1.26
– *Kann ich ihn ansehen*?	—

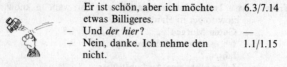

Er ist schön, aber ich möchte etwas Billigeres. 6.3/7.14

– Und *der hier*? —

– Nein, danke. Ich nehme den nicht. 1.1/1.15

Kann ich ihn ansehen (Can I look at it). *der hier* (this one here).

11 How to cope with

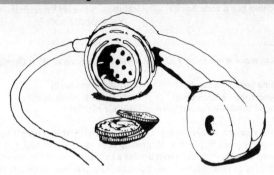

11.1 The telephone

Where to find a phone: In cities – in the same places as in Britain. Look out for yellow call boxes.

Money: For call boxes and pay phones you need 10 pfennig, 50 pfennig and 1 mark pieces.

Inland calls (Inlandsgespräche): See list of codes (Vorwählnummer) in call box. Note: If you know an internal extension number, you can often dial straight through to a particular person, by adding it on to the ordinary number.

International calls (Auslandsgespräche): Most international calls can be dialled direct. See code list. To call Britain from West Germany, dial the code 00 44, then the code for the British town and then the number.
NB If the British code starts with 0, omit it – eg to dial London (code 01), dial 00 44 1, followed by the number.

General Expressions

Where's the (nearest) phone please? | Wo gibt es hier ein Telefon, bitte?
May I use your phone please? | Darf ich bitte telefonieren?

Have you got a telephone directory?	Haben Sie ein Telefonbuch?
Have you got a code book?	Haben Sie ein Verzeichnis der Vorwählnummern?

How to make a telephone call from a public telephone in West Germany

Dialling tone (Freizeichen)	tüt-tüüüt tüt-tüüüt
Ringing tone (Rufzeichen)	tüüüt tüüüt tüüüt tüüüt
Engaged tone (Besetztzeichen)	tüt tüt tüt tüt

Lift the receiver. A sign saying 'Geld einwerfen' ('put in money') lights up. Insert coins (10 pfennig, 50 pfennig or 1 mark piece) and dial the number. 20 pfennig is the minimum for a call within West Germany, 30 pfennig for an international call. You can either put in more money than you expect to spend (unspent money is automatically returned when the receiver is replaced), or you can add more money as it is used up. For local calls there is no time restriction (20 pfennig). For long distance calls, when the orange sign saying 'Bitte zahlen' (please pay) lights up on the phone, put in more money.

Directory Enquiries (Fernsprechauskunft)
Directory enquiries within West Germany (Fernsprechauskunft – Inland) dial.01 18.
International directory enquiries (Fernsprechauskunft – Ausland) dial 0 01 18.

Note that the word 'zwo' is often used on the phone instead of 'zwei' ('two'). This is to distinguish it clearly from 'drei' ('three').

Directory Enquiries	Auskunft
I'd like a telephone number in /Nördlingen in Bavaria/	Ich möchte eine Nummer in /Nördlingen in Bayern/
Name?	Name? /Brandt/
First name?	Vorname? /Otto/
Street?	Straße? /Leuschnerstraße 25/
What is the code for /Bonn/ please?	Was ist die Vorwählnummer für /Bonn/, bitte?

Dial 0 10 for the operator for inland numbers (Fernvermittlungsstelle – Fernamt).
Dial 00 10 for the international operator (Fernvermittlungsstelle – Ausland).

Number please?	Welche Nummer möchten Sie? /Bingen 3 52 61/
What's your number please?	Ihre Nummer, bitte? /Berlin 7 43 10 26/
I'd like a personal call to /Mr Cook/, /Oxford 56762/	Ich möchte ein Gespräch mit Voranmeldung mit /Herrn Cook/, /Oxford 56762/, bitte
I'd like a transferred charge call to /York 33582/	Ich möchte ein R-Gespräch nach /York 33582/
Can I have a line please?	Ein Amt, bitte
Could you call me at /7 o'clock/ please?	Bitte rufen Sie mich um /7 Uhr/ an
Hold the line please	Bleiben Sie bitte am Apparat
The line's engaged	Die Nummer ist besetzt
There's no reply	Es meldet sich niemand

Difficulties
Dial the operator (0 10 or 00 10 – as above).

I want /London 327 5389/. I can't get through	Ich möchte /London 327 5389/. Ich komme nicht durch
I was speaking to /Hanover 1 43 96 47/. I was cut off	Mein Gespräch mit /Hannover 1 43 96 47/ wurde unterbrochen

PHONE CALLS
In Germany answer the phone by giving your name rather than your number. If you are at someone else's house, say 'bei /Schmidt/' (if you are staying at the /Schmidts'/ house). Note also at the end of a telephone call, you say 'Auf Wiederhören' rather than 'Auf Wiedersehen'.

1 *Informal*

/Frisch/ speaking	/Frisch/
Hello. Is that /Mr Frisch/?	Hallo! Ist das /Herr Frisch/?
Speaking	Am Apparat

This is /Jane Butcher/ here. May I speak to /Mrs Frisch/?	/Jane Butcher/ hier. Kann ich bitte /Frau Frisch/ sprechen?
She's out at the moment	Sie ist im Moment nicht da
I'll ring back later	Ich rufe später noch einmal an

2 *Wrong number*

Hello. May I speak to /John/ please?	Hallo! Kann ich bitte /Johann/ sprechen?
I'm sorry. There's no /John/ here. This is /41 36 24/	Es tut mir leid! Hier ist kein /Johann/. Hier ist /41 36 24/
Sorry. Wrong number	Entschuldigung. Ich habe die falsche Nummer

3 *Business*

This is /Meyer's Furniture/. Good morning	/Möbel Meyer/. Guten Tag!
Can I speak to /Mr Braun/ please? Extension 56	Kann ich bitte /Herrn Braun/ sprechen? Apparat 56
Hold the line please	Bleiben Sie am Apparat
I'm putting you through	Ich verbinde
Hello. /Mr Braun's/ office	/Vorzimmer /von Herrn Braun/
Hello. Can I speak to /Mr Braun/ please?	Kann ich bitte /Herrn Braun/ sprechen?
I'm sorry. He's /in a meeting/	Es tut mir leid. Er ist /in einer Sitzung/
Would you please take a message?	Würden Sie bitte etwas ausrichten?
Yes, of course	Ja, natürlich
Could you tell him /Mr Cook/ called?	Könnten Sie ihm sagen, daß /Herr Cook/ angerufen hat?
Yes, certainly	Ja, natürlich
Thank you. Goodbye	Danke. Auf Wiederhören!
Goodbye	Auf Wiederhóren!

11.2 Emergencies

Dial 1 10 in an emergency. For the Fire Brigade dial 1 12. In certain public telephone boxes there is an automatic device for summoning the fire brigade or the police. It is called a 'Notrufmelder'. It is a small box with a handle which can be moved to the left or right. If moved to the left (towards the sign 'Feuerwehr') the Fire Brigade will reply. If moved to the right (towards the sign 'Notruf') the police will reply.

Emergency calls (Notrufe)

Police	Polizei
Fire brigade	Feuerwehr
Ambulance	Rettungsdienst
There's been an accident on /Lindenstraße/	In /der Lindenstraße/ ist ein Unfall passiert
Where exactly?	Wo genau?
Near the /post office/	Beim /Postamt/
There's a fire on /Friedrichstraße/	In /der Friedrichstraße/ brennt es
Please send an ambulance to /9, Ludwigstraße/	Bitte schicken Sie einen Krankenwagen zur /Ludwigstraße, 9/
What's your number please?	Was ist Ihre Nummer, bitte?

General expressions

Where's the /British/ Embassy?	Wo ist die /britische/ Botschaft?
Help!	Hilfe!
Help me please!	Helfen Sie mir, bitte!
Quick!	Schnell!
Look out!	Paß auf!
Careful!	Vorsicht!
Call the /police/	Rufen Sie die /Polizei/!
Call the /fire brigade/	Rufen Sie die /Feuerwehr/!
Call /an ambulance/	Rufen Sie /einen Krankenwagen/!
Call /a doctor/	Rufen Sie /einen Arzt/!
Are you insured?	Sind Sie versichert?
Please give me your name and address	Bitte geben Sie mir Ihren Namen und Ihre Adresse

At the Hospital

Should you have an accident in West Germany, you can be confident that the highest standards of medical care exist. You would be taken by ambulance to the casualty ward ('Unfallstation') of the nearest hospital. Your British National Health contributions are valid there providing you have Form No. E111 with you (see below), as both countries are members of the EEC and ambulance services and hospital treatment are covered by the reciprocal National Health Service arrangements. Before travelling, contact your nearest Social Security office to inform them of the dates of your visit and obtain Form No. E111.

Where's /the nearest hospital/ please?	Wo gibt es hier /ein Krankenhaus/, bitte?
I'm /diabetic/ (male)	Ich bin /Diabetiker/
I'm /diabetic/ (female)	Ich bin /Diabetikerin/
I'm /pregnant/	Ich bin /schwanger/
(I think) it's /my heart/	(Ich glaube) es ist /mein Herz/
Is it broken?	Ist es gebrochen?
I'd like /a painkiller/	Ich möchte ein /schmerzstillendes Mittel/
I'm allergic to /penicillin/	Ich bin allergisch gegen /Penizillin/
Please notify /Mr Davis/ at the /Hotel Bristol/	Bitte, benachrichtigen Sie /Herrn Davis/ im /Hotel Bristol/

At the Police Station
If you've lost somebody or something go to the nearest police station.

Where's /the nearest police station/ please?	Wo gibt es hier /eine Polizeiwache/, bitte?
I've lost /my passport/	Ich habe /meinen Paß/ verloren
I've lost /my wallet/	Ich habe /meine Brieftasche/ verloren
/My handbag/ has been stolen	/Meine Handtasche/ wurde mir gestohlen
/My luggage/ has been stolen	/Mein Gepäck/ wurde mir gestohlen
I've run out of money	Ich habe kein Geld mehr
I want /a lawyer/	Ich möchte /einen Rechtsanwalt/

PART B
REFERENCE SECTION

Pronunciation key

Sounds you don't have to worry about – they're very close to English sounds:

[b]	bath	Bad (bath)
[d]	date	Datum (date)
[e]	bed	Bett (bed), Apfel (apples)
[f]	fire	Feuer (fire)
[g]	game	Garten (garden)
[h]	hard	hart (hard)
[i]	with	mit (with)
[k]	climb	klettern (climb)
[ks]	export	exakt (exact)
[l]	lemon	letzt (last)
[m]	me	mich (me)
[n]	nose	Nase (nose)
[n̄g]	sing	Ding (thing), singen (sing)
[o]	home	wohnen (live)
[p]	place	Platz (square)
[r]	red	rot (red), Radio (radio)
[s]	sausage	ist (is)
[sh]	shoe	Schuh (shoe)
[t]	tea	Tee (tea), und (and)

Sounds which are also close to English sounds but which may look different when written in German:

[a]	cat	Hand (hand) – a short 'a' sound, more like the 'u' in 'under'
[ā]	father	Vater (father)
[āy]	hate	geben (give)
[ch]	choose	tschüs (goodbye)
[ee]	she	sie (she)
[ə]	daughter	Karte (ticket)
[ī]	sign	Zeichen (sign)
[ɔ]	knot	Koffer (suitcase)
[ōō]	zoo	du (you)
[oy]	boy	heute (today), Fräulein (Miss)
[ow]	brown	braun (brown)

62

[shp]	fi**sh**pond	**sp**ät (late)
[sht]	wa**shed**	**St**adt (town)
[ts]	ca**ts**	**z**u (to)
[ŭ]	p**u**t	**u**nd (and)
[v]	**v**eal	**W**ein (wine)
[w]	**w**orry	**T**oilette (toilet)
[y]	**y**es	**j**a (yes), **Y**acht (yacht)
[z]	**z**oo	**s**ie (she)

There are a few extra sounds which you will meet only in words which have been borrowed from other languages:

[j]	mas**s**age	Mas**s**age (massage)
[ã]	as in French 'or**an**ge' (orange)	Or**an**ge (orange)
[ẽ]	as in French 'p**ain**' (bread)	Souter**rain** (basement)
[õ]	as in French 'b**on**b**on**' (sweet)	B**on**b**on** (sweet)

Difficult sounds – see 'A few sounds'

[ēy]		sp**ät** (late), K**ä**se (cheese)
[kh]	– as in Scottish 'lo**ch**'	a**ch**t (eight), no**ch** (still)
[h]		i**ch** (I), hungri**g** (hungry)
[œ]		w**ö**chentlich (weekly)
[œ]		sch**ö**n (beautiful)
[ü]		f**ü**nf (five), h**ü**bsch (pretty)
[üh]		T**ü**r (door), f**ü**r (for)

NB 'd' and 'b' are pronounced as in English except where they come at the end of a word, when the 'd' is pronounced like 't' and the 'b' is pronounced like 'p'.

'g' when it comes after the letter 'i' at the end of a word is pronounced like 'ch' in 'ich'.

63

Mini Dictionary

The words in this Mini Dictionary have been selected to fit into the key sentence patterns in the Study Section. The more familiar you are with the Study Section the more you will get out of the Mini Dictionary. Here are a few notes which will help you.

1 How to get the most out of the Mini Dictionary

1.1 *Abbreviations*

(adj)	adjective
(adv)	adverb
(n)	noun
(prep)	preposition
(vb)	verb
(s)	for words used in the singular in German although they are plural in English eg '*Hose*' (s) (trousers)
(pl)	for words which have no singular, eg '*Ferien*' (pl) (holidays) or which are usually used in the plural, eg '*Sachen*' (pl) (belongings)
(no pl)	for words which have no plural, eg '*Handgepäck*' (hand luggage)
(infml)	for colloquial expressions used in everyday or informal speech, eg '*das Hinterteil*' (infml) (bottom)
(tdmk)	for trademark names of products which are commonly used as ordinary words eg '*die Kornflakes*' (tdmk) (cornflakes)

1.2 *Plurals*

Plurals are indicated as follows:

(–)	Plural form is the same as the singular form
(–e)	Plural made by adding –e: *der Tag, die Tage* (day)
(–̈e)	Plural made by adding –e + Umlaut: *die Hand, die Hände* (hand)
(–er)	Plural made by adding –er: *das Kind, die Kinder* (child)
(–̈er)	Plural made by adding –er + Umlaut: *der Mann, die Männer* (man)
(–n)	Plural made by adding –n: *der Junge, die Jungen* (boy)
(–en)	Plural made by adding –en: *der Mensch, die Menschen* (person)
(–s)	Plural made by adding –s: *das Auto, die Autos* (car)
(–̈)	Plural made by adding Umlaut: *der Vater, die Väter* (father)

As many words in German are made up of two separate words, eg '*Flughafen*' (airport) is made up of '*Flug*' (flight) and '*Hafen*' (port), the part of the word which changes is written out in full eg '*Flughafen*' (*–häfen*).

NB It is only 'a', 'o' and 'u' which can take an Umlaut. It alters the pronunciation of the vowel. See pronunciation key on p62.

1.3 *Gender*

'The' – '*der*' (masculine), '*die*' (feminine) or '*das*' (neuter) is given before every noun eg '*der Zug*' (train), '*die Karte*' (ticket), '*das Telefon*' (telephone). If you want to say '*a* train' etc, substitute '*ein*' (masculine), '*eine*' (feminine) or '*ein*' (neuter).

1.4 *Substitutions*

Oblique lines / / show that the words within the obliques can be substituted by others eg '*ein Glas /Wein/*' (a glass of wine); '*ein Glas /Wasser/*' (a glass of water).

1.5 *Verbs*

The use of the past tense is beyond the scope of the Survival Kit. That is why the past form of verbs is not given. What you will find is the infinitive form which you can fit into various patterns you have learnt in the Study Section. Note that the infinitive always comes at the end of the sentence:

Könnten Sie das (mir) /schreiben/?	Could you /write/ this (for me)?
Ich möchte das /sehen/	I'd like to /see/ this

If the verb isn't in the infinitive, it always comes second:

Ich möchte nur ein paar Äpfel	I only want a few apples

Some verbs always need the German equivalent of 'myself' 'yourself' etc even if they don't in English:

Ich möchte /mich beschweren/	I'd like to /make a complaint/

The '*mich*' (myself) form is given in the Mini Dictionary because this will be the form which you will be most likely to need. But, for example, if you are talking to someone else and using '*Sie*', then you must change '*mich*' to '*sich*':

Möchten Sie /sich beschweren/?	Would you like to /make a complaint/?

For more information about these 'reflexive verbs' see the Mini Grammar (p288).

65

The first person singular form of some other verbs is given where their use is not immediately obvious. For example, some verbs are made up of two parts:

zurückkommen   return
Ich komme am Montag zurück   I return on Monday

Note that the second part of the verb always goes to the end of the sentence. For a full explanation of 'separable' verbs, see the Mini Grammar (p288).

2 A note on quantity

How to indicate quantity is fully covered in Section 7. There is no equivalent to 'some' and 'any' to indicate a quantity in a *general* way in German.

Ich möchte Kaffee, bitte (I'd like some coffee please)
Haben Sie Postkarten, bitte? (Have you got any postcards please?)

However, the Mini Dictionary will enable you to indicate very precise amounts. Thus if you look up 'matches' (*die Streichhölzer*) you will find 'box of matches' (*die Schachtel Streichhölzer*) beneath the main entry, thus enabling you to say:

Ich möchte Streichhölzer, bitte (I'd like some matches please)
Ich möchte eine Schachtel Streichhölzer, bitte (I'd like a box of matches please)

Quantity can also be indicated very precisely in terms of volume or weight eg 20 litres of petrol, a kilo of tomatoes, etc. See Equivalents p298.

Remember these six 'quantity words' and you will be able to ask for almost anything:

eine Flasche /Bier/   a bottle of /beer/
ein Glas /Milch/   a glass of /milk/
eine Schachtel /Zigaretten/   a packet of /cigarettes/
ein Stück /Kuchen/   a piece of /cake/
eine Scheibe /Schinken/   a slice of /ham/
eine Dose /Tomaten/   a tin of /tomatoes/

NB When the 'quantity word' itself is in the plural you don't have to worry about changing the noun unless it's feminine:

zwei Flaschen /Bier/   two bottles of /beer/

If the 'quantity word' is masculine or neuter, it stays the same:

zwei Glas /Wein/   two glasses of /wine/
zwei Stück /Kuchen/   two pieces of /cake/

A

about (=approximately)	ungefähr	ŭngəfeȳr
about (=concerning)	über	ühbər
above	oben	obən
abroad	im Ausland	im owslant
he's a.	er ist im A.	āyr ist im owslant
accept	annehmen	annāymən
	ich nehme an	ih nāymə an
accident	der Unfall (–fälle)	der unfal (–felə)
accommodation	die Unterkunft	dēē ŭntərkŭnft
accountant	der Bücherrevisor (–en)	der bühkhərrevēēzor (–ən)
ache	die Schmerzen (mpl)	dēē shmertsən
I've got backache	ich habe Rückenschmerzen	ih hābə rükənshmertsən
I've got earache	ich habe Ohrenschmerzen	ih hābə orənshmertsən
I've got stomachache	ich habe Magenschmerzen	ih hābə māgənshmertsən
across	über	ühbər
walk a. /the street/	ü. /die Straße/ gehen	ühbər /dēē shtrasə/ gāyən
actor	der Schauspieler	der showshpēēlər
actress	die Schauspielerin (–nen)	dēē showshpēēlərin (–ən)
adaptor plug	der Zwischenstecker (–)	der tsvishənshtekər
add	hinzufügen	hintsōōfügən
	ich füge hinzu	ih fügə hintsōō
address	die Adresse (–n)	dēē adresə (–n)
temporary a.	die zeitweilige A.	dēē tsītvīligə adresə
adjust	anpassen	anpasən
	ich passe / / an	ih pasə / / an
admission (=cost)	die Eintrittsgebühr (–en)	dēē īntritsgəbühr (–ən)
adult	der Erwachsene (–n)	der ervaksənə (–n)
adults only	nur für Erwachsene	nōōr führ ervaksənə
advance (a. of money)	die Vorausbezahlung (–en)	dēē forowsbətsālŭng (–ən)
in a.	im voraus	im forows
a. booking	die Reservierung (–en)	dēē rezervēērŭng (–ən)
advantage	der Vorteil (–e)	der fortīl (–ə)
advertise	annoncieren	anonsēērən

67

advertisement	die Anzeige (–n)	dēē **ant**sīgə (–n)
advice	der Rat (Ratschläge)	der rat (**ratsh**lēygə)
I'd like some a.	ich möchte Ihren R.	ih **mœh**tə **ēē**rən rat
advise a rest	Ruhe empfehlen	**rōō**ə empf**ā**ylən
	ich empfehle Ruhe	ih empf**ā**ylə **rōō**ə
aerial	die Antenne (–n)	dēē ant**e**nə (–n)
aeroplane	das Flugzeug (–e)	das **flōō**ktsoyk (–tsoygə)
by air	mit dem F.	mit d**ā**ym **flōō**ktsoyk
aerosol	die Sprühdose (–n)	dēē **shprüh**dozə (–n)
afraid		
be a. (of / /)	Angst haben (vor / /)	**angst** habən (for / /)
I'm a. of / /	ich habe Angst vor / /	ih **ha**bə **ang**st for / /
after	nach	n**ā**kh
afternoon	der Nachmittag (–e)	der **nākh**mitāk (–tagə)
this a.	heute n.	**hoy**tə **nākh**mitāk
tomorrow a.	morgen n.	**mor**gən **nākh**mitāk
yesterday a.	gestern n.	**ge**stərn **nākh**mitāk
aftershave lotion	das Rasierwasser (–)	das raz**ēē**rvasər
afterwards	danach	dan**ākh**
again	wieder	v**ēē**dər
against	gegen	**gāy**gən
age	das Alter (–)	das **al**tər
agenda	die Tagesordnung	dēē **tā**gəsordnŭng
agree	einverstanden sein	**īn**fershtandən zīn
a. to / /	mit / / e. s.	mit / / **īn**fershtandən zīn
	ich bin mit / / e.	ih bin mit / / **īn**fershtandən zīn
I a.	ich bin damit e.	ih bin damit **īn**fershtandən
ahead	voraus	for**ows**
air	die Luft ("-e)	dēē lŭft (**lŭf**tə)
a. pressure	der Luftdruck	der **lŭft**drŭk
by a.	mit dem Flugzeug	mit d**ā**ym **flōō**ktsoyk
some fresh a.	frische L.	**fri**shə lŭft
air conditioning	die Klimaanlage (–n)	dēē **klēē**maanlāgə (–n)
air letter	der Brief (–e) per Luftpost	der br**ēē**f (–ə) per **lŭft**post

airline	die Fluggesellschaft (–en)	dēē flo͞okgəzelshaft (–ən)
airmail	die Luftpost	dēē lŭftpɔst
by a.	per L.	per lŭftpɔst
airport	der Flughafen (–häfen)	der flo͞okhāfən (–hēyfən)
a. bus	der Flughafenbus (–se)	der flo͞okhāfənbŭs (–ə)
alarm clock	der Wecker (–)	der vekər
alcohol	der Alkohol	der alkɔhol
alcoholic (adj)	alkoholisch	alkɔholish
alive	lebend	lāybənt
he's a.	er lebt	āyr lāybt
all	alle	alə
all /the children/	all /die Kinder/	al /dēē kindər/
allergic	allergisch	alergish
I'm a. to /penicillin/	ich bin a. gegen /Penizillin/	ih bin alergish gāygən /penitsilēēn/
allow	erlauben	erlowbən
a. /smoking/	/das Rauchen/ e.	/das rowkhən/ erlowbən
	ich erlaube /das Rauchen/	ih erlowbə/ das rowkhən/
allowed	erlaubt	erlowbt
almost	fast	fast
alone	allein	alīn
alphabet	das Alphabet (–e)	das alfabāyt (–ə)
already	schon	shon
also	auch	owkh
alter (change)	ändern	endərn
alter (=clothes)	ändern	endərn
alternative (n)	die Alternative (–n)	dēē alternatēēvə (–n)
always	immer	imər
a.m	morgens	mɔrgəns
/4/ a.m.	/4 Uhr/ m.	/fēēr o͞or/mɔrgəns/
ambassador	der Botschafter (–)	der botshaftər
ambulance	der Krankenwagen (–)	der krangkənvāgən
amenities	die Vorzüge (pl)	dēē fortsühgə
among	unter	ŭntər
a. /my friends/	u. /meinen Freunden/	ŭntər/ mīnən froyndən/
amusement arcade	der Spielsalon (–s)	der shpēēlsalon (–s)

	masculine	feminine	neuter
the/a (subject)	der/ein	die/eine	das/ein
the/a (object)	den/einen	die/eine	das/ein
the (plural, subject/object)	die	die	die

amusing	amüsant	am**ü**z**ant**
anaemic	anämisch	an**ēy**mish
anaesthetic (n)	das Betäubungsmittel	das bətoyb**ŭ**ŋgsmitəl
anchor	der Anker (–)	der **ank**ər
angry	böse	b**ōē**zə
I'm a. with /him/	ich bin b. mit /ihm/	i**h** bin b**ōē**zə mit /**ēē**m/
animal	das Tier (–e)	das t**ēē**r (–ə)
ankle	das Fußgelenk (–e)	das f**oo**sgələŋgk (–ə)
a. socks	die Socken (pl)	d**ēē** zɔkən
anniversary	der Gedenktag (–e)	der gəde**ŋk**t**ā**k (–tagə)
wedding a.	der Hochzeitstag (–e)	der h**ɔ**khts**ī**tst**ā**k (–tagə)
announcement	die Ansage (–n)	d**ēē** **anz**āgə (–n)
make an a.	eine A. machen	**ī**nə **anz**āgə makhən
	ich mache eine A.	i**h** makhə **ī**nə **anz**āgə
annoying	ärgerlich	**erg**ərli**h**
annual	jährlich	**yēy**rli**h**
anorak	der Anorak (–s)	der **a**norak (–s)
another (= additional)	noch	no**kh**
a. /glass of wine/	n. /ein Glas Wein/	no**kh** /**ī**n gl**ā**s v**ī**n/
another (different)	ein anderer (m) eine andere (f) ein anderes (n)	**ī**n **and**ərər **ī**nə **and**ərə **ī**n **and**ərəs
answer (n)	die Antwort (–en)	d**ēē antv**ɔrt (–ən)
answer (vb)	antworten	**antv**ɔrtən
ant	die Ameise (–n)	d**ēē** am**ī**zə (–n)
antibiotic	das Antibiotikum (–biotika)	das antibiotik**ŭ**m (antibiotika)
antique (n)	die Antiquität (–en)	d**ēē** antikvit**ēy**t (–ən)
antique shop	die Antiquitätenhandlung (–en)	d**ēē** antikvit**ēy**tənhandl**ŭ**ŋg (–ən)
antiseptic	antiseptisch	antize**pt**ish
a. cream	die antiseptische Salbe	d**ēē** antize**pt**ishə zalbə
tube of a. (cream)	eine Tube (–n) antiseptische Salbe	**ī**nə t**oo**bə antize**pt**ishə zalbə
aperitif	der Aperitif (–s)	der **a**perit**ēē**f (–s)
apologise	mich entschuldigen	mi**h** ents**h**ŭldigən
	ich entschuldige mich	i**h** ents**h**ŭldigə mi**h**
apology	die Entschuldigung (–en)	d**ēē** ents**h**ŭldig**ŭ**ŋg (–ən)

appendicitis	die Blinddarm-entzündung	dēē **blint**därm-entsündŭng
apple	der Apfel (¨)	der **apf**əl (**epf**əl)
a. juice	der Apfelsaft	der **apf**əlzaft (–zeftə)
application form	das Antragsformular (–e)	das **an**traksfərmoolār (–ə)
apply for /petrol coupons/	/Benzingutscheine/ bestellen	/bents**ēē**ngootshīnə/ bəshtelən
	ich bestelle /Benzingutscheine/	ih bəshtelə /bents**ēē**ngootshīnə/
a. for /a job/	mich um /eine Stelle/ bewerben	mih ŭm /īnə **shtel**ə/ bəverbən
	ich bewerbe mich bei /ihm/ um /eine Stelle/	ih bəverbə mih bī /**ēē**m/ ŭm /īnə **shtel**ə/
appointment	der Termin	der ter**mēē**n
make an a.	einen T. vereinbaren	**ī**nən ter**mēē**n fer**ī**nbārən
	ich vereinbare einen T.	ih fer**ī**nbārə **ī**nən ter**mēē**n
I've got an a.	ich bin bestellt	ih bin bəshtelt
apricot	die Aprikose (–n)	dēē aprikozə (–n)
April	der April	der **a**pril
aqualung	das Tauchgerät (–e)	das **towkh**gərēyt (–ə)
architect	der Architekt (–en)	der ar**h**itekt (–ən)
area (of town or country)	die Gegend (–en)	dēē **gāy**gənt (**gāy**gəndən)
argue	streiten	**shtrī**tən
argument	der Streit (no pl)	der shtrīt
arm	der Arm (–e)	der arm (–ə)
army	das Heer (–e)	das hāyr (–ə)
around	um	ŭm
a. /the table/	um /den Tisch/	ŭm /dāyn tish/
arrange	vereinbaren	fer**ī**nbārən
a. /a meeting/	/ein Treffen/ v.	/īn trefən/ fer**ī**nbārən
	ich vereinbare /ein Treffen/	ih fer**ī**nbarə /īn trefən/
arrangement	die Vereinbarung (–en)	dēē fer**ī**nbārŭng (–ən)
arrival	die Ankunft	dēē **an**kŭnft
time of a.	die Ankunftszeit (–en)	dēē **an**kŭnftstsīt (–ən)
arrive on /Monday/	am /Montag/ ankommen	am /**mon**tāk/ **an**kəmən
	ich komme am /Montag/ an	ih **kə**mə am /**mon**tāk/ **an**

71

a. at /4.30/ p.m.	um /16.30 Uhr/ ankommen	ŭm/zehtsayn oor drīsih/ankɔmən
a. in /July/	im /Juli/ a.	im /yooli/ ankɔmən
arrow	der Pfeil (–e)	der pfīl (–ə)
art gallery	die Kunstgalerie (–n)	dee kŭnstgalərēe (–ən)
artichoke	die Artischocke (–n)	dee artishɔkə (–n)
artificial	künstlich	kŭnstlih
artificial respiration	die künstliche Beatmung	dee kŭnstlihə bəātmŭng
artist	der Künstler (–) die Künstlerin (–nen)	der kŭnstlər/dee kŭnstlərin (–ən)
ashamed		
be a. (of / /)	mich schämen (wegen / /) ich schäme mich (wegen /meines/ Freundes/	mih sheymən (vāygən / /) ih sheymə mih (vāygən /mīnəs/ froyndəs/
ashtray	der Aschenbecher (–)	der ashənbehər
ask	fragen	frāgən
please a. how much it is	bitte fragen Sie, was es kostet	bitə frāgən zee vas es kɔstət
ask (a favour)	bitten	bitən
asleep		
he's a.	er schläft	ayr shleyft
asparagus	der Spargel (–)	der shpargəl
a. tips	die Spargelköpfe (mpl)	dee shpargəlkœpfə
aspirin	das Aspirin	das aspireen
a bottle of aspirins	eine Flasche (–n) A.	īnə flashə (–n) aspireen
a packet of aspirins	eine Schachtel (–n) A.	īnə shakhtəl (–n) aspireen
assistant		
shop a.	der Verkäufer (–) die Verkäuferin (–nen)	der ferkoyfər/dee ferkoyfərin (–ən)
asthma	das Asthma	das astma
at	um/in/an	ŭm/in/an
a. /7.30/	um /7.30/	ŭm /zeebə oor drīsih/
a. /the hotel/	im /Hotel/	im /hotel/
a. /the corner/	an /der Ecke/	an /der ekə/
atlas	der Atlas (–se)	der atlas (–ə)

Remember: [kh] as in acht (eight) [h] as in hungrig (hungry)
[œ] as in schön (beautiful) [üh] as in Tür (door)

attack (n)	der Angriff (–e)	der angrif (–ə)
an a. of /coughing/	ein /Husten/anfall	īn /hōōstən/anfal
attend	besuchen	bəzōōkhən
a. a /Catholic/ service	einen /katholischen/ Gottesdienst b.	īnən /katolishən/ gotəsdēēnst bəzōōkhən
	ich besuche einen /katholischen/ Gottesdienst	ih bəzōōkhə īnən /katolishən/ gotəsdēēnst
attendant	der Angestellte (–n)	der angəshteltə (–n)
attractive	hübsch	hüpsh
aubergine	die Aubergine (–n)	dēē obərjēēnə (–n)
auction (n)	die Versteigerung (–en)	dēē fershtīgərŭng (–ən)
auction (vb)	versteigern	fershtīgərn
audience	das Publikum	das pōōblikŭm
August	der August	der owgŭst
aunt	die Tante (–n)	dēē tantə (–n)
au pair	das Au-pair-Mädchen	das o-pāyrmēythən
author	der Autor (–en)	der owtor (owtorən)
authorities	die Behörden (fpl)	dēē bəhœrdən
automatic	automatisch	owtomātish
autumn	der Herbst	der herpst
in a.	im H.	im herpst
available	erhältlich	erheltlih
avalanche	die Lawine (–n)	dēē lavēēnə (–n)
average (n)	der Durchschnitt (–e)	der dŭrhshnit (–ə)
avocado	die Avocato (–s)	dēē avokāto (–z)
avoid	vermeiden	fermīdən
awake	wach	vakh
he's a.	er ist w.	er ist vakh
away	fort	fort
he's a.	er ist f.	āyr ist fort
away (absent)	abwesend	apvāyzənt
awful (of people)	schrecklich	shreklih
awful (of things)	schrecklich	shreklih

B

baby	das Baby (–s)	das bāybēē (–s)
baby-sit	Kinder hüten	kindər hühtən
baby-sitter	der Babysitter (–) die Babysitterin (–nen)	der bāybizitər/dēē bāybizitərin (–ən)

back	der Rücken (–)	der rükən
backache	die Rückenschmerzen (mpl)	dee rükənshmertsən
back door	die Hintertür (–en)	dee hintərtühr (–ən)
backwards	rückwärts	rükverts
bacon	der Schinken	der shingkən
bad	schlecht	shleht
badly	schlecht	shleht
b. hurt	schwer verletzt	shvayr ferletst
badminton	das Federballspiel	das faydərbalshpeel
play a game of b.	Federball spielen	faydərbal shpeelən
	ich spiele F.	ih shpeelə faydərbal
bag	die Tasche (–n)	dee tashə (–n)
carrier b.	die Tragtasche (–n)	dee trägtashə (–n)
paper b.	die Papiertüte (–n)	dee papeertühtə (–n)
plastic b.	der Plastikbeutel (–)	der plasteekboytəl
string b.	das Netz (–e)	das nets (–ə)
bake	backen	bakən
baker's	der Bäcker	der bekər
balcony	der Balkon (–s)	der balkon (–s)
bald		
I'm b.	ich habe eine Glatze	ih häbə īnə glatsə
ball	der Ball (–̈e)	der bal (belə)
b. of /string/	die Rolle /Bindfaden/	dee rolə /bintfädən/
beach b.	der Strandball (–bälle)	der shtrantbal (–belə)
footb.	der Fußball (–bälle)	der foosbal (–belə)
golf b.	der Golfball (–bälle)	der golfbal (–belə)
squash b.	der Squashball (–bälle)	der skvashbal (–belə)
table tennis b.	der Tischtennisball (–bälle)	der tishtenisbal (–belə)
tennis b.	der Tennisball (–bälle)	der tenisbal (belə)
ball (=dance)	der Ball (–̈e)	der bal (belə)
ballet	das Ballett (–e)	das balet (–ə)
b. dancer	der Ballettänzer (–) die Ballettänzerin (–nen)	der balettentsər/dee balettentsərin (–ən)

74

balloon	der Ballon (–e)	der balon (–ə)
ballpoint pen	der Kugelschreiber (–)	der kōōgəlshrībər
ballroom	der Balsaal (–säle)	der balzāl (–zelə)
banana	die Banane (–n)	dēē banānə (–n)
band (=orchestra)	die Band (–s)	dēē bant (–s)
bandage (n)	der Verband (¨e)	der ferbant (–bendə)
bandage (vb)	verbinden	ferbindən
bank	die Bank (–en)	dēē bangk (–ən)
bank account	das Bankkonto (–konten)	das bangkkonto (–kontən)
current account	das Girokonto (–konten)	das jēērokonto (–kontən)
bar (=for drinks)	die Bar (–s)	dēē bār (–s)
barbecue	der Grill (–s)	der gril (–s)
bare (=naked)	nackt	nakt
bare (of room etc)	kahl	kāl
bargain (n)		
it's a b.	es ist spottbillig	es ist shpotbilih
bargain (vb)	handeln	handəln
b. with /him/	mit /ihm/ h.	mit /ēēm/ handəln
	ich handle mit /ihm/	ih handlə mit /ēēm/
barrel	das Faß (Fässer)	das fas (fesər)
b. of / /	F. / /	fas / /
barrier	die Sperre (–n)	dēē shperə (–n)
basement	das Souterrain (–s)	das zōōterē
basket	der Korb (¨e)	der korp (kœrbə)
a b. of / /	ein K. / /	īn korp / /
shopping b.	der Einkaufskorb (–körbe)	der īnkowfskorp (–kœrbə)
waste paper b.	der Papierkorb (–körbe)	der papēērkorp (–kœrbə)
basketball (=game)	der Basketball (no pl)	das baskətbal
play b.b.	B. spielen	baskətbal shpēēlən
	ich spiele B.	ih shpēēlə baskətbal
bat (cricket)	der Schläger (–)	der shlāygər
bath	das Bad (¨er)	das bāt (bāydər)
have a b.	mich baden	mih bādən
	ich bade mich	ih bādə mih
Turkish b.	das türkische Bad	das türkishə bad
bathe (eyes etc)	baden	bādən

	masculine	feminine	neuter
the/a (subject)	der/ein	die/eine	das/ein
the/a (object)	den/einen	die/eine	das/ein
the (plural, subject/object)	die	die	die

bathe (in the sea etc)	baden	**bā**dən
bathing cap	die Bademütze (–n)	dee **bā**dəmütsə (–n)
bathing costume (one piece)	der Badeanzug (–züge)	der **bā**dəantsook (–tsügə)
bathing trunks	die Badehose (s)	dee **bā**dəhozə
bath mat	die Badematte (–n)	dee **bā**dəmatə (–n)
bathroom	das Badezimmer (–)	das **bā**dətsimər
bath salts	das Badesalz	das **bā**dəzalts
battery (car)	die Batterie (–n)	dee batə**ree** (–ən)
battery (radio)	die Batterie (–n)	dee batə**ree** (–ən)
bay (=part of sea)	die Bucht (–en)	dee bükht (–ən)
be	sein	zīn
beach	der Strand (–̈e)	der shtrant (**shtrendə**)
b. hut	die Strandhütte (–n)	dee **shtrant**hütə (–n)
b. umbrella	der Sonnenschirm (–e)	der **zɔnən**shirm (–ə)
beads	die Glasperlen (fpl)	dee **glās**perlən
string of b.	die Perlenkette (–n)	dee **perlən**ketə (–n)
beans	die Bohnen (fpl)	dee bonən
broad b.	die Brechbohnen (fpl)	dee **brekh**bonən
french b.	die grünen Bohnen (fpl)	dee **grühnən** bonən
beautiful	schön	shœn
beauty salon	der Kosmetiksalon	der kɔs**māy**tikzalon
because	weil	vīl
b. of /the weather/	wegen /des Wetters/	**vāy**gən /des vetərs/
bed	das Bett (–en)	das bet (–ən)
b. and beakfast	Übernachtung und Frühstück	ühbər**nakh**tüng ünt **früh**shtük
double b.	das Doppelbett (–en)	das **dɔpəl**bet (–ən)
go to b.	zu B. gehen	tsoo bet **gāy**ən
	ich gehe zu B.	ih **gāy**ə tsoo **bet**
in b.	im B.	im bet
make the b.	das B. machen	das bet **makh**ən
	ich mache das B.	ih **makh**ə das bet
single b.	das Einzelbett (–en)	das **īntsəl**bet (–ən)
bed clothes	die Bettlaken (npl)	dee **bet**lākən
bedpan	der Nachttopf (–töpfe)	der **nakht**tɔpf (–tœpfə)
bedroom	das Schlafzimmer (–)	das **shlāf**tsimər

bee	die Biene (–n)	dēē bēēnə (–n)
b. sting	der Bienenstich (–e)	der bēēnənshtih (–ə)
beef	das Rindfleisch	das rintflīsh
b. sandwich	ein mit R. belegtes Brot	īn mit rintflīsh bəlayhtəs brot
beer	das Bier	das bēer
a b.	ein B.	īn bēer
a bottle of b.	eine Flasche (–n) B.	īnə flashə (–n) bēer
a can of b.	eine Dose (–n) B.	īnə dozə (–n) bēer
a pint of b.	ein Halbes	īn halbəs
beetroot	die rote (–n) Rübe (–n)	dēē rotə (–n) rübə (–n)
before	bevor	bəfor
behalf		
on b. of / /	für / /	führ / /
behaviour	das Benehmen	das bənāymən
behind (prep)	hinter	hintər
b. /the house/	h. /dem Haus/	hintər /daym hows/
beige	beige	bāyjə
believe	glauben	glowbən
b. /me/	/mir/ g.	/mēer/ glowbən
I don't b. it	das glaube ich nicht	das glowbə ih niht
bell (large)	die Glocke (–n)	dēē glɔkə (–n)
bell (small)	die Klingel (–)	dēē kliṉgəl
belongings	die Sachen (pl)	dēē zakhən
below	unter	üntər
b. /the chair/	u. /dem Stuhl/	üntər /daym shtōōl/
belt	der Gürtel (–)	der gürtəl
bend (in a road)	die Kurve (–n)	dēē kürvə (–n)
bend (vb)	biegen	bēēgən
bent (adj)	krumm	krüm
beret	die Mütze (–n)	dēē mütsə (–n)
berth	das Bett (–en)	das bet (–ən)
/four/-b. cabin	die /Vier/bett-kabine (–n)	dēē /fēer/bet-kabēēnə (–n)
lower b.	das untere B. (–en)	das üntərə bet (–ən)
upper b.	das obere B. (–en)	das obərə bet (–ən)
beside	neben	nāybən
b. /her/	n. /ihr/	nāybən /ēer/
best	best	best
the b. /hotel/	das beste /Hotel/	das bestə /hotel/
bet (n)	die Wette	dēē vetə

bet (vb)	wetten	vetən
better	besser	besər
he's b. (health)	es geht ihm b.	es gāyt eem besər
it's b. (things)	es ist b.	es ist besər
betting shop	die Wettannahme-stelle (–n)	dee vetannāməshtelə (–n)
between /London/ and /Berlin/	zwischen /London/ und /Berlin/	tsvishən /londn/ ŭnt /berleen/
beyond	jenseits	yāynzīts
b. /the station/	j. /des Bahnhofs/	yāynzīts /des bānhofs/
bib	das Lätzchen (–)	das lēythən
bible	die Bibel (–n)	dee beebəl (–n)
bicycle/bike	das Rad (–̈er)	das rāt (rēydər)
on a b.	auf einem R.	owf īnəm rāt
big	groß	gros
bikini	der Bikini (–s)	der bikeeni (–s)
bill (for food, hotel, etc)	die Rechnung (–en)	dee rehnŭng (–ən)
billiards	das Billard (s)	das bilyart
play a game of b.	B. spielen	bilyart shpeelən
	ich spiele B.	ih shpeelə bilyart
bingo	das Lotto	das lotto
binoculars	das Feldstecher (s)	das feltshtehər
a pair of b.	ein F.	īn feltshtehər
bird	der Vogel (–̈)	der fogəl (fœgəl)
biro (tdmk)	der Kugelschreiber (–)	der koogəlshrībər
birth certificate	die Geburtsurkunde (–n)	dee gəboortsoorkŭndə (–n)
date of b.	das Geburtsdatum (–daten)	das gəboortsdātŭm (–dātən)
place of b.	der Geburtsort	der gəboortsort
birthday	der Geburtstag (–e)	der gəboortstāk (–tāgə)
biscuit	der Keks (–e)	der kāyks (–ə)
bite (=insect b.)	der Biß (Bisse)	der bis (–ə)
bitter (adj)	bitter	bitər
black	schwarz	shvarts
b. coffee	schwarzer Kaffee	shvartsər kafāy
blackberry	die Brombeeren (fpl)	dee brombāyrən
blackcurrant	die schwarzen Johannisbeeren (fpl)	dee shvartsən yohanisbāyrən
blanket	die Decke (–n)	dee dekə (–n)

Remember: [kh] as in acht (eight) [h] as in hungrig (hungry)
[œ] as in schön (beautiful) [üh] as in Tür (door)

bleach (n) (hair)	die Blondierung	dee blondeerüng
bleach (n) (laundry)	die Bleiche	dee blīhə
bleach (vb) (hair)	blondieren	blondeerən
bleach (vb) (laundry)	bleichen	blīhən
bleed	bluten	blootən
my nose is bleeding	meine Nase blutet	mīnə nāzə blootət
stop the bleeding	die Blutung stoppen	dee blootüng shtopən
blind (adj)	blind	blint
blinds (=Venetian-type)	die Jalousien (fpl)	dee jalüzeeən
blister	die Blase (–n)	dee blāzə (–n)
block of flats	der Wohnblock (–blöcke)	der vonblok (–blœkə)
blocked (eg drain)	verstopft	fershtopft
blonde	blond	blont
blood	das Blut	das bloot
b. group	die Blutgruppe (–n)	dee blootgrüpə (–n)
b. pressure	der Blutdruck	der blootdrük
blotting paper	das Löschpapier	das lœshpapeer
blouse	die Bluse (–n)	dee bloozə (–n)
blue	blau	blow
blunt (eg knife)	stumpf	shtümpf
board (n) (=cost of meals)	die Pension	dee pentsyon
full b.	Vollpension	folpentsyon
half b.	Halbpension	halppentsyon
board (vb) (eg a plane)	an Bord gehen	an bort gāyən
	ich gehe a. B.	ih gāyə an bort
boarding card	die Bordkarte (–n)	dee bortkartə (–n)
boat	das Boot (–e)	das bot (–ə)
by b.	mit dem B.	mit dāym bot
b. train	die Eisenbahnfähre (–n)	dee īzənbānfeyrə (–n)
lifeb.	das Rettungsboot (–e)	das retüngsbot (–ə)
motor-b.	das Motorboot (–e)	das motorbot (–ə)
body	der Körper (–)	der kœrpər
boil (vb)	kochen	kokhən
hardboiled egg	ein hartgekochtes Ei (–er)	īn hartgəkokhtəs ī (–ər)
softboiled egg	ein weichgekochtes Ei (–er)	īn vīhgəkokhtəs ī (–ər)
bomb	die Bombe (–n)	dee bombə (–n)
bone	der Knochen (–)	der knokhən

book	das Buch (¨-er)	das **bōokh** (**bühkh**ər)
guide b.	der Reiseführer (–)	der **rī**zəführər
paperback	das Taschenbuch (¨-er)	das **ta**shənbōokh (–**bühkh**ər)
booking	die Reservierung (–en)	dēē rezervēērűng (–ən)
advance b.	die Vorbestellung (–en)	dēē fɔrbəshtelűng (–ən)
booking office	die Kasse (–n)	dēē **ka**sə (–n)
bookmaker	der Buchmacher (–)	der **bōokh**makhər
bookshop	die Buchhandlung (–en)	dēē **bōokh**handlűng (–ən)
boots	die Stiefel (mpl)	dēē **shtēē**fəl
a pair of b.	ein Paar S.	īn pār **shtēē**fəl
rubber b.	die Gummistiefel (mpl)	dēē gŭmi**shtēē**fəl
ski-b.	die Skistiefel (mpl)	dēē **shēē**shtēēfəl
border (=frontier)	die Grenze (–n)	dēē **grent**sə (–n)
bored	gelangweilt	gəlang**vī**lt
I'm b.	ich langweile mich	ih **lang**vīlə mih
borrow /a pen/	/einen Füller/ borgen	/īnən fülər/ bɔrgən
both	beide	**bī**də
b. /sides/	b. /Seiten/	**bī**də /**zī**tən/
bother (vb)	stören	**shtœr**ən
don't b.	machen Sie sich keine Mühe	**makh**ən zēē zih **kī**nə mühə
I'm sorry to b. you	es tut mir leid, Sie zu s.	es tōot mēēr līt zēē tsōō **shtœr**ən
bottle	die Flasche (–n)	dēē **fla**shə (–n)
a b. of / /	eine F. / /	**ī**nə flashə / /
b.-opener	der Flaschenöffner (–)	der **fla**shənœfnər
feeding b.	die Babyflasche (–n)	dēē **bāy**biflashə (–n)
bottom (part of body)	das Hinterteil (infml)	das **hint**ərtīl
the b. of / /	die Unterseite von / /	dēē **ünt**ərzītə fɔn / /
bowl	die Schüssel (–n)	dēē **shüs**əl (–n)
bowling (=ten pin bowling)	das Kegeln	das **kāy**gəln
b. alley	die Kegelbahn (–en)	dēē **kāy**gəlbān (–ən)
bows (of ship)	der Bug (s)	der **bōok**
bow tie	die Fliege (–n)	dēē **flēē**gə (–n)
box	die Schachtel (–n)	dēē **shakht**əl (–n)
a b. of / /	eine S. / /	**ī**nə shakhtəl / /
boxer	der Boxer (–)	der **bɔks**ər

boxing	das Boxen	das bɔksən
b. match	der Boxkampf (–kämpfe)	der bɔkskampf (–kempfə)
box office	die Kasse (–n)	dee kasə (–n)
boy	der Junge (–n)	der yūŋə (–n)
boyfriend	der Freund (–e)	der froynt (froyndə)
bra	der Büstenhalter (–)	der büstənhaltər
bracelet	der Armreif (–e)	der armrīf (–ə)
silver b.	der Silberarmreif	der silbərarmrīf
braces	die Hosenträger (pl)	dee hozəntreÿgər
a pair of b.	ein Paar H.	īn pār hozəntreÿgər
branch (of company)	die Filiale (–n)	dee filyālə (–n)
brand (= of make)	die Marke (–n)	dee markə (–n)
b. name	das Warenzeichen (–)	das vārəntsīhən
brandy	der Kognak	der kɔnyak
a bottle of b.	eine Flasche (–n) K.	īnə flashə (–n) kɔnyak
a b.	ein K.	īn kɔnyak
bread	das Brot (–e)	das brot (–ə)
a loaf of b.	ein Laib (–e) B.	īn līp (lībə) brot
a slice of b.	eine Scheibe (–n) B.	īnə shībə (–n) brot
b. and butter	das Butterbrot	das bütərbrot
brown b.	das Schwarzbrot	das shvartsbrot
b. roll	das Brötchen (–)	das brœthən
sliced b.	das Scheibenbrot	das shībənbrot
white b.	das Weißbrot	das vīsbrot
break (vb)	brechen	**brekh**ən
breakfast	das Frühstück	das **frühshtük**
bed and b.	Übernachtung und F.	ühbər**nakh**tūng ünt **frühshtük**
b. for /2/	F. für /2/	**frühshtük führ /tsvī/**
b. in my room	F. auf meinem Zimmer	**frühshtük** owf mīnəm tsimər
continental b.	das Kaffeefrühstück	das kafaÿ**frühshtük**
English b.	das englische F.	das eŋglishə **frühshtük**
have b.	frühstücken	**frühshtük**ən
serve b.	das F. servieren	das **frühshtük** zervēērən

	masculine	feminine	neuter
the/a (subject)	der/ein	die/eine	das/ein
the/a (object)	den/einen	die/eine	das/ein
the (plural, subject/object)	die	die	die

breast	die Brust (¨-e)	dee brüst (brüstə)
breast-feed	stillen	**shtil**ən
breath	der Atem	der **āt**em
out of b.	außer A.	owsər **āt**əm
breathe	atmen	**āt**mən
bride	die Braut (¨-e)	dee browt (**broyt**ə)
bridegroom	der Bräutigam (–e)	der **broyt**igam (–ə)
bridge	die Brücke (–n)	dee **brük**ə (–n)
toll b.	die Zollbrücke (–n)	dee **tsɔl**brükə (–n)
bridge (=card game)	das Bridge	das britsh
a game of b.	eine Runde B.	īnə **rŭnd**ə britsh
bridle	der Zügel	der **tsüh**gəl
briefcase	die Aktentasche (–n)	dee **akt**əntashə (–n)
bring	bringen	**bring**ən
broadcast (n)	die Sendung (–en)	dee **zend**ŭng (–ən)
broadcast (vb)	senden	**zend**ən
broccoli	die Brokkoli (pl)	dee **brɔk**oli
brochure	die Broschüre (–n)	dee brɔ**shüh**rə (–n)
broken	kaputt	ka**pŭt**
brooch	die Brosche (–n)	dee **brɔsh**ə (–n)
cameo b.	die Kamee (–n)	dee ka**māy** (–ən)
silver b.	die Silberbrosche (–n)	dee **zilb**ərbrɔshə (–n)
brother	der Bruder (¨)	der **brōō**dər (**brüh**dər)
brother-in-law	der Schwager (¨)	der **shvā**gər (**shvēy**gər)
brown	braun	brown
bruise (n)	die Quetschung (–en)	dee **kvets**hŭng (–ən)
bruised	wund	vŭnt
brush	die Bürste (–n)	dee **bürst**ə (–n)
clothes b.	die Kleiderbürste (–n)	dee **klī**dərbürstə (–n)
hair-b.	die Haarbürste	dee **hār**bürstə (–n)
nail-b.	die Nagelbürste (–n)	dee **nāg**əlbürstə (–n)
paint-b.	der Pinsel (–n)	der **pinz**əl (–n)
shaving b.	der Rasierpinsel (–n)	der ra**zeer**pinzəl (–)
shoe-b.	die Schuhbürste (–n)	dee **shōō**bürstə (–n)
tooth-b.	die Zahnbürste (–n)	dee **tsān**bürstə (–n)
bucket	der Eimer (–)	der **īm**ər
b. and spade	ein E. und Schaufel	īn **īm**ər ŭnt **show**fəl
buckle	die Schnalle (–n)	dee **shnal**ə (–n)
Buddhist	der Buddhist (–en)	der **bŭd**ist (–ən)
buffet car	der Buffetwagen	der bü**faÿ**vāgən

builder	der Bauunternehmer (–)	der **bow**ŭntərn**ay**mər
building	das Gebäude (–)	das gə**boyd**ə
public b.	das öffentliche G.	das **œf**əntlihə gə**boyd**ə
bulb (=light b.)	die Glühbirne (–n)	dēē **glüh**birnə (–n)
40/60/100/200	40/60/100/200	f**ēē**rtsih/**zeh**tsih/ **hŭnd**ərt/**tsv**ī**hŭnd**ərt/ vat
watt	Watt	
bun (bread)	das Brötchen (–)	das **brœth**ən
bun (hair)	der Knoten (–)	der **knot**ən
in a b. (hair)	in einem K.	in **ī**nəm **knot**ən
bunch	der Strauß (–̈e)	der shtrows (–**shtroys**ə)
a b. of /flowers/	ein /Blumen/strauß (–̈e)	īn /**blüm**ən/shtrows (–**shtroys**ə)
bungalow	der Bungalow (–s)	der **bŭng**alo (–z)
bunk bed	das Etagenbett (–en)	das et**āj**ənbet (–ən)
buoy	die Boje (–n)	dēē **boy**ə (–n)
burglary	der Einbruch (–̈e)	der **ī**nbrŭkh (–brükhə)
burn (n)	der Brand (–̈e)	der brant (**brend**ə)
burn (vb)	brennen	**bren**ən
burnt	verbrannt	fer**brant**
burst (adj)	geplatzt	gə**platst**
a b. pipe	ein geplatztes Rohr	īn gə**platst**əs ror
bury	begraben	bə**grāb**ən
bus	der Bus (Busse)	der bŭs (–ə)
by b.	mit dem B.	mit d**āy**m bŭs
b. stop	die Bushaltestelle (–n)	dēē **bŭs**haltəshtelə (–n)
the b. for / /	der B. nach / /	der bŭs nākh / /
bus driver	der Autobusfahrer (–)	der **ow**tobŭsfārər
businessman	der Geschäftsmann (Geschäftsleute)	der gə**sheft**sman (gə**sheft**sloytə)
busy	fleißig	**flī**sih
butane	das Butangas	das bŭt**āng**ās
butcher's	der Fleischer (–) (der Metzger (–))	der **flīsh**gər (der **metsg**ər)
butter	die Butter	dēē **bŭt**ər
butterfly	der Schmetterling (–e)	der **shmet**erlin̄g (–ə)
button	der Knopf (–̈e)	der knɔpf (**knœpf**ə)
buy /an umbrella/	/einen Regenschirm/ kaufen	/**ī**nən **rāy**gənshirm/ kowfən
bypass (n)	die Umgehungsstraße (–n)	dēē ŭmg**āyŭng**s- shtrāsə (–n)

cabbage	der Kohl (Kohlköpfe)	der kol (**kolkœpfə**)
cabin	die Kabine (–n)	dēē kab**ēē**nə (–n)
c. cruiser	das Kabinenboot (–e)	das kab**ēē**nənbot (–ə)
/four/ berth c.	die /Vier/bett-kabine (–n)	dēē /**fēēr**/betkab**ēē**nə (–n)
cable (n)	das Kabel (–)	das **kā**bəl
cable car	die Drahtseilbahn (–en)	dēē **drāt**zīlbān (–ən)
café	das Café (–s)	das kaf**āy** (–z)
caffeine	das Koffein	das kɔfe**ēēn**
cake	der Kuchen (–)	der **kōō**khən
a piece of c.	ein Stück (–) K.	īn shtük **kōō**khən
cake shop	die Konditorei (–en)	dēē kɔnditor**ī** (–ən)
calculate /the cost/	/die Kosten/ ausrechnen	/dēē kɔstən/ **ows**rehnən
	ich rechne /die Kosten/ aus	ih rehnə /dēē kɔstən/ ows
calculator	der Taschenrechner (–)	der **tash**ənrehnər
calendar	der Kalender (–)	der kal**end**ər
call (n) (telephone c.)	der Anruf (–e)/das Telefongspräch (–e)	der **an**rōōf (–ə)/das telefong**esh**preh (–ə)
alarm c.	der Notruf (–e)	der **not**rōōf (–ə)
c. box	die Telefonzelle (–n)	dēē telefon**tsel**ə (–n)
early morning c.	ein A. früh am Morgen	īn **an**rōōf früh am mɔrgən
international c.	ein internationales Telefongespräch (–e)	īn internatsyon**āl**əs telefong**esh**preh (–ə)
local c.	ein Ortsgespräch (–e)	īn **ɔrts**gəshpreh (–ə)
long distance c.	ein Ferngespräch (–e)	īn **ferng**əshpreh (–ə)
make a c.	anrufen	**an**rōōfən
	ich rufe an	ih **rōōf**ə an
personal c.	ein persönlicher A. (–e)	īn perz**œn**lihər **an**rōōf (–ə)

Remember:[kh] as in acht (eight) [h] as in hungrig (hungry)
[œ] as in schön (beautiful) [üh] as in Tür (door)

transferred charge c.	ein R-Gespräch (–e)	īn **āyr**-geshpreh (–ə)
call (vb) (=telephone)	anrufen	**an**roofən
c. again later	zurückrufen ich rufe zurück	tsŭrük**roo**fən ih **roo**fə tsŭrük
c. /the police/	/die Polizei/ a.	/dee polit**sī**/ **an**roofən
	ich rufe /die Polizei/ an	ih **roo**fə /dee polit**sī**/ an
call on / / (=visit)	/ / besuchen	/ / bə**zoo**khən
calm (of sea)	ruhig	**roo**ih
calor gas	das Campinggas	das **kamp**inggās
calories	die Kalorien (fpl)	dee kalor**ee**ən
cameo	die Kamee (–n)	dee kam**āy** (–ən)
camera	der Fotoapparat (–e)	der **fo**toaparat (–ə)
cine c.	die Filmkamera (–s)	dee **film**kamera (–s)
35 mm c.	35 Millimeterkamera (–s)	fünfunt**drī**sih mili**māy**tərkamera
camera shop	das Fotogeschäft (–e)	das **fo**togəsheft (–ə)
camp (n)	das Zeltlager (–)	das **tselt**lāgər
holiday c.	das Ferienlager (–)	das **fāy**riənlāgər
camp bed	das Feldbett (–en)	das **felt**bet (–ən)
campfire	das Lagerfeuer (–)	das **lā**gərfoyər
camping	zelten	**tselt**ən
go c.	z. gehen ich gehe z.	**tselt**ən **gāy**ən ih **gāy**ə **tselt**ən
campsite	der Campingplatz (–plätze)	der **kamp**ingplats (–pletsə)
can (n)	die Dose (–n)	dee **doz**ə (–n)
a c. of /beer/	eine D. (–n) /Bier/	īnə **doz**ə (–n) /beer/
can (vb)	können	**kœn**ən
canal	der Kanal (Kanäle)	der kan**āl** (kaneylə)
cancel /my flight/	/meinen Flug/ absagen ich sage /meinen Flug/ ab	/mīnən **flook**/ **ap**zāgən ih **zā**gə /mīnən **flook**/ ap
cancellation	die Absage (–n)	dee **ap**zāgə (–n)
make a c.	eine A. machen ich mache eine A.	īnə **ap**zāgə makhən ih **makh**ə īnə **ap**zagə
cancelled	abgesagt	**ap**gəzaht
candle	die Kerze (–n)	dee **kerts**ə (–n)
canoe (n)	das Kanu (–s)	das kan**oo** (–s)
canoeing	das Paddeln	das **pad**əln
go c.	paddeln gehen	**pad**əln **gāy**ən

	ich gehe p.	ih gāyə padəln
canvas (=material)	der Kanevas	der kanevas
c. bag	die Leinentasche (–n)	dee līnəntashə (–n)
cap (= hat)	die Mütze (–n)	dee mütsə (–n)
shower c.	die Bademütze (–n)	dee bādəmütsə (–n)
swimming c.	die Bademütze (–n)	dee badəmütsə (–n)
cap (n) (for tooth)	die Zahnkrone (–n)	dee tsānkronə (–n)
cap (vb) (tooth)	eine Zahnkrone bekommen	īnə tsānkronə bəkomən
	ich bekomme eine Z.	ih bəkomə īnə tsānkronə
cape (=cloak)	der Umhang (–hänge)	der ŭmhang (–hengə)
cape (eg Cape of Good Hope)	das Kap (–s)	das kap (–s)
captain	der Kapitän (–e)	der kapitēyn (–ə)
car	das Auto (–s)	das owto (–z)
by c.	mit dem A.	mit daym owto
buffet c.	der Speisewagen (–)	der shpīzəvāgən
c. ferry	die Autofähre (–n)	dee owtofeyrə (–n)
c. hire	der Autoverleih (–e)	der owtoferlī (–ə)
c. park	der Parkplatz (–plätze)	der parkplats (–pletse)
c. wash	die Autowaschanlage (–n)	dee owtovashanlāgə (–n)
sleeping c.	der Schlafwagen (–)	der shlāfvāgən
carafe	die Karaffe (–n)	dee karafə (–n)
a c. of /wine/	eine K. /Wein/	īnə karafə /vīn/
carat	das Karat	das karāt
/9/ c. gold	/neun/karätig	/noyn/karēytih
caravan	der Wohnwagen (–)	der vonvāgən
c. site	der Campingplatz (–plätze)	der kampingplats (–pletse)
/four/ berth c.	der /Vier/bett-wohnwagen (–)	der /feer/betvonvāgən
card (business c.)	die Geschäftskarte (–n)	dee gəsheftskārtə (–n)
birthday c.	die Geburtstagskarte (–n)	dee gəboortstākskārtə (–n)
cardigan	die Strickjacke (–n)	dee shtrikyakə (–n)
cards	die Karten (fpl)	dee kārtən
a game of c.	ein Kartenspiel (–e)	īn kārtənshpeel (–ə)

a pack of c.	ein Spiel (–e) K.	īn shpeel (–ə) kārtən
careful	vorsichtig	forzihtih
careless	unvorsichtig	ŭnforzihtih
caretaker	der Hausmeister (–)	der howsmīstər
carnation	die Nelke (–n)	dee nelkə (–n)
carnival	der Karneval	der karnəval
car park	der Parkplatz (–plätze)	der parkplats (–pletsə)
carpet	der Teppich (–e)	der tepih (–ə)
fitted c.	ein Auslegeteppich (–e)	īn owslaygətepih(–ə)
carriage (in a train)	der Wagen (–)	der vāgən
carrier bag	die Einkaufstasche (–n)	dee īnkowfstashə (–n)
carrot	die Karotte (–n)	dee karətə (–n)
carry	tragen	trāgən
carrycot	die Babytragtasche (–n)	dee baybeetrāgtashə (–n)
carton of /cigarettes/ (=200)	die Stange (–n) /Zigaretten/	dee shtangə (–n) /tsigaretən/
a c. of /milk/	eine Tüte (–n) /Milch/	īnə tühtə (–n) /milh/
cartridge (=film c.)	die Kassette (–n)	dee kasetə (–n)
cartridge (for gun)	die Patrone (–n)	dee patronə (–n)
case (=suitcase)	der Koffer (–)	der kəfər
cigarette c.	das Zigarettenetui (–s)	das tsigarətənetvee (–s)
cash (n)	das Bargeld	das bārgelt
c. payment	die Barzahlung (–en)	dee bārtsālŭng (–ən)
c. price	der Barzahlungspreis (–e)	der bārtsālŭngsprīs (–prīzə)
pay by c.	bar zahlen	bār tsālən
cash (vb)	einlösen	īnlœezən
c. /a traveller's cheque/	/einen Reise–scheck/ e.	/īnən rīzəshek/ īnlœezən
	ich löse /einen R./ ein	ih lœezə /īnən rīzəshek/ īn
cash desk	die Kasse (–n)	dee kasə (–n)
cashier	der Kassierer (–) die Kassiererin (–nen)	der kaseerər/dee kaseerərin (–ən)

	masculine	feminine	neuter
the/a (subject)	der/ein	die/eine	das/ein
the/a (object)	den/einen	die/eine	das/ein
the (plural, subject/object)	die	die	die

cashmere	der Kaschmir	der **kash**mēēr
c. sweater	der Kaschmirpullover (–)	der **kash**mēērpülovər
casino	das Kasino (–s)	das kazēēno (–z)
casserole (container)	der Topf (¨e)	der tɔpf (tœpfə)
casserole (meal)	der Eintopf (¨e)	der **ī**ntɔpf (–tœpfə)
cassette	die Kassette (–n)	dēē kasetə (–n)
c. player	der Kassetten-recorder (–)	der kasetənrekɔrdər
c. recorder	der Kassetten-recorder (–)	der kasetənrekɔrdər
pre-recorded c.	die bespielte (–n) Kassette (–n)	dēē bəshpēēltə (–n) kasetə (–n)
c60/90/120	die 60/90/120 Minutenkassette (–n)	dēē **zeh**tsih/**noyn**tsih/ hündərttsvantsih minootənkasetə (–n)
castle	das Schloß (¨sser)	das shlɔs (**shlœ**sər)
cat	die Katze (–n)	dēē **kat**sə (–n)
catalogue	der Katalog (–e)	der katalok (katalogə)
catch /an illness/	mir /eine Krankheit/ holen	mēēr /īnə **krang**khīt/ holən
	ich hole mir /eine Krankheit/	ih holə mēēr /īnə **krang**khīt/
catch /the train/	/den Zug/ erreichen	/dāyn tsōōk/ erīhən
	ich erreiche /den Zug/	ih er**īh**ə /dāyn tsōōk/
cathedral	der Dom (–e)	der dom (–ə)
Catholic (adj)	katholisch	katolish
cattle	das Vieh (s)	das fēē
cauliflower	der Blumenkohl (–e)	der **blōō**mənkol (–ə)
cause (n)	die Ursache (–n)	dēē **ōōr**zakhə (–n)
cave	die Höhle (–n)	dēē hœlə (–n)
ceiling	die Decke (–n)	dēē dekə (–n)
celery	der Selleri	der zelərēē
a head of c.	ein Kopf S.	in kɔpf zelərēē
cellar	der Keller (–)	der kelər
cement (n)	der Zement	der tse**ment**
cemetery	der Friedhof (–höfe)	der **frēēt**hof (–hœfə)
centimetre	das Zentimeter (–)	das tsentimāytər
central heating	die Zentralheizung	dēē tsen**tral**hītsüng
centre	das Zentrum (die Zentren)	das **tsen**trüm (dēē **tsen**trən)
in the c.	im Z.	im **tsen**trüm

88

shopping c.	das Einkaufszentrum (–zentren)	das īnkowfstsentrŭm (–tsentrən)
town c.	die Stadtmitte (–n)	dēē shtatmitə (–n)
century	das Jahrhundert (–e)	das yārhŭndərt (–ə)
ceramic	die Keramik	dēē kerāmik
cereal (=breakfast c.)	die Frühstücks-flocken (pl)	dēē frühshtüksflɔkən
a bowl of c.	eine Portion (–en) F.	īnə pɔrtsyon (–ən) frühshtüksflɔkən
ceremony	die Feier (–n)	dēē fīər (–n)
certain	sicher	zihər
I'm c.	ich bin s.	ih bin zihər
certainly	sicher	zihər
certificate	das Zeugnis (–se)	das tsoygnis (–ə)
chain	die Kette (–n)	dēē ketə (–n)
chain store	der Kettenladen (–läden)	der ketənlādən (–lēydən)
chair	der Stuhl (·̈e)	der shtool (–shtühlə)
high c.	der Babystuhl (–stühle)	der bāybēēshtool (–shtühlə)
wheel c.	der Rollstuhl (–stühle)	der rɔlshtool (–shtühlə)
c. lift	die Sesselbahn (–en)	dēē zesəlbān (–ən)
chairman	der Vorsitzende (–n)	der forzitsəndə (–n)
chalet	das Chalet (–s)	das shalāy (–s)
chambermaid	das Zimmermädchen (–)	das tsimərmēythən
champagne	der Sekt	der zekt
a bottle of c.	eine Flasche (–n) S.	īnə flashə (–n) zekt
change (n) (= alteration)	die Änderung (–en)	dēē enderŭng (–ən)
change (n) (=money)	das Wechselgeld	das veksəlgelt
small c.	das Kleingeld	das klīngelt
change (vb)	wechseln	veksəln
I'd like to c. /some traveller's cheques/	ich möchte /Reiseschecks/ w.	ih mœhtə /rīzəsheks/ veksəln
change at / / (of train)	in / / umsteigen	in / / ŭmshtīgən
	ich steige in / / um	ih shtīgə in / / ŭm
do I have to change?	muß ich u.?	mŭs ih ŭmshtīgən
changing room	der Umkleideraum (–räume)	der ŭmklīdərowm (–roymə)

89

charcoal	die Holzkohle (–n)	dee holtskolə (–n)
charge (n) (=payment)	der Preis (–e)	der prīs (prīzə)
charge (vb) (=payment)	kosten	kostən
charming	charmant	sharmānt
chart (= sea map)	die Karte (–n)	dee kārtə (–n)
charter flight	der Charterflug (–flüge)	der shartərflook (–flühgə)
chauffeur	der Chauffeur (–e)	der shofoer (–ə)
cheap	billig	bilih
cheat (vb)	betrügen	bətrühgən
check (vb)	prüfen	prühfən
check in (vb) (=of hotel/plane)	mich anmelden	mih anmeldən
	ich melde mich an	ih meldə mih an
check out (vb) (=of hotel)	mich abmelden	mih apmeldən
	ich melde mich ab	ih meldə mih ap
check up (n) (=of health)	die Untersuchung (–en)	dee üntərzookhüng (–ən)
cheek (of face)	die Wange (–n)	dee vangə (–n)
cheese	der Käse (–sorten)	der keyzə (–zortən)
c. /omelette/	die K./omelett/	dee keyzə/omlet/
chemist's	die Apotheke (–n)	dee apotaykə (–n)
cheque	der Scheck (–s)	der shek (–s)
c. book	das Scheckbuch (¨er)	das shekbookh (–bühkhər)
c. card	die Scheckkarte (–n)	dee shekkartə (–n)
traveller's c.	der Reisescheck (–s)	der rīzəshek (–s)
pay by c.	mit S. zahlen	mit shek tsālən
cherry	die Kirsche (–n)	dee kirshə (–n)
chess	das Schach (no pl)	das shakh
play c.	S. spielen	shakh shpeelən
	ich spiele S.	ih shpeelə shakh
chest (part of body)	die Brust (¨e)	dee brüst (brüstə)
chestnuts	die Kastanien (fpl)	dee kastānyən
chest of drawers	die Kommode (–n)	dee komodə (–n)
chewing gum	der Kaugummi	der kowgümi
chicken	das Huhn (¨er)	das hoon (hühnər)
chicken pox	die Windpocken (pl)	dee vintpokən
chilblain	die Frostbeule (–n)	dee frostboylə (–n)
child	das Kind (–er)	das kint (kindər)
chill	kühlen	kühlən

Remember:[kh] as in acht (eight) [h] as in hungrig (hungry)
[œ] as in schön (beautiful) [üh] as in Tür (door)

chimney	der Schornstein (–e)	der **shorn**sht**ī**n (–ə)
chin	das Kinn (–e)	das kin (–ə)
china	das Porzellan	das portsel**ā**n
chips	die Pommes frites (pl)	d**ē**e pom **frits**
chiropodist	der Fußpfleger (–) die Fußpflegerin (–nen)	der f**oo**spfl**ā**yg**ə**r/ d**ē**e f**oo**spfl**ā**yg**ə**rin (–ən)
chocolate	die Schokolade (–n)	d**ē**e sh**ɔ**kol**ā**də (–n)
a bar of c.	eine Tafel (–n) S.	**ī**nə **tā**fəl (–n) sh**ɔ**kol**ā**də
a box of chocolates	eine Schachtel (–n) Pralinen	**ī**nə **shakh**tel (–n) pral**ē**enən
choice	die Wahl (–en)	d**ē**e v**ā**l (–ən)
c. between / / and / /	die W. zwischen / / und / /	d**ē**e v**ā**l tsvishən / / ünt / /
choir	der Chor (–̈e)	der kor (k**ō̈**rə)
choose	wählen	v**ē**ylən
c. between / / and / /	w. zwischen / / und / /	v**ē**ylən tsvishən / / ünt / /
chop (n)	das Kotelett (–s)	das kotəlet (–s)
lamb c.	das Lammkotelett (–s)	das **lam**kotəlet (–s)
pork c.	das Schweinekotelett (–s)	das **shvī**nəkotəlet (–s)
chop (vb)	hacken	hakən
chopsticks	die Eßstäbchen (npl)	d**ē**e essht**ē**yphən
Christ	Christus	krist**ü**s
Christian	der Christ (–en)	der krist (–ən)
Christmas	Weihnachten	v**ī**nakhtən
C. card	die Weihnachts- karte (–n)	d**ē**e v**ī**nakhtsk**ā**rtə (–n)
C. Day	der erste Weihnachtstag	der **ā**yrstə v**ī**nakhtstäk
church	die Kirche (–n)	d**ē**e **kir**hə (–n)
a /Protestant/ C.	eine /evangelische/ K.	**ī**nə /eva**n**gg**ā**ylishə/ **kir**hə
cider	der Apfelwein	der **apf**əlv**ī**n
a bottle of c.	eine Flasche (–n) A.	**ī**nə flashə (–n) apfəlv**ī**n
a c.	ein Glas (–) A.	**ī**n gl**ā**s (–) **apf**əlv**ī**n
cigar	die Zigarre (–n)	d**ē**e tsigarə (–n)
a box of cigars	eine Kiste (–n) Zigarren	**ī**nə kistə (–n) tsigarən

91

a Havana c.	eine Havanna-zigarre (–n)	ĭnə havanatsigarə (–n)
cigarette (American type)	die milde (n) Zigarette (–n)	dēē mildə (–n) tsigaretə (–n)
c. (French type)	die starke (–n) Zigarette (–n)	dēē shtārkə (–n) tsigaretə (–n)
smoke a c.	eine Z. rauchen	ĭnə tsigaretə rowkhən
	ich rauche eine Z.	ih rowkhə ĭnə tsigaretə
cigarette case	das Zigarettenetui (–s)	das tsigaretənetvēē (–s)
cigarette lighter	das Feuerzeug (–e)	das foyərtsoyk (–tsoygə)
gas lighter	das Gasfeuerzeug (–e)	das gāsfoyərtsoyk (–tsoygə)
cigarette paper	das Zigarettenpapier (–e)	das tsigaretənpapēēr (–ə)
cigarettes	die Zigaretten (fpl)	dēē tsigaretən
a carton of c. (= 200)	eine Stange (–n) Z.	ĭnə shtāngə (–n) tsigaretən
a packet of c.	eine Schachtel (–n) Z.	ĭnə shakhtəl (–n) tsigaretən
filter-tipped c.	die Filterzigaretten (fpl)	dēē filtərtsigaretən
cinema	das Kino (–s)	das kēēno (–s)
circus	der Zirkus (–se)	der tsirkŭs (–ə)
citizen	der Bürger (–)	der bürgər
city	die Stadt (–̈e)	dēē shtat (stetə)
the new part of the c.	der neue Teil der S.	der noyə tīl der shtat
the old part of the c.	die Altstadt	dēē altshtat
civilisation	die Zivilisation (–en)	dēē tsivilizatsyon (–ən)
civil servant	der Beamte (–n)	der bəamtə (–n)
claim /damages/	/Schadenersatz/ fordern	/shādənerzats/ fordərn
	ich fordere /Schadenersatz/	ih fordərə /shādənerzats/
claim on /the insurance/	Schadenersatz von /der Versicherung/ fordern	shādənerzats fon /der ferzihərŭng/ fordərn
	ich fordere Schadenersatz von /der Versicherung/	ih fordərə shādənerzats fon /der ferzihərŭng/
clarify	klären	klēyrən

class	die Klasse (–n)	dēē klasə (–n)
cabin c.	die Kabinenklasse	dēē kabēēnənklasə
/first/ c.	die /erste/ K.	dēē /āyrstə/ klasə
tourist c.	die Touristenklasse	dēē tŭristənklasə
class (in a school)	die Klasse (–n)	dēē klasə (–n)
classical (eg music)	klassisch	klasishə
c. music	klassische Musik	klasishə mŭzēēk
clean (adj)	sauber	zowbər
clean (vb)	reinigen	rīnigən
cleaner's	die Reinigung (–en)	dēē rīnigŭng (–ən)
cleansing cream	die Reinigungskreme (–s)	dēē rīnigŭngskrāym (–s)
clear (=obvious)	klar	klār
clear (=transparent)	durchsichtig	dŭrḫzihtih
clear goods through Customs	Waren durch den Zoll bringen	vārən dŭrḫ dāyn tsol bringən
	ich bringe Waren durch den Zoll	ih bringə vārən dŭrḫ den tsol
clever (of people)	geschickt	gəshikt
client	der Klient (–en)	der klient (–ən)
cliff	die Klippe (–n)	dēē klipə (–n)
climate	das Klima	das klēēma
climb (vb) (=c. mountains)	klettern	kletərn
climbing	das Bergsteigen	das berkshtīgən
go c.	bergsteigen gehen	berkshtīgən gāyən
	ich gehe bergsteigen	ih gāyə berkshtīgən
clinic	die Klinik (–en)	dēē klēēnik (–ən)
private c.	die Privatklinik (–en)	dēē prēēvatklēēnik (–ən)
cloakroom	die Garderobe (–n)	dēē gardərobə (–n)
clock	die Uhr (–en)	dēē ōōr (–ən)
alarm c.	der Wecker (–)	der vekər
clogs	die Holzschuhe (–)	dēē holtsshōōə
a pair of c.	ein Paar H.	īn pār holtsshōōə
close (vb)	schließen	shlēēsən
closed (adj)	geschlossen	gəshlosən
cloth (=dishcloth)	das Tuch (¨-er)	das tōōkh (tühkhər)
clothes	die Kleider (pl)	dēē klīdər
c. brush	die Kleiderbürste (–n)	dēē klīdərbürstə (–n)
c. line	die Wäscheleine (–n)	dēē veshəlīnə (–n)

	masculine	feminine	neuter
the/a (subject)	der/ein	die/eine	das/ein
the/a (object)	den/einen	die/eine	das/ein
the (plural, subject/object)	die	die	die

c. peg	die Wäsche- klammer (–n)	dee veshəklamər (–n)
cloud	die Wolke (–n)	dee volkə (–n)
cloudy	wolkig	volkih
club	der Klub (–s)	der klŭp (–s)
gambling c.	der Spielklub (–s)	der shpeelklŭp (–s)
golf c. (institution)	der Golfklub (–s)	der golfklŭp (–s)
golf c. (object)	der Golfschläger (–)	der golfshleygər (–)
coach	der Bus (–se)	der bŭs (–ə)
by c.	mit dem B.	mit daym bŭs
c. (on a train)	der Wagen	der vāgən
coal	die Kohle (–n)	dee kolə (–n)
coarse (of person)	grob	grop
coast (n)	die Küste (–n)	dee küstə (–n)
coastguard	die Küstenwache (–n)	dee küstənvakhə (–n)
coastline	die Küstenlinie (–n)	dee küstənleenyə (–n)
coat	der Mantel (¨)	der **mant**əl (**ment**əl)
coat hanger	der Kleiderbügel (–)	der klīdərbühgəl
cockroach	die Küchenschabe (–n)	dee kühənshābə (–n)
cocktail	der Cocktail (–s)	der koktāyl (–s)
cocoa	der Kakao	der kakow
a cup of c.	eine Tasse (–n) K.	īnə tasə (–n) kakow
coconut	die Kokosnuß (–nüsse)	dee kokosnŭs (–nüsə)
cod	der Kabeljau (–e)	der kābəlyow (–ə)
code	die Zahl (–en)	dee tsāl (–ən)
dialling c.	die Vorwählnummer (–n)	dee forveylnŭmər (–n)
postal c.	die Postleitzahl (–en)	dee postlīttsāl (–ən)
codeine	das Kodein	das kodeeen
coffee	der Kaffee	der **kaf**ay
a cup of c.	eine Tasse (–n) K.	īnə tasə (–n) **kaf**ay
a percolated c.	der Filterkaffee	der **filt**ərkafay
a pot of c.	eine Kanne (–n) K.	īnə kanə (–n) **kaf**ay
black c.	schwarzer K.	**shvarts**ər kafay
decaffeinated c.	der koffeinfreie K.	der **kof**eeeenfriə kafay
ground c.	gemahlener K.	gə**mā**lənər **kaf**ay
instant c.	der Pulverkaffee	der **pŭlf**ərkafay
white c.	K. mit Milch	**kaf**ay mit **milh**

coffeepot	die Kaffeekanne (–n)	dee kafaykanə (–n)
coffin	der Sarg (–̈e)	der zark (zergə)
coin	die Münze (–n)	dee müntsə (–n)
cold (adj)	kalt	kalt
I'm c.	mir ist k.	mir ist **kalt**
it's c. (of things)	es ist k.	es ist **kalt**
it's c. (of weather)	es ist k.	es ist **kalt**
cold (n)	der Schnupfen	der **shn**üpfən
I've got a c.	ich habe einen S.	ih **hā**bə **ī**nən **shn**üpfən
collar	der Kragen (–)	der **krā**gən
c. bone	das Schlüsselbein	das **shl**üsəlbīn
dog c.	das Halsband (–bänder)	das **hal**sbant (–bendər)
colleague	der Kollege (–n) die Kollegin (–nen)	der kə**lā**ygə (–n)/dee kə**lā**ygin (–ən)
collect /from/	holen /von/	**hol**ən fon / /
c. /my luggage/	/mein Gepäck/ h. ich hole /mein Gepäck/	/mīn gəpek/ **hol**ən ih **hol**ə /mīn gəpek/
collection (in a church)	die Kollekte (–n)	dee kə**lek**tə (–n)
collection (of objects)	die Sammlung (–en)	dee **zam**lüng (–ən)
last c. (of post)	die letzte Leerung	dee letstə **lāy**rüng
college	das Institut (–e)	das insti**tōō**t (–ə)
cologne	das Kölnische Wasser	das **kœl**nishə vasər
colour	die Farbe (–n)	dee **fār**bə (–n)
comb (n)	der Kamm (–̈e)	der kam (kemə)
come /from/	kommen /aus/	**kom**ən fon / /
I come /from Nuremberg/	ich komme /aus Nürnberg/	ih **kom**ə /ows **nürn**berk/
comfortable	bequem	bə**kvāy**m
comic (=funny paper)	die Comics (pl)	dee komiks
commerce	der Handel	der **hand**əl
commission (=payment)	die Gebühr (–en)	dee gə**bühr** (–ən)
common (=usual)	gewöhnlich	gə**vœn**lih
company (=firm)	die Gesellschaft (–en)	dee gə**zel**shaft (–ən)
compartment (in train)	das Abteil (–e)	das ap**tī**l (–ə)
non-smoking c.	das Nichtraucherabteil (–e)	das **niht**rowhər-ap**tī**l (e–)
smoking c.	das Raucherabteil (–e)	das **row**khərap**tī**l (–ə)
compass	der Kompaß (–sse)	der **kom**pas (–ə)

compensation	die Entschädigung (–en)	dēē entsh**ēy**digŭng (–ən)
competition	der Wettkampf (¨e)	der **vet**kampf (–kempfə)
complain /to the manager/	mich /bei der Direktion/ beschweren	mih /bī der direktsyon/ bəshv**āy**rən
	ich beschwere mich /bei der Direktion/	ih bəshv**āy**rə mih /bī der direktsyon/
c. about /the noise/	mich über /den Lärm/ b.	mih **ü**hbər /d**āy**n lerm/ bəshv**āy**rən
	ich beschwere mich über /den Lärm/	ih bəshv**āy**rə mih **ü**hbər /d**āy**n lerm/
complaint	die Beschwerde (–n)	dēē bəshv**āy**rdə (–n)
complete (adj)	ganz	gants
compulsory	obligatorisch	obligat**ō**rish
computer	der Computer (–)	der kɔmpy**ōō**tər
concert	das Konzert (–e)	das kɔnt**sert** (–ə)
concert hall	der Konzertsaal (–säle)	dēē kɔnt**sert**sal (–s**ēy**lə)
condition	der Zustand (–stände)	der ts**ōō**shtant (–shtendə)
in bad c.	in schlechtem Z.	in shl**eh**tem ts**ōō**shtant
in good c.	in gutem Z.	in g**ōō**təm ts**ōō**shtant
conditioner (for hair)	die Haarkur	dēē **har**k**ōō**r
a bottle of hair c.	eine Flasche (–n) H.	īnə flashə (–n) **har**k**ōō**r
conducted tour	die Führung (–en)	dēē **fü**hrŭng (–ən)
go on a c. t.	eine F. mitmachen	īnə **fü**hrŭng mitmakhən
	ich mache eine F. mit	ih makhə īnə **fü**hrŭng mit
conference	die Konferenz (–en)	dēē kɔnfer**ents** (–ən)
confirm /my flight/	/meinen Flug/ bestätigen	/mīnən fl**ōō**k/ bəsht**ēy**tigən
	ich bestätige /meinen Flug/	ih bəsht**ēy**tigə /mīnən **fl**ōōk/
confused	verwirrt	fer**virt**
I'm c.	ich bin v.	ih bin fer**virt**
congratulate /you/ on / /	/Ihnen/ zu / / gratulieren	/**ēē**nən/ ts**ōō** / / gratŭl**ēē**rən
congratulations	herzliche Glückwünsche!	**herts**lihə gl**ü**kvünshə

Remember: [kh] as in acht (eight) [h] as in hungrig (hungry)
[œ̄] as in schön (beautiful) [üh] as in Tür (door)

connect	verbinden	ferbindən
connecting flight	der Anschlußflug (–flüge)	der anshlusflook (–flühgə)
constipated	verstopft	fershtopft
consul	der Konsul (–en)	der konzül (–ən)
consulate	das Konsulat (–e)	das konzülāt (–ə)
the /British/ C.	das /britische/ K.	das /britishə/ konzülāt
contact lenses	die Kontaktlinsen	dee kontaktlinzən
contagious	ansteckend	anshtekent
contents (eg of a parcel)	der Inhalt (s)	der inhalt
continental	kontinental	kontinentāl
c. breakfast	das normale Frühstück	das normālə frühshtük
continual	ständig	shtendih
continue /a journey/	/eine Reise/ fortsetzen	/īnə rīzə/ fortzetsən
	ich setze /meine Reise/ fort	ih zetsə /mīnə rīzə/ fort
contraceptives	die Verhütungsmittel (npl)	dee ferhühtüngsmitəl
the Pill	die Antibabypille (–n)	dee antibaybeepilə (–n)
a packet of sheaths (=Durex)	ein Päckchen Kondome	īn pekhən kondomə
contract (n)	der Vertrag (–̈e)	der fertrāg (–treygə)
convenient (of time and distance)	passend	pasent
cook (vb)	kochen	kokhən
cooked	gekocht	gəkokht
cooker	der Herd (–e)	der hayrt (hayrdə)
electric c.	der elektrische H.	der elektrishə hayrt
gas c.	der Gasherd (–e)	der gāshayrt (–hayrdə)
cooking	das Kochen	das kokhən
do the c.	kochen	kokhən
cool (adj)	kühl	kühl
cool (vb)	kühlen	kühlən
copper	das Kupfer	das küpfər
copy (n)	die Kopie (–n)	dee kopee (–ən)
copy (vb)	kopieren	kopeerən
coral	die Koralle (–n)	dee koralə (–n)
cord	der Strick (–e)	der shtrik (–ə)
corduroy	der Manchester	der manshestər
cork	der Korken	der korkən
corkscrew	der Korkenzieher (–)	der korkəntseeər

97

corn	das Korn /der Maiskolben (–)	das kɔrn/der mīskɔlbən
sweet c.	der Mais	der mīs
corn (eg on a toe)	das Hühnerauge (–n)	das hühnərowgə (–n)
c. pads	das Hühneraugen-pflaster (–)	das hühnərowgən-pflastər
corner	die Ecke (–n)	dēē ekə (–n)
cornflakes	die Kornflakes (pl) (tdmk)	dēē kɔrnflāyks
correct (adj)	richtig	rihtih
correct (vb)	korrigieren	kɔrigēērən
correction	die Korrektur (–en)	dēē kɔrektōōr (–ən)
corridor	der Korridor (–e)	der kɔridor (–ə)
corset	das Korsett (–e)	das kɔrzet (–ə)
cost (n)	der Preis (–e)	der prīs (prīsə)
cost (vb)	kosten	kɔstən
cot	das Kinderbett (–en)	das kindərbet (–ən)
cottage	das Haus (¨er)	das hows (hoyzər)
cotton	die Baumwolle	dēē bowmvɔlə
a reel of c.	ein Knäuel (–) B.	īn knoyəl bowmvɔlə
cotton wool	die Watte	dēē vatə
couchette	der Liegewagenplatz (–plätze)	der lēēgəvāgənplats (–pletsə)
cough (n)	der Husten	der hōōstən
cough (vb)	husten	hōōstən
cough mixture	der Hustensaft (–säfte}	der hōōstənzaft (–zeftə)
a bottle of c. m.	eine Flasche (–n) H.	īnə flashə (–n) hōōstənzaft
cough pastilles	die Hustenbonbons (mpl)	dēē hōōstənbōbō
count (vb)	zählen	tsēylən
country (=countryside)	das Land (no pl)	das lant
in the country	auf dem L.	owf dāym lant
country (=nation)	das Land (¨er)	das lant (lendər)
countryside	die Landschaft	dēē lantshaft
couple (married c.)	das Paar (–e)	das pār (–ə)
coupon	der Schein (–e)	der shīn (–ə)
/petrol/ c.	der /Benzin-/gutschein (–e)	der /bentsēēn /-gōōtshīn (–ə)
courrier	der Reiseführer (–)	der rīzəführər
course (of food)	der Gang (¨e)	der gang (gengə)
first c.	der erste G.	der āyrstə gang
main c.	das Hauptgericht (–e)	das howptgəriht (–ə)

last c.	der letzte G.	der letstə gaṅg
court (law)	das Gericht (–e)	das gəriht (–ə)
tennis c.	der Tennisplatz (–plätze)	der tenisplats (–pletsə)
cousin	der Vetter (–n) die Kusine (–n)	der fetər (–n)/deē küzeēnə (–n)
cow	die Kuh (ᵁe)	deē koō (kühə)
crab	die Krabbe (–n)	deē krabə (–n)
crack (n)	der Sprung (ᵁe)	der shprüṅg (shprüṅgə)
it's cracked	es hat einen S.	es hat īnən shprüṅg
cramp (n)	der Krampf (ᵁe)	der krampf (krempfə)
crash (car c.)	der Unfall (ᵁe)	der ŭnfal (–felə)
crash helmet	der Sturzhelm (–e)	der shtŭrtshelm (–ə)
crayon	der Buntstift (–e)	der bŭntshtift (–ə)
cream (from milk)	die Sahne	deē zānə
cream (=lotion)	die Kreme (–s)	deē krāym (–s)
crease (vb)	knittern	knitərn
does it c.?	knittert es?	knitərt es
credit	der Kredit	der kredeēt
on c.	auf K.	owf kredeēt
c. terms	die Kreditbedingungen (fpl)	deē kredeēt bədiṅg ṅgən
credit card	die Kreditkarte (–n)	deē kredeētkartə (–n)
crew	die Mannschaft (–en)	deē manshaft (–ən)
air c.	die Besatzung (–en)	deē bəzatsüṅg (–ən)
ground c.	das Bodenpersonal (no pl)	das bodənpersɔnāl
ship's c.	die Schiffsbesatzung (–en)	deē shifsbəzatsüṅg (–ən)
cricket	das Kricket	das krikət
play c.	K. spielen	krikət shpeēlən
	ich spiele K.	ih shpeēlə kriket
crime	das Verbrechen (–)	das ferbrehən
criminal	der Verbrecher (–)	der ferbrehər
crisps	die Chips (mpl)	deē ships

	masculine	feminine	neuter
the/a (subject)	der/ein	die/eine	das/ein
the/a (object)	den/einen	die/eine	das/ein
the (plural, subject/object)	die	die	die

crocodile (leather)	das Krokodilleder	das krokodeellāydər
c. bag	die Krokodil-lederhandtasche (–n)	dee krokodeel-lāydərhanttashə (–n)
cross /the road/	/die Straße/ überqueren	/dee shtrāsə / ühbərkvāyrən
	ich überquere /die Straße/	ih ühbərkvāyrə /dee shtrāsə/
crossed (eg a cheque)	der Verrechnungs-scheck (–s)	der ferrehnŭngsshek (–s)
crossroads	die Kreuzung (–en)	dee krōytsŭng (–ən)
crossword puzzle	das Kreuzworträtsel (–)	das kroystsvort-rēytsəl
crowd	die Menge (–n)	dee mengə (–n)
crowded	überfüllt	ühbərfült
crown (vb) (tooth)	eine Zahnkrone bekommen	īnə tsānkronə bəkəmən
cruise	die Kreuzfahrt (–en)	dee krōytsfārt (–ən)
go on a c.	eine K. machen	īnə krōytsfārt makhən
	ich mache eine K.	ih makhə īnə krōytsfārt
cry (vb)	weinen	vīnən
the baby's crying	das Baby weint	das bāybee vīnt
cucumber	die Gurke (–n)	dee gŭrkə (–n)
cuff links	die Manschettenknöpfe (mpl)	dee manshetənknœpfə
a pair of c. l.	ein Paar M.	īn pār manshetənknœpfə
cup	die Tasse (–n)	dee tasə (–n)
a c. of / /	eine T. / /	īnə tasə (–n) / /
/plastic/ c.	ein Plastikbecher (–)	īn /plastik/behər
cupboard	der Schrank (:-e)	der shrangk (shrengkə)
cure (n) (health)	die Kur (–en)	dee kōor (–ən)
cure (vb) (health)	heilen	hīlən
curl (vb)	locken	ləkən
curlers	die Lockenwickler (mpl)	dee ləkənviklər
currants	die Rosinen (fpl)	dee rozēenən
currency	die Währung (–en)	dee vēyrŭng (–ən)
current (=electric c.)	der Strom (:-e)	der shtrom (shtrœmə)
A.C.	der Wechselstrom	der veksəlshtrom
D.C.	der Gleichstrom	der glīhshtrom

120/240 volt	120/240 Volt	hŭndərt
		tsvantsih/tsvī
		hŭndərt**feer**tsih
		volt
current (of water)	die Strömung (–en)	dēē **shtrœ**mŭng (–ən)
strong c.	die starke S.	dēē **shtark**ə **shtrœ**mŭng
curry	der Curry	der **kari**
c. powder	das Currypulver	das **kari**pŭlfər
curtain	der Vorhang (–hänge)	der **for**hang (–hengə)
cushion	das Kissen (–)	das **kis**ən
custom	die Sitte (–n)	dēē **zit**ə (–n)
Customs	der Zoll (s)	der **tsol**
c. declaration form	das Zollformular (–e)	das **tsol**formŭlār (–ə)
cut (n)	der Schnitt (–e)	der **shnit** (–ə)
c. and blow dry	Fönschnitt	**fœn**shnit
cut (vb)	schneiden	**shnī**dən
cutlery	das Besteck (–e)	das bə**shtek** (–ə)
cutlet	das Kotelett (–s)	das **kot**əlet (–s)
lamb c.	das Lammkotelett (–s)	das **lam**kotəlet (–s)
veal c.	das Kalbskotelett (–s)	das **kalps**kotəlet (–s)
cut off (eg of telephone)	unterbrechen	ŭntər**breh**ən
I've been c. o.	ich bin unterbrochen worden	ih bin ŭntər**bro**khən vordən
cycling	das Radfahren	das **rāt**fārən
go c.	r. gehen	**rāt**fārən gāyən
	ich gehe r.	ih gāyə **rāt**fārən

D

daily	täglich	**tēyk**lih
damage (n)	der Schaden (–)	der **shā**dən (sh**ēy**dən)
damaged	beschädigt	bə**shēy**diht
damages (=compensation)	die Entschädigung (–en)	dēē ent**shēy**digŭng (–ən)
damn!	verdammt!	fer**damt**
damp (adj)	feucht	**foyht**
dance (n)	der Tanz (–e)	der **tants** (**tents**ə)
dance (vb)	tanzen	**tant**sən
dance hall	der Balsaal (–säle)	der **bal**zāl (–zēylə)

dancer	der Tänzer (–) die Tänzerin (–nen)	der tentsər/dēē tentsərin (–ən)
dancing	das Tanzen	das tantsən
go d.	t. gehen	tantsən gāyən
	ich gehe t.	ih gāyə tantsən
dandruff	die Haarschuppen (pl)	dēē härshŭpən
danger	die Gefahr (–en)	dēē gəfār (–ən)
dangerous	gefährlich	gəfeyrlih
dark (=d. haired)	dunkel	dŭngkəl
dark (=d. skinned)	farbig	färbih
dark (of colour)	dunkel	dŭngkəl
d. /green/	d./grün/	dŭngkəl/grühn/
dark (=time of day)	dunkel	dŭngkəl
it's d.	es wird d.	es virt dŭngkəl
darn (vb)	stopfen	shtɔpfən
dartboard	die Zielscheibe (–n)	dēē tsēēlshībə (–n)
darts	die Wurfpfeile (mpl)	dēē vōōrfpfīlə
	ich spiele W.	ih shpēēlə vōōrfpfīlə
play d.	W. spielen	vōōrfpfīlə shpēēlən
date (calendar)	das Datum (Daten)	das dātŭm (dātən)
d. of birth	das Geburtsdatum (–daten)	das gəbōōrtsdātŭm (–dātən)
dates (=fruit)	die Datteln (pl)	dēē datəln
daughter	die Tochter (¨)	dēē tɔkhtər (tœkhtər)
daughter-in-law	die Schwiegertochter (¨)	dēē shvēēgərtɔkhtər (–tœkhtər)
dawn (n)	die Morgen- dämmerung (–en)	dēē mɔrgəndemərŭng (–ən)
day	der Tag (–e)	der tāk (tāgə)
every d.	jeden T.	yāydən tāk
dead	tot	tot
deaf	taub	towp
decaffeinated	koffeinfrei	kɔfeēēnfrī
December	der Dezember	der detsembər
decide	mich entschlieöen	mih entshlēēsən
d. on /a plan/	mich zu /einem Plan/ entschließen	mih tsōō /īnəm plān/ entshlēēsən
	ich entschließe mich zu /einem Plan/	ih entshlēēsə mih tsōō /īnəm plān/
deck	das Deck (–s)	das dek (–s)
lower d.	das untere D.	das ŭntərə dek
upper d.	das Hauptdeck (–s)	das howptdek (–s)

Remember: [kh] as in acht (eight) [h] as in hungrig (hungry)
[œ] as in schön (beautiful) [üh] as in Tür (door)

deckchair	der Liegestuhl (ˍe)	der **lee**gəsht<u>oo</u>l (–shtül̄ə)
declare /this watch/	/diese Uhr/ verzollen	/**dee**zə **oor**/ fert**so**lən
deduct	abziehen	**ap**ts<u>ee</u>ən
d. /50 marks/ from /the bill/	/50 Mark/ von /der Rechnung/ a.	/**fünf**tsih mārk/ fon /der **reh**nū̄ng/ **ap**ts<u>ee</u>ən
	ich ziehe /50 Mark/ von /der Rechnung/ ab	ih ts<u>ee</u>ə /**fünf**tsih mārk/ fon /der **reh**nū̄ng/ ap
deep	tief	t<u>ee</u>f
deep freeze (=machine)	die Kühltruhe (–n)	d<u>ee</u> **kühl**trōōə (–n)
definite	bestimmt	bə**shtimt**
definitely	bestimmt	bə**shtimt**
degree (=university d.)	das Diplom (–e)	das di**plom** (–ə)
degrees Centigrade Fahrenheit	der Grad (–e) G. Celsius G. Fahrenheit	der grād (–ə) grāt **tsel**ziŭs grāt **fā**rənhīt
delay (n)	der Verzug (no pl)	der fert**sook**
delayed (of people)	verspätet	fer**shpey**tət
delayed (of things)	verzögert	fert**sœ**gərt
delicate (health)	zart	tsart
delicatessen (=food shop)	das Delikatessen-geschäft (–e)	das delik**ā**tesən-gəsheft (–ə)
deliver to	liefern an	**lee**fərn an
denim (=material) a pair of d. jeans	der Jeansstoff ein Paar Jeans	der **djeen**shtof īn pār **djeens**
dentist	der Zahnarzt (–ärzte)	der **tsān**ārtst (–eyrtstə)
I must go to the dentist's	ich muß zum Z. gehen	ih müs tsüm **tsān**ārtst gāyən
dentures	das Gebiß (–sse)	das gə**bis** (–ə)
deodorant	das Deodorant (–s)	das deodo**rant** (–s)
depart on /Monday/	am /Montag/ abfahren ich fahre am /Montag/ ab	am /**mon**tāk/ **ap**fārən ih fārə am /**mon**tāk/ ap
d. at /4.30 p.m./	um /sechzehn Uhr dreißig/ a.	üm /**zehts**āyn oor **drī**sih/ **ap**fārən
d. in /July/	im /Juli/ a.	im /**yoo**li/ **ap**fārən

department	die Abteilung (–en)	dēē aptīlŭng (–ən)
children's d.	Kinderkleidung	kindərklīdŭng
men's d.	Herrenkleidung	herənklīdŭng
women's d.	Damenmode	dāmənmodə
department store	das Kaufhaus (–häuser)	das kowfhows (–hoyzər)
departure lounge	die Abflughalle (–n)	dēē abflookhalə (–n)
departure time	die Abfahrtszeit (–en)	dēē apfārtstsīt (–ən)
depend /on the weather/	/vom Wetter/ abhängen	/fom vetər/ aphengən
it depends on /the weather/	das hängt /vom Wetter/ ab	das hengt /fom vetər/ ap
deposit (n)	die Anzahlung (–en)	dēē antsālŭng (–ən)
deposit /some money/	/Geld/ deponieren	/gelt/ deponēērən
d. /these valuables/	/diese Wertsachen/ d.	/dēēzə vertzakhən/ deponēērən
	ich möchte /diese Wertsachen/ d.	ih mœhtə /dēēzə vertzakhən/ deponēērən
depth	die Tiefe (–n)	dēē tēēfə (–n)
describe	beschreiben	bəshrībən
description	die Beschreibung (–en)	dēē bəshrībŭng (–ən)
design (n)	die Zeichnung (–en)	dēē tsīhnŭng (–ən)
design (vb)	zeichnen	tsīhnən
desk	der Schreibtisch (–e)	der shrīptish (–ə)
dessert	der Nachtisch (–e)	der nakhtish (–ə)
dessertspoonful of / /	ein Teelöffel (–) / /	īn tāylœfəl / /
destination	das Ziel (–e)	das tsēēl (–ə)
detail	die Einzelheit (–en)	dēē īntsəlhīt (–ən)
detergent	das Waschmittel (–)	das vashmitəl
detour	der Umweg (–e)	der ŭmvek (–vegə)
make a d.	einen U. machen	īnən ŭmvek makhən
	ich mache einen U.	ih makhə īnən ŭmvek
develop	entwickeln	entvikəln
d. and print (a film)	e. und abziehen	entvikəln ŭnt aptsēēən
diabetes	die Zuckerkrankheit	dēē tsŭkərkrangkhīt
diabetic	der Diabetiker	der dēēabāytikər
dial	wählen	vēylən
diamond	der Diamant (–en)	der diamant (–ən)
diarrhoea	der Durchfall	der dŭrhfal

104

diary	das Tagebuch (–bücher)	das **tag**əb$\overline{oo}$kh (–b**ü**khər)
dice	der Würfel (–)	der **vür**fəl
dictionary	das Wörterbuch (–bücher)	das **vœrt**ərb$\overline{oo}$kh (–b**ü**hkhər)
English/German d.	ein Englisch/Deutsches W.	$\overline{i}$n **en**glish/**doyts**həs **vœrt**ərb$\overline{oo}$kh
German/English d.	ein Deutsch/Englishes W.	$\overline{i}$n **doytsh**/**en**glishəs **vœrt**ərb$\overline{oo}$kh
pocket d.	ein Taschen-wörterbuch	$\overline{i}$n **tash**ən-**vœrt**ərb$\overline{oo}$kh
die (vb)	sterben	**shter**bən
diet (=slimming d.)	die Diät	dee di**ey**t
be on a d.	D. halten	di**ey**t **halt**ən
	ich halte D.	ih **halt**ə di**ey**t
difference	der Unterschied (–e)	der **ünt**ərsh**ee**t (–sh**ee**də)
different	verschieden	fersh**ee**dən
d. from / /	v. von / /	fersh**ee**dən fɔn / /
difficult	schwierig	shv**ee**rih
difficulty	die Schwierigkeit (–en)	dee shv**ee**rihk$\overline{i}$t (–ən)
dig	graben	**grāb**ən
dinghy	das Dingi (–s)	das **dīngg**i (–s)
rubber d.	das Schlauchboot (–e)	das **shlowkh**bot (–ə)
sailing d.	das Segelboot (–e)	das **zāyg**əlbot (–ə)
dining room	das Eßzimmer	das **ests**imər
dinner (=evening meal)	das Essen	das **es**ən
d. jacket	die Smokingjacke (–n)	dee **smokīngg**yakə (–n)
have d.	essen	**es**ən
diplomat	der Diplomat (–en)	der diplom**āt** (–ən)
direct (adj)	direkt	dir**ekt**
d. line	die direkte Linie	dee dir**ekt**ə **lee**nyə
d. route	der direkte Weg	der dir**ekt**ə vek
direction	die Richtung (–en)	dee **riht**üngg (–ən)
director	der Direktor (–en)	der dir**ekt**ɔr (–ən)

	masculine	feminine	neuter
the/a (subject)	der/ein	die/eine	das/ein
the/a (object)	den/einen	die/eine	das/ein
the (plural, subject/object)	die	die	die

directory	das Adreßbuch (–bücher)	das adresbo͞okh (–bühkhər)
telephone d.	das Telefonbuch (–bücher)	das telefonbo͞okh (–bühkhər)
D. Enquiries	die Auskunft	de͞e owskünft
dirty	schmutzig	shmütsih̠
disagree with		
it disagrees with /me/ (food)	das bekommt /mir/ nicht	das bəkomt /me͞er/ niht
I d. with /you/	ich bin mit /Ihnen/ nicht einverstanden	ih̠ bin mit /e͞enən/ niht i͞nfershtandən
disappointed	enttäuscht	enttoysht
disc	die Schallplatte (–n)	de͞e shalplatə (–n)
a slipped d.	ein Bandscheiben- vorfall (–fälle)	i͞n bantshi͞bənforfal (–felə)
disco	die Diskothek (–en)	de͞e diskota͞yk (–ən)
disconnect	unterbrechen	üntərbreh̠ən
discount (n)	der Rabatt (–e)	der rabat (–ə)
disease	die Krankheit (–en)	de͞e kra͞ngkhi͞t (–ən)
disembark	aussteigen ich steige aus	owsshti͞gən ih̠ shti͞gə ows
disgusting	entsetzlich	entzetslih̠
dish (container for food)	die Schüssel (–n)	de͞e shüsəl (–n)
dish (food)	das Gericht (–e)	das gəriht (–ə)
dishcloth	das Geschirrtuch (¨er)	das gəshirto͞okh (–tühkhər)
dishonest	unehrlich	üna͞yrlih̠
dishwasher	die Spülmaschine (–n)	de͞e shpühlmashe͞enə (–n)
disinfectant	das Desinfektionsmittel (–)	das desinfektsyonsmitəl
a bottle of d.	eine Flasche (–n) D.	i͞nə flashə (–n) desinfektyons- mitəl
disposable		
d. lighter	das Einweg- /feuerzeug (–e)	das i͞nver- foyərtsoyk (–tsoygə)
d. nappies	die Wegwerf- windeln (fpl)	de͞e vekverf/vindəln/
distance	die Entfernung (–en)	de͞e entfernüng (–ən)
dive into /the water/	/ins Wasser/ tauchen ich tauche /ins Wasser/	/ins vasər/ towkhən ih̠ towkhə /ins vasər/

diversion	die Umleitung (–en)	dēē ŭmlītŭng (–ən)
divide (vb)	trennen	trenən
diving	das Tauchen	das towkhən
go d.	tauchen	towkhən
skin-d.	das Sporttauchen	das shporttowkhən
divorced	geschieden	gəsheedən
dizzy	schwindlig	shvindlih
I feel d.	mir ist s.	meer ist shvindlih
do	tun	tōōn
d. /some shopping/	/einkaufen/ gehen	/īnkowfən/ gāyən
	ich gehe /einkaufen/	ih gāyə /īnkowfən/
d. /me/ a favour	/mir/ einen Gefallen tun	/meer/ īnən gəfalən tōōn
could you do /me/ a favour?	könnten Sie /mir/ einen Gefallen tun?	kœnten zee /meer/ īnən gəfalən tōōn?
docks	der Hafen (–̈)	der hafən (heyfən)
doctor	der Arzt (–̈e)	der artst (eyrtstə)
I must go to the doctor's	ich muß zum A. gehen	ih mŭs tsŭm artst gāyən
documents	die Papiere (npl)	dēē papeerə
travel d.	die Reisepapiere	dēē rīzəpapeerə
car d.	die Wagenpapiere	dēē vāgənpapeerə
dog	der Hund (–e)	der hŭnt (hŭndə)
d. collar	das Halsband (–bänder)	das halsband (–bendər)
doll	die Puppe (–n)	dēē pŭpə (–n)
dollar	der Dollar (–s)	der dolar (–s)
domestic help	die Hausgehilfin (–nen)	dēē howsgəhilfin (–ən)
dominoes	die Dominos (npl)	dēē dominos
play d.	Domino spielen	domino shpeelən
	ich spiele D.	ih shpeelə domino
donkey	der Esel (–)	der āyzəl
door	die Tür (–en)	dēē tühr (–ən)
back d.	die Hintertür (–en)	dēē hintərtühr (–ən)
front d.	die Haustür (–en)	dēē howstühr (–ən)
doorbell	die Klingel (–)	dēē klingəl (–n)
doorman	der Portier (–s)	der portyāy (–s)
dose of /medecine/	eine Dosis (Dosen) /Medizin/	īnə dozis (dozən) /meditseen/
double	doppelt	dopəlt
a d. room	ein Doppelzimmer (–)	īn dopəltsimər

a d. whisky	ein doppelter Whisky	īn **d**ɔpəltər vis**kēē**
pay d.	zweimal soviel zahlen	tsv**ī**mal zo**fēēl** zahlen
doubt (vb)	zweifeln	tsv**ī**fəln
I d. it	das möchte ich bezweifeln	**das** mœhtə ih bətsv**ī**fəln
down	unter	**ŭn**tər
are you going down?	gehen sie hinunter?	g**āy**ən z**ēē** hin**ŭn**tər
downstairs	unten	**ŭn**tən
	ich gehe hinunter	ih g**āy**ə hin**ŭn**tər
dozen	das Dutzend (–e)	das **dŭt**sent (**dŭt**sendə)
a d. /eggs/	ein D. /Eier/	īn **dŭt**sent /**ī**ər/
half a d.	ein halbes D.	īn **hal**bəs **dŭt**sənt
drains (=sanitary system)	die Kanalisation (–en)	d**ēē** kanalizatsyon (–ən)
the drain's blocked	das Abflußrohr ist verstopft	das **ap**flŭsror ist fer**sht**ɔpft
draught (of air)	der Luftzug (–züge)	der **lŭft**ts**ōō**k (–ts**üh**gə)
draughts (game)	das Damespiel	das **dā**məshp**ēē**l
a game of d.	eine Partie Dame	**ī**nə part**ēē dā**mə
draughty	zugig	ts**ōō**gih
it's d.	es ist z.	es ist ts**ōō**gih
draw (a picture)	zeichnen	ts**ī**hnən
drawer	die Schublade (–n)	d**ēē shŭp**lādə (–n)
dreadful	furchtbar	**fŭrh**tbār
dress (n)	das Kleid (–er)	das kl**ī**t (kl**ī**dər)
dress (vb) (a wound)	verbinden	fer**bin**dən
dressing (medical)	der Verband (¨e)	der fer**bant** (–bendər)
dressing (=salad d.)	die Salatsoße (–n)	d**ēē** zal**ā**tzosə (–n)
dressing gown	der Morgenrock (–röcke)	der **mɔr**gənrɔk (–rœkə)
dressmaker	der Schneider (–) die Schneiderin (–nen)	der **shnī**dər/d**ēē shnī**dərin (–ən)
dress /oneself/	/mich/ anziehen	/mih/ **ant**s**ēē**ən
	ich ziehe /mich/ an	ih ts**ēē**ə /mih/ an
d. /the baby/	/das Baby/ anziehen	/das **bāy**b**ēē**/ **ant**s**ēē**ən
	ich ziehe /das Baby/ an	ih ts**ēē**ə /das **bāy**b**ēē**/**an**
dress shop	das Modegeschäft (–e)	das **mo**dəgəsheft (–ə)

Remember: [kh] as in acht (eight) [h] as in hungrig (hungry)
[œ] as in schön (beautiful) [üh] as in Tür (door)

drink (n) (usually alcoholic)	das Getränk (–e)	das gətreŋk (–ə)
soft d.	das alkoholfreie G.	das alkɔholfrīə gətreŋk
drink (vb)	trinken	triŋkən
drip-dry	bügelfrei	bühgəlfrī
a d.-d. shirt	ein bügelfreies Hemd (–en)	īn bühgəlfrīəs hemt (hemdən)
drive (n) (=entrance)	die Einfahrt (–en)	dee īnfart (–ən)
drive (vb)	fahren	fārən
go for a d.	ausfahren	owsfārən
	ich fahre aus	ih fārə ows
driver	der Fahrer (–)	der fārər
driving licence	der Führerschein (–e)	der führərshīn (–ə)
international d. l.	der internationale F.	der intərnatsyonālə führərshīn
drop /of water/	der /Wasser/tropfen (–)	der /vasər/trɔpfən
drug	die Droge (–n)	dee drogə (–n)
drunk (adj) (=not sober)	betrunken	bətruŋkən
dry (adj) (of drinks)	herb	herp
dry (adj) (of the weather)	trocken	trɔkən
dry (adj) (of things)	trocken	trɔkən
dry (vb)	trocknen	trɔknən
dry cleaner's	die Reinigung (–en)	dee rīniguŋ (–ən)
dryer		
hair d.	der Fön (–e)	der fœn (–ə)
dual carriageway	die Schnellstraße (–n)	dee shnelshtrāsə (–n)
duck/duckling	die Ente (–n)	dee entə (–n)
due (to arrive)		
/the train/'s d. /at 2 p.m./	/der Zug /kommt /um 14 Uhr/ an	der tsook kɔmt /ŭm feertsayn oor/ an
dull (of people and entertainments)	langweilig	laŋvīlih
dull (of the weather)	trüb	trühp
dummy (baby's d.)	der Schnuller (–)	der shnŭlər
during /the night/	während /der Nacht/	vēyrənt /der nakht/
dusk	die Abenddämmerung (–en)	dee ābəntdemərŭŋ (–ən)
dust	der Staub (no pl)	der shtowp
dustbin	der Mülleimer (–)	der mülīmər

dustman	der Müllfahrer (–)	der **mül**färər
duty (= obligation)	die Pflicht (–en)	dēē pfliht (–ən)
duty (= tax)	der Zoll (¨e)	der tsɔl (**tsœlə**)
duty-free goods	die zollfreien Waren (fpl)	dēē **tsɔl**frīən **vā**rən
duty-free shop	das Duty Free Shop	das **dü**tēē frēē shop
duvet	das Federbett (–en)	das **fay**dərbet (–ən)
d. cover	der Bettbezug (¨e)	der **bet**bətsōōk (–tsühgə)
dye (vb)	färben	**fer**bən
d. /this sweater/ /black/	/diesen Pullover/ /schwarz/ f.	/dēēzən pŭlovər/ /shvārts/ ferbən
dysentry	die Ruhr	dēē rōōr

E

each	jeder/jede/jedes	**yay**dər/**yay**də/**yay**dəs
e. /of the children/	jedes /der Kinder/	**yay**dəs /der kindər/
ear	das Ohr (–en)	das or (–ən)
earache	die Ohrenschmerzen (mpl)	dēē **or**ənshmertsən
early	früh	frǖh
e. train	der frühe Zug	der **frǖ**hə tsōōk
leave e.	f. abreisen	frǖh ap**rī**zən
	ich reise f. ab	ih̲ **rī**zə frǖh **ap**
earn	verdienen	fer**dēē**nən
earplugs	die Ohrenstopfen (mpl)	dēē **or**ənshtopfən
earrings	der Ohrring (–e)	der **or**ing̲ (–ə)
clip-on e.	der Ohrklips (–e)	der **or**klips (–ə)
e. for pierced ears	der Steckohrring (–e)	der **shtek**oring̲ (–ə)
earth (= the e.)	die Erde	dēē **ayr**də
easily	leicht	lī̲ht
east	der Osten	der **ɔs**tən
Easter	das Ostern	das **os**tərn
easy	leicht	lī̲ht
eat	essen	**es**ən
eau-de-Cologne	das Kölnischwasser	das **kœl**nishvasər
a bottle of e.-d.-C.	eine Flasche (–n) K.	**ī**nə flashə (–n) **kœl**nishvasər
education	die Erziehung	dēē ert**sēē**ŭng̲
educational	Erziehungs/ /	ert**sēē**ŭng̲s/ /
efficient	tüchtig	**tüh**ti̲h̲

110

egg	das Ei (–er)	das ī (–ər)
boiled e.	ein gekochtes Ei (–er)	īn gəkokhtəs ī (–ər)
fried e.	ein Spiegelei (–er)	īn shpeegəlī (–ər)
poached e.	ein pochiertes Ei (–er)	īn posheertəs ī (–ər)
scrambled eggs	das Rührei (s)	das rührī
elaborate (adj)	kompliziert	komplitseert
elastic (n)	der Gummizug (–züge)	der gŭmitsōok (–tsühgə)
elastic band	das Gummiband (–bänder)	das gŭmibant (–bendər)
Elastoplast (tdmk)	das Hansaplast (tdmk)	das hanzaplast
elbow	der Ellbogen	der elbogən
election	die Wahl (–en)	dee vāl (–ən)
electric	elektrisch	elektrish
e. shock	der Schlag (¨e)	der shlāk (shleygə)
electrical appliance shop	das Elektrogeschäft (–e)	das elektrogəsheft (–ə)
electrician	der Elektriker (–)	der elektrikər
electricity	die Elektrizität	dee elektritsiteyt
elsewhere	anderswo	andersvo
embarcation	die Einschiffung	dee īnshifūng
embark	einsteigen	īnshtīgən
	ich steige ein	ih shtīgə īn
embassy	die Botschaft (–en)	dee botshaft (–ən)
the /British/ E.	die /britische/ B.	dee /britishə/ botshaft
embroidery	die Stickarbeit	dee shtikārbīt
emergency	der Notfall (–fälle)	der notfal (–felə)
emergency exit	der Notausgang (–gänge)	der notowsgāng (–gengə)
emotional	gefühlsbetont	gəfühlsbətont
she's very e.	sie ist sehr emotionell	zee ist zāyr emotsyonel
employed by / /	beschäftigt bei / /	bəsheftiht bī / /
empty (adj)	leer	lāyr
empty (vb)	leeren	lāyrən
enclose	beilegen	bīlāygən
please find enclosed	als Anlage senden wir Ihnen	als anlāgə zendən veer eenən
	ich lege bei	ih lāygə bī
end (n)	das Ende (–n)	das endə (–n)

	masculine	feminine	neuter
the/a (subject)	der/ein	die/eine	das/ein
the/a (object)	den/einen	die/eine	das/ein
the (plural, subject/object)	die	die	die

end (vb)	enden	endən
endorse	stempeln	**shtemp**əln
e. my ticket to / /	meine Fahrkarte nach / / s.	mīnə fārkārtə nakh / / **shtemp**əln
e. /my passport/	/mein Paß/ s.	/mīn pās/ **shtemp**əln
engaged (telephone)	besetzt	bəzetst
engaged (to be married)	verlobt	ferlobt
engaged (toilet)	besetzt	bəzetst
engagement ring	der Verlobungsring (–e)	der ferlob**ū̄ng**sring (–ə)
engine (eg for a car)	der Motor (–en)	der motɔr (–ən)
engineer	der Ingenieur (–e)	der injāynyœ̄r (–ə)
engrave	gravieren	gravēērən
enjoyable	amüsant	amüzant
enjoy oneself	mich amüsieren ich amüsiere mich	mih amüzēērən ih amüzēērə mih
e. /swimming/	gern /schwimmen/ ich /schwimme/ gern	gern /shvimən/ ih /shvimə/ gern
enlarge	vergrößern	fergrœ̄sərn
enough	genug	gənōōk
e. money	g. Geld	gənōōk gelt
fast e.	schnell g.	shnel gənōōk
enroll	mich einschreiben ich schreibe mich ein	mih īnshrībən ih shrībə mih īn
enter	einreisen	īnrīzən
e. /a country/	in /ein Land/ einreisen ich reise in /ein Land/ ein	in /īn lant/ īnrīzən ih rīzə in /īn lant/ īn
entertaining	amüsant	amüzant
entitled		
be e. to /petrol coupons/	/benzingutschein/– berechtigt sein	/bentsēēn– gōōtshīn/– bərehtikt zīn
entrance	der Eingang (–̈e)	der īngang (–gengə)
e. fee	die Eintrittsgebühr (–en)	dēē īntritsgəbühr (–ən)
main e.	der Haupteingang (–̈e)	der **howpt**īngang (–gengə)
side e.	der Nebeneingang (–̈e)	der **nāy**bənīngang (–gengə)

envelope	der Umschlag (–schläge)	der ŭmshlāk (–shlēygə)
a packet of envelopes	ein Paket Umschläge	īn pakāyt ŭmshlēygə
airmail e.	der Luftpostumschlag (–schläge)	der lŭftpɔstŭmshlāk (–shlēygə)
epidemic (n)	die Epidemie (–n)	dēē epidemēē (–ən)
epileptic (adj)	epileptisch	epileptish
equal	gleich	glīh
equip	ausrüsten ich rüste aus	owsrüstən ih rüstə ows
equipment	die Ausrüstung	dēē owsrüstŭng
photographic e.	die fotografische A.	dēē fotogrāfishə owsrüstŭng
eraser	der Radiergummi (–s)	der radēērgŭmi (–s)
escape from / /	entkommen aus / / ich entkomme aus / /	entkɔmən ows / / ih entkɔmə ows / /
escort (n)	der Begleiter (–)	der bəglītər
escort (vb)	begleiten	bəglītən
espresso coffee	der Espresso (–s)	der espreso (–s)
estate agent	der Immobilienmakler (–)	der imobēēlyenmāklər
estimate (n)	die Schätzung (–en)	dēē shetsŭng (–en)
even (surface)	eben	āybən
evening	der Abend (–e)	der ābənt (ābəndə)
this e.	heute a.	hoytə ābənt
tomorrow e.	morgen a.	mɔrgən ābənt
yesterday e.	gestern a.	gestərn ābənt
evening dress (for men)	der Smoking (–s)	der smokīng (–s)
evening dress (for women)	das Abendkleid (–er)	das ābəntklīt (–klīdər)
every	jeder/jede/jedes	yāydər/yāydə/yāydəs
every day	jeden Tag	yāydən tāk
everyone	jedermann	yāydərman
everything	alles	aləs
everywhere	überall	ühbəral
exact	genau	gənow
exactly	genau	gənow
examination	die Untersuchung (–en)	dēē ŭntərzōōkhŭng (–ən)
medical e.	die ärztliche U.	dēē ēyrtstlihə ŭntərzōōkhŭng

113

examine (medically)	untersuchen	ŭntərz<u>oo</u>khən
example	das Beispiel (–e)	das b<u>i</u>shp<u>ee</u>l (–ə)
for e.	zum B.	tsŭm b<u>i</u>shp<u>ee</u>l
excellent	ausgezeichnet	owsgəts<u>i</u><u>h</u>nət
except	außer	owsər
excess	das Übermaß	das ühbərmās
e. baggage	das Übergepäck	das ühbərgəpek
e. fare	der Zuschlag (–schläge)	der ts<u>oo</u>shlāk (–shl<u>ey</u>gə)
exchange	umtauschen	ŭmtowshən
e. /this sweater/	/diesen Pullover/ u.	/d<u>ee</u>zən pŭlovər ŭmtowshənɪwshən
	ich tausche /diesen Pullover/ um	ih towshə /d<u>ee</u>zən pŭlovər/ ŭm
exchange rate	der Wechselkurs (–e)	der veksəlkŭrs (–ə)
excited	aufgeregt	owfgər<u>ay</u>ht
exciting	spannend	shpanent
excursion	der Ausflug (–flüge)	der owsfl<u>oo</u>k (–flühgə)
go on an e.	einen A. machen	<u>i</u>nən owsfl<u>oo</u>k makhən
	ich mache einen A.	ih makhə <u>i</u>nən owsfl<u>oo</u>k
excuse (n)	die Entschuldigung (–en)	d<u>ee</u> entsh<u>ŭ</u>ldig<u>ŭ</u>ng (–ən)
make an e.	mich entschuldigen	mih entsh<u>ŭ</u>ldigən
	ich entschuldige mich	ih entsh<u>ŭ</u>ldigə mih
excuse (vb)	entschuldigen	entsh<u>ŭ</u>ldigən
exhibition	die Ausstellung (–en)	d<u>ee</u> owsshtelüng (–ən)
exit	der Ausgang (–gänge)	der owsgang (–gengə)
emergency e.	der Notausgang (–gänge)	der notowsgang (–gengə)
expedition	die Expedition (–en)	d<u>ee</u> ekspeditsyon (–ən)
expensive	teuer	toyər
experienced	erfahren	erfārən
expert (adj)	sachkundig	zakhkündih
expert (n)	der Fachmann (Fachleute)	der fakhman (fakhloytə)
expire (= run out)	verfallen	ferfalən
/my visa/ has expired	/mein Visum/ ist v.	/m<u>i</u>n v<u>ee</u>zŭm/ ist ferfalən
explain	erklären	erkl<u>ey</u>rən

Remember: [kh] as in acht (eight) [h] as in hungrig (hungry)
[œ] as in schön (beautiful) [üh] as in Tür (door)

explanation	die Erklärung (–en)	dee erkleyrüng (–ər.)
export (vb)	exportieren	eksporteerən
exposure meter	der Belichtungs-messer (–)	der bəlih̲tüngzmesər
express		
e. letter	der Eilbrief (–e)	der īlbreef (–ə)
e. mail	der Eilboten	der īlbotən
e. service	der Schnelldienst (–e)	der shneldeenst (–ə)
e. train	der Schnellzug (-̈e)	der shneltsook (–tsühgə)
extension (telephone)	der Nebenanschluß (–schlüsse)	der naybənanshlüs (–shlüsə)
extra	extra	ekstra
extras	die Extras (pl)	dee ekstras
eye	das Auge (–n)	das owgə (–n)
eyebrow	die Augenbraue (–n)	dee owgənbrowə (–n)
eyelid	das Augenlid (–er)	das owgənleet (–leedər)
eye make-up	das Augen-Make-up	das owgən-mayk-ap

F

face	das Gesicht (–er)	das gəziht (–ər)
facecloth	der Waschlappen (–)	der vashlapən
facial (=face massage)	die Gesichtsmassage (–n)	dee gəzihtsmasājə (–n)
fact	die Tatsache (–n)	dee tātzahə (–n)
factory	die Fabrik (–en)	dee fabreek (–ən)
factory worker	der Fabrikarbeiter (–)	der fabreekārbītər
faded	verwelkt	fervelkt
faint (vb)	in Ohnmacht fallen	in onmakht falən
I fell f.	ich fühle mich matt	ih fühlə mih mat
fair (adj) (hair)	blond	blont
fair (adj) (=just)	billig	bilih̲
that's not f.	das ist nicht b.	das ist niht bilih̲
fair (adj) (skin)	hell	hel
fair (=entertainment)	der Jahrmarkt (-̈e)	der yārmārkt (–ə)
fall (n)	der Fall (-̈e)	der fal (felə)
fall (vb)	fallen	falən
I fell downstairs	ich bin die Treppe hinuntergefallen	ih bin dee trepə hinüntərgəfalən
false	falsch	falsh
f. teeth	die Zahnprothese (–n)	dee tsānprotayzə (–n)

115

family	die Familie (–n)	dēē famēēlyə (–n)
famous	berühmt	bərühmt
fan (n) (electric)	der Ventilator (–en)	der ventilātor (ventilātorən)
fan (n) (sports)	der Anhänger (–)	der anhengər
fancy dress	das Maskenkostüm	das maskənkostühm
far	weit	vīt
fare	der Fahrpreis (–e)	der fārprīs (–prīzə)
air f.	der Flugpreis (–e)	der flookprīs (–prīzə)
bus f.	der Busfahrpreis (–e)	der busfārprīs (–prīzə)
full f.	der volle F.	der folə fārprīs
half f.	der halbe F.	der halbə fārprīs
return f.	der Rückfahrpreis	der rükfārprīs (–prīzə)
single f.	der einfache F.	der īnfakhə fārprīs
train f.	der Zugfahrpreis (–e)	der tsookfārprīs (–prīzə)
farm	der Bauernhof (–höfe)	der bowərnhof (–hōēfə)
farmer	der Bauer (–n)	der bowər (–n)
farmhouse	das Bauernhaus (–häuser)	das bowərnhows (–hoyzər)
fashionable	modisch	modish
fast	schnell	shnel
f. train	der Schnellzug (–züge)	der shneltsook (–tsühgə)
fasten	mich anschnallen ich schnalle mich an	mih anshnalən ih shnalə mih an
fat (adj)	dick	dik
father	der Vater (–̈)	der fātər (feytər)
father-in-law	der Schwiegervater (–̈)	der shvēēgərfātər (–feytər)
fattening	daß dick macht	das dik makht
fatty (of food)	fett	fet
fault	die Schuld	dēē shult
it's my f.	das ist meine Schuld	das ist mīnə shult
faulty	fehlerhaft	faylərhaft
favour	der Gefallen	der gəfalən
do me a f.	mir einen G. tun	koentən zēē mēēr īnən gefalən toon
could you do me a f.?	könnten Sie mir einen G. tun?	koentən zēē mēēr īnən gəfalən toon
favourite (adj)	Lieblings/ /	lēēplings/ /
feather	die Feder (–n)	dēē faydər (–n)

February	der Februar	der **fáy**brūar
fed up		
be f. u.	es satt haben	es **zat** hābən
I'm f. u.	ich habe es satt	ih hābə es **zat**
feeding bottle	die Babyflasche (–n)	dēē **báy**bēēflashə (–n)
feel	mich fühlen	mih **fǖh**lən
I f. ill	ich bin krank	ih bin **kra͞ngk**
I f. sick	mir ist schlecht	mēer ist **shleht**
felt (material)	der Filz (–e)	der filts (–ə)
felt-tip pen	der Filzstift (–e)	der **filts**shtift (–ə)
feminine	weiblich	**vī**plih
ferry	die Fähre (–n)	dēē **fēy**rə (–n)
by f.	mit der F.	mit der **fēy**rə
festival	das Festspiel (–e)	das **fest**shpēēl (–e)
fetch	holen	**hol**ən
fever	das Fieber	das **fēē**bər
feverish	fieberhaft	**fēē**bərhaft
few	wenig	**váy**nik
a f.	einige	**ī**nigər
f. /people/	wenige /Leute/	**váy**nigə /loytə/
fewer	weniger	**váy**nigər
fiancé	der Verlobte (–n)	der ferlobtə (–n)
fiancée	die Verlobte (–n)	dēē ferlobtə (–n)
field (n)	das Feld (–er)	das felt (feldər)
fig	die Feige (–n)	dēē **fī**gə (–n)
fight (n)	der Kampf (–̈e)	der kampf (**kemp**fə)
fight (vb)	kämpfen	**kemp**fən
figure (=body)	die Figur (–en)	dēē fig**ōō**r (–ən)
fill in (form)	ausfüllen	**ows**fülən
fill in /a form/	/ein Formular/ ausfüllen	/īn fɔrmu**lār**/ **ows**fülən
	ich fülle /ein Formular/ aus	ih fülə /īn fɔrmu**lār**/ ows
fill (tooth)	plombieren	plɔmb**ēē**rən
fill (vessel)	füllen	**fül**ən
fillet (n)	das Filet (–s)	das fi**lāy** (–s)
fillet (vb)	als Filet herrichten	als fi**lāy** herrihtən
filling (tooth)	die Plombe (–n)	dēē **plɔm**bə (–n)
filling station	die Tankstelle (–n)	dēē **ta͞ngk**shtelə (–n)
film	der Film	der film (–ə)
ASA (tdmk)	ASA (tdmk)	**ā** es **ā**

	masculine	feminine	neuter
the/a (subject)	der/ein	die/eine	das/ein
the/a (object)	den/einen	die/eine	das/ein
the (plural, subject/object)	die	die	die

black and white f.	der Schwarzweißfilm (–e)	der **shvarts**vīsfilm (–ə)
cartridge f.	der Kassettenfilm (–e)	der kaset**ə**nfilm (–ə)
colour f.	der Farbfilm (–e)	der **fārb**film (–ə)
DIN (tdmk)	DIN (tdmk)	dēen
Polaroid f. (tdmk)	der Polaroidfilm (–e)(tdmk)	der **polaroyd**film (–ə)
Super 8	Super-8	zōopər-**akht**
16mm	16mm	**zehts**āyn mili**māy**tər
35mm 20/36 exposures	35mm 20 oder 36 Aufnahmen	**fünf**üntdr**ī**sih mili**māy**tər **tsvants**ih odər zeks**ünt**dr**ī**sih owf**nā**mən
120, 127, 620	120/127/620	hŭndərt**tsvants**ih/ hŭndərt**zēeb**ənŭnt-**tsvants**ih/ zekshŭndərt **tsvants**ih
film (=entertainment)	der Film (–e)	der film (–ə)
horror f.	der Horrorfilm (–e)	der **hor**ərfilm (–ə)
pornographic f.	der Pornofilm (–e)	der **por**nofilm (–ə)
thriller	der Abenteuerfilm (–e)	der **ab**əntoyərfilm (–ə)
Western	der Wildwestfilm (–e)	der **vilt**vestfilm (–ə)
filter-tipped cigarettes	die Filterzigaretten (fpl)	dēe **filt**ərtsigaretən
find	finden	**find**ən
f. /this address/	/diese Adresse/ f.	/dēezə adresə/ findən
	ich finde /diese Adresse/	ih **find**ə /dēezə adresə/
fine (adj) (of weather)	schön	shēen
it's f.	es ist s.	es ist **shēen**
fine (n) (=sum of money)	die Geldstrafe (–n)	dēe **gelt**shtrāfə (–n)
pay a f.	eine G. zahlen	īnə **gelt**shtrāfə **tsāl**ən
finger	der Finger (–)	der **fing**ər
finish	fertig sein	**fert**ih zīn
f. /my breakfast/	mit /meinem Frühstück/ f. s.	mit /mīnəm **früh**shtük/ **fert**ih zīn
	ich bin mit /meinem Frühstück/ fertig	ih bin mit /mīnəm **früh**stük/ **fert**ih

fire (n)	das Feuer (–)	das foyər
on f.	es brennt	es brent
fire alarm	der Feueralarm (–e)	der foyəralarm (–ə)
fire brigade	die Feuerwehr (–en)	dē foyərvāyr (–ən)
fire engine	das Feuerwehrauto (–s)	das foyərvāyrowto (–s)
fire escape	die Feuerleiter (–)	dē foyərlītər
fire extinguisher	der Feuerlöscher (–)	der foyərlœshər
fireman	der Feuerwehrmann (–leute)	der foyərvāyrman (foyərvāyrloytə)
fireworks (pl)	das Feuerwerk	das foyərverk
firework display	ein F.	īn foyərverk
firm (n) (=company)	die Firma (Firmen)	dē firma (firmən)
first	erster	āyrstər
at f.	zuerst	tsūāyrst
f. of all	erstens	āyrstəns
first aid	die erste Hilfe	dē ayrstə hilfə
f. a. kit	der Verbandskasten (–kästen)	der ferbantskastən (–kestən)
first class (adj)	erstklassig	āyrstklasih
first class (n)	die erste Klasse	dē ayrstə klasə
first name	der Vorname (–n)	der fornāmə (–n)
fish	der Fisch (–e)	der fish (–ə)
f. and chips	F. und Pommes frites	fish ŭnt pom frits
fishing	das Angeln	das angəln
go f.	a. gehen	angəln gāyən
	ich gehe a.	ih gāyə angəln
fishing line	die Angelschnur (–schnüre)	dē angəlshnōōr (–shnührə)
fishing rod	die Angelrute (–n)	dē angəlrōōtə (–n)
fishmonger's	der Fischhändler (–)	der fishhendlər
fit (adj)	fit	fit
he's f.	er ist in Form	er ist in form
fit (n) (=attack)	der Anfall (–fälle)	der anfal (–felə)
fit (vb)	sitzen	zitsən
it doesn't f. me	es paßt nicht	es past niht
it's a good f.	es sitzt gut	es zitst gōōt
fitting room (in shop)	der Umkleideraum (¨e)	der ŭmklīdərowm (–roymə)
fix (vb) (=mend)	ausbessern	owsbesərn
	ich bessere aus	ih besərə ows
fizzy	sprüdelnd	shprōōdəlnt
flag	die Fahne (–n)	dē fānə (–n)
flame (n)	die Flamme (–n)	dē flamə (–n)
flannel (=cloth)	der Flanell	der flanel

flash	das Blitzlicht (–er)	das **blits**li̱ht (–ər)
f. bulb	die Blitzlichtbirne (–n)	de̱e̱ **blits**li̱htbirnə (–n)
f. cube	der Blitzwürfel (–)	der **blits**würfəl
flask (vacuum f.)	die Thermosflasche (–n)	de̱e̱ termɔsflashə (–n)
flat (adj)	flach	flakh
flat (n)	die Wohnung (–en)	de̱e̱ vonu̱ng (–ən)
furnished f.	eine möblierte W.	ı̱nə mœble̱e̱rtə vonu̱ng
unfurnished f.	eine unmöblierte W.	ı̱nə ŭnmœble̱e̱rtə vonu̱ng
flavour	der Geschmack (·̈e)	der gəshmak (–shmekə)
banana f.	Banane	banānə
blackcurrant f.	schwarze Johannisbeere	**schvarts**ə johanisbāyrə
chocolate f.	Schokolade	shokolādə
strawberry f.	Erdbeere	ā̱yrdbāyrə
vanilla f.	Vanille	vanilyə
flea	der Floh (–e)	der flo (**flœ̱**ə)
fleabite	der Flohbiß (–bisse)	der **flo**bis (–ə)
flea market	der Flohmarkt (·̈e)	der **flo**markt (–merktə)
flea powder	das Flohpulver	das **flo**pŭlfər
flight	der Flug (·̈e)	der flo̱o̱k (**flü̱h**gə)
charter f.	der Charterflug (–flüge)	der **shart**ərflo̱o̱k (–flü̱hgə)
connecting f.	der Anschlußflug (–flüge)	der **anshlüs**flo̱o̱k (–flü̱hgə)
scheduled f.	der planmäßige F.	der **planmēy**sigə flo̱o̱k
student f.	der Studentenflug (–flüge)	der **shtŭdent**ənflo̱o̱k (–flü̱hgə)
flippers	die Schwimmflossen (fpl)	de̱e̱ **shvim**flɔsən
a pair of f.	ein Paar S.	ı̱n pār **shvim**flɔsən
float (vb)	treiben	trı̱bən
flood (n)	die Überschwemmung (–en)	de̱e̱ ü̱hbərshvemu̱ng (–ən)
flooded	überschwemmt	ü̱hbərshvemt
floor (of building)	der Stock (Stockwerke)	der shtɔk (**shtɔk**verkə)
basement (B)	das Souterrain (–s)	das zŭterē̱

Remember: [kh] as in acht (eight) [h] as in hungrig (hungry)
[œ̈] as in schön (beautiful) [üh] as in Tür (door)

ground f. (G)	das Erdgeschoß (–schösse)	das **āyr**dgəshɔs (–shɔsə)
/first/ f.	der /erste/ S.	der / **āy**rstə / shtɔk
top f.	der oberste S.	der oberstə shtɔk
floor (of room)	der Boden (¨)	der bodən (**bē**dən)
floor (=the ground)	der Boden (¨)	der bodən (**bē**dən)
florist's	das Blumengeschäft (–e)	das **blōō**məngəsheft (–ə)
flour	das Mehl	das **māy**l
flower	die Blume (–n)	dēē **blōō**mə (–n)
a bunch of flowers	ein Blumenstrauß (–sträusse)	īn **blōō**mənshtrows (–shtröysə)
flower pot	der Blumentopf (–töpfe)	der **blōō**məntɔpf (–tœpfə)
flu	die Grippe	dēē **gri**pə
fly (=insect)	die Fliege (–n)	dēē **flēē**gə (–n)
fly spray	das Fliegenspray (–s)	das **flēē**gənshprāy (–s)
flying	das Fliegen	das **flēē**gən
go f.	f. gehen	**flēē**gən **gāy**ən
	ich gehe f.	ih **gāy**ə **flēē**gən
fly to / /	fliegen nach / /	**flēē**gən nākh / /
fog	der Nebel	der **nāy**bəl
foggy	neblig	**nāy**blih
it's f.	es ist n.	es ist **nāy**blih
fold	falten	**fal**tən
folding /bed/	das Klapp/bett/ (–en)	das **klap**/bet/(–ən)
folk (adj)	volks/ /	**fɔl**ks/ /
f. art	die Volkskunst	dēē **fɔl**kskünst
f. dancing	das Volkstanzen	das **fɔl**kstantsən
f. music	die Volksmusik	dēē **fɔl**ksmüzēēk
folklore	die Folklore	dēē **fɔl**klorə
follow	folgen	**fɔl**gən
fond		
be f. of	gern haben	**gern** hābən
i'm f. of /him/	ich habe /ihn/ gern	ih hābə /ēēn/ **gern**
food	die Lebensmittel (npl)	dēē **lāy**bənsmitəl
where can I get some f.?	wo kann ich L. kaufen?	vo kan ih **lāy**bənsmitəl kowfən
f. poisoning	die Lebensmittel-vergiftung (–en)	dēē **lāy**bənsmitəl-fergiftüng (–ən)
health f.	die Reformkost	dēē re**fɔrm**kɔst
fool (n)	der Dummkopf (–köpfe)	der **dŭm**kɔpf (–kœpfə)

foolish	dumm	dŭm
foot (distance)	der Fuß (¨e)	der fōōs (fühsə)
foot (=part of body)	der Fuß (¨e)	der fōōs (fühsə)
on f.	zu F.	tsōō fōōs
football (=ball)	der Fußball (–bälle)	der fōōsbal (–belə)
football (=game)	der Fußball	der fōōsbal
play f.	F. spielen	fōōsbal shpēēlən
	ich spiele F.	ih shpēēlə fōōsbal
footpath	der Gehweg (–e)	der gāyvek (–vāygə)
for (prep)	für	führ
forehead	die Stirn (–en)	dēē shtirn (–ən)
foreign	ausländisch	owslendish
foreigner	der Ausländer (–) die Ausländerin (–nen)	der owslendər/dēē owslendərin (–ən)
forest	der Wald (¨er)	der valt (veldər)
forget	vergessen	fergesən
forgive	vergeben	fergāybən
fork (cutlery)	die Gabel (–n)	dēē gābəl
form (=document)	das Formular (–e)	das formūlār (–ə)
fortunately	glücklicherweise	glüklihərvīzə
forward to	nachsenden	nākhzendən
	ich sende nach	ih zendə nākh
please forward	bitte n.!	bitə nākhzendən
fountain	der Brunnen (–)	der brŭnən
fountain pen	der Füller (–)	der fülər
foyer (in hotels and theatres)	das Foyer (–s)	das fwayāy (–s)
fragile	zerbrechlich	tserbrehlīh
f. with care (=on labels)	vorsicht! z.!	forziht tserbrehlih
frame (n) (=picture f.)	der Rahmen (–)	der rāmən
frame (vb)	einrahmen	īnrāmən
	ich rahme ein	ih rāmə īn
free (=unconstrained)	frei	frī
free (=without payment)	gratis	gratēēs
freeze	frieren	frēērən
it's f.	es friert	es frēērt
frequent (adj)	häufig	hoyfih
fresh	frisch	frish
f. food (not stale, not tinned)	die frischen Lebensmittel (npl)	dēē frishən lāybənsmitəl
f. water (ie not salt)	das Süßwasser	das zühsvasər
Friday	der Freitag (–e)	der frītāk (–tāgə)
on Friday	am F.	am frītāk
on Fridays	freitags	frītāks

fridge	der Kühlschrank (–̈e)	der **kühl**shra̅n̅gk (–shrenkə)
friend	der Freund (–e)	der froynt (**froynd**ə)
friendly	freundlich	**froynt**li<u>h</u>
fringe (hair)	der Pony	der **pɔn**i
from	von	fɔn
front		
in f. of / /	vor / /	for / /
frontier	die Grenze (–n)	de̅e̅ **grent**sə (–n)
frost	der Frost	der frɔst
frosty	frostig	**frɔst**ih
frozen (=deep f.)	tiefgekühlt	te̅e̅fgəkühlt
f. /food/	die Tiefkühlkost (no pl)	de̅e̅ **te̅e̅f**kühlkɔst
fruit	das Obst (no pl)	das ɔpst
fresh f.	frisches O.	**frish**əs ɔpst
tinned f.	die Obstkonserven (fpl)	de̅e̅ **ɔpst**kɔnzervən
fruit juice (see also under juice)	der Obstsaft (–säfte)	der **ɔpst**zaft (–zeftə)
a bottle of f. j.	eine Flasche (–n) O.	i̅nə flashə (–n) **ɔpst**zaft
a glass of f. j.	ein Glas (–) O.	i̅n gla̅s **ɔpst**zaft
fry	braten	**bra̅t**ən
frying pan	die Bratpfanne (–n)	de̅e̅ **bra̅t**pfanə (–n)
full	voll	fɔl
f. board	die Vollpension	de̅e̅ **fɔl**pentsyon
fun	der Spaß	der shpa̅s
have f.	S. machen	shpa̅s **makh**ən
	das macht mir S.	das ma<u>kh</u>t me̅e̅r shpa̅s
funeral	das Begräbnis (–se)	das bəgre̅ypnis (–ə)
funicular	die Drahtseilbahn (–en)	de̅e̅ **dra̅t**zi̅lba̅n (–ən)
funny (=amusing)	komisch	**ko**mish
fur	der Pelz (–e)	der pelts (–ə)
f. coat	der Pelzmantel (–̈)	der **pelts**mantəl (–mentəl)
lined with f.	mit P. gefüttert	mit **pelts** gəfütərt
furnish	möblieren	mœble̅e̅rən
furnished /flat/	die möblierte /Wohnung/	de̅e̅ mœble̅e̅rtə /vonu̅n̅g/
furniture	die Möbel (npl)	de̅e̅ **mœ**bəl

	masculine	feminine	neuter
the/a (subject)	der/ein	die/eine	das/ein
the/a (object)	den/einen	die/eine	das/ein
the (plural, subject/object)	die	die	die

furniture shop	das Möbelgeschäft (–e)	das **mȫ**bəlgəsheft (–ə)
further	weiter	**vī**tər
fuse (n)	die Sicherung (–en)	dēē **zi**hərüng (–ən)
the lights have fused	wir haben einen Kurzschluß	vīr **hā**bən **ī**nən **kŭrts**shlŭs
/3 / amp f.	/drei/ Ampère S.	/drī/ am**pāy**r **zi**hərüng
f. wire	der Sicherungsdraht	der **zi**hərüngsdrāt
future (adj)	künftig	**künf**tih
future (n)	die Zukunft	dēē **tsŭ**künft

G

gabardine coat	der Gabardinenmantel (–mäntel)	der gabardēēnən**man**təl (–**men**təl)
gadget	das Gerät (–e)	das gə**rēy**t (–ə)
gale	der Sturm (¨e)	der **shtŭr**m (**shtür**mə)
gallery	die Galerie (–n)	dēē galə**rēē** (–ən)
art g.	die Kunstgalerie (–n)	dēē **künst**galərēē (–ən)
gallon	4 Liter	fēēr **lēē**tər
gallop	galoppieren	galo**pēē**rən
gamble (vb)	spielen	**shpēē**lən
gambling	das Spielen	das **shpēē**lən
gambling club	der Spielklub (–s)	der **shpēē**lklüp (–s)
game	das Spiel (–e)	das **shpēē**l (–ə)
play /tennis/	/Tennis/ spielen ich spiele /Tennis/	/tenis/ **shpēē**lən ih **shpēē**lə /tenis/
game (animals)	das Wild	das vilt
grouse	das schottische Moorhuhn (–hühner)	das **sho**tishə **mor**hōōn (–**hüh**nər)
hare	der Hase (–n)	der **hā**zə (–n)
partridge	das Rebhuhn (–hühner)	das **ray**phōōn (–**hüh**nər)
pheasant	der Fasan (–en)	der fa**zān** (–ən)
pigeon	die Taube (–n)	dēē **tow**bə (–n)
quail	die Wachtel (–n)	dēē **vakh**təl (–n)
wild boar	das Wildschwein (–e)	das **vilt**shvīn (–ə)
gaol	das Gefängnis (–se)	das gə**feyng**nis (–sə)
in g.	im G.	im gə**feyng**nis
garage	die Garage (–n)	dēē ga**rā**jə (–n)
garden	der Garten (¨)	der **gar**tən (**ger**tən)

124

garlic	der Knoblauch (no pl)	der **knoplowkh**
gas	das Gas (–e)	das gās (–ə)
gate (=airport exit)	der Ausgang (–gänge)	der **owsgang** (–gengə)
gate (=door)	das Tor (–e)	das tor (–ə)
gear	die Ausrüstung (–en)	dee **owsrüstüng** (–ən)
climbing g.	die Bergsteigerausrüstung (–en)	dee **berkshtīgər**-**owsrüstüng** (–ən)
diving g.	die Taucherausrüstung (–en)	dee **towkhər**-**owsrüstüng** (–ən)
general (adj)	allgemein	algəmīn
generator	der Generator (–en)	der generātor (generātorən)
generous	großzügig	**grostsühgih**
Gent's (lavatory)	die Herrentoilette (–n)	dee herəntwaletə (–n)
genuine	echt	eht
germ	der Keim (–e)	der kīm (–ə)
German measles	die Röteln (pl)	dee rœtəln
get /a taxi/	/ein Taxi/ rufen	/īn taksi/ rōōfən
get off at / /	an / / aussteigen ich steige an / / aus	an / / **owsshtīgən** ih shtīgə an / / ows
get on at / /	an / / einsteigen ich steige an / / ein	an / / **īnshtīgən** ih shtīgə an / / īn
gift	das Geschenk (–e)	das gəshengk (–ə)
gift shop	der Geschenkladen (¨)	der gəshengklādən (–leydən)
gin	der Gin (–s)	der djin (–s)
a bottle of g.	eine Flasche G.	īnə flashə (–n) **djin**
a g.	ein G.	īn djin
a g. and tonic	ein Gin-Tonic	īn djintonik
ginger (flavour)	der Ingwer	der **ing**vər
g. bread	der Pfefferkuchen (–)	der pfefərkōōkhən
girl	das Mädchen (–)	das **mey**thən
girlfriend	die Freundin (–nen)	dee froyndin (–ən)
give	geben	**gay**bən
g. it to /me/ please	g. Sie es /mir/ bitte	**gay**bən zee es /meer/ bitə
glacier	der Gletscher (–)	der gletshər
glad	froh	fro
he's g.	er ist f. darüber	er ist fro darühbər
glass	das Glas (¨er)	das glās (**gley**zər)
a g. of /water/	ein Glas /Wasser/	īn glās /vasər/

a wine g.	ein Weinglas (⁻er)	īn vīnglās (–glēȳzər)
glass (=substance)	das Glas	das glās
glasses	die Brille (–n) (s)	dēē brilə (–n)
a pair of g.	eine B.	īnə brilə
glassware shop	der Porzellanladen (–läden)	der portselānlādən (–lēȳdən)
gliding	das Segelfliegen	das zāȳgəlflēēgən
go g.	s. gehen	zāȳgəlflēēgən gāȳən
	ich gehe s.	ih gāȳə zāȳgəlflēēgən
gloves	die Handschuhe (mpl)	dēē hantshōōə
a pair of g.	ein Paar H.	īn pār hantshōōə
glue	der Klebstoff (–e)	der klāȳbshtof (–ə)
go	gehen	gāȳən
g. /home/	/nach Hause/ g.	/nākh howzə/ gāȳən
	ich gehe /nach Hause/	ih gāȳə /nākh howzə/
g. on a picnic	picknicken	piknikən
g. out with / /	mit / / ausgehen	mit / / owsgāȳən
	ich gehe mit / / aus	ih gāȳə mit / / ows
g. /shopping/	/Einkäufe/ machen	/īnkoyfə/ makhən
	ich mache /Einkäufe/	ih makhə /īnkoyfə/
let's g.	g. wir?	gāȳən wēēr
go to /a conference/	auf /eine Konferenz/ gehen	owf /īnə konferents/ gāȳən
	ich gehe auf /eine Konferenz/	ih gāȳə owf /īnə konferents/
goal	das Tor (–e)	das tor (–ə)
goalkeeper	der Torwart (–e)	der torvart (–ə)
goat	die Ziege (–n)	dēē tsēēgə (–n)
godfather	der Pate (–n)	der pātə (–n)
God/god	Gott/der Gott (⁻er)	got/der got (gœtər)
godmother	die Patin (–nen)	dēē pātin (–ən)
goggles	die Schutzbrille (–n) (s)	dēē shütsbrilə (–n)
underwater g.	die Taucherbrille (–n)(s)	dēē towkhərbrilə (–n)
go-kart	das Go-Kart (–s)	das go-kart (–s)
gold (adj)	golden	goldən
gold (n)	das Gold (no pl)	das golt

Remember: [kh] as in acht (eight) [h] as in hungrig (hungry)
[œ] as in schön (beautiful) [üh] as in Tür (door)

golf	das Golf	das gɔlf
a round of g.	eine Runde (–n) G.	īnə r**ŭ**ndə (–n) g**ɔ**lf
g. ball	der Golfball (–bälle)	der g**ɔ**lfbal (–belə)
g. club (=institution)	der Golfklub (–s)	der g**ɔ**lfklŭp (–s)
g. club (=object)	der Golfschläger (–)	der g**ɔ**lfshlēygər
g. course	der Golfplatz (–plätze)	der g**ɔ**lfplats (–pletsə)
good	gut	gōōt
good-looking	gutaussehend	gōōtowszāyənt
a g.-l. man	ein gutaussehender mann	īn gōōtowszāyəndər man
a g.-l. woman	eine hübsche Frau	īnə h**ü**pshə frow
goods (=merchandise)	die Waren (fpl)	dēē vārən
goods train	der Güterzug (–züge)	der g**ü**htərtsōōk (–tsühgə)
goose	die Gans (–̈e)	dēē gans (gensə)
wild geese	die Wildgans (–̈e)	dēē viltgans (–gensə)
government	die Regierung (–en)	dēē rəgēērŭng (–ən)
grade (=level)	der Grad (–e)	der grāt (grēydə)
gradually	allmählich	almēylih
graduate of / /	der Absolvent (–en) von / /	der apzɔlvent (–ən) fɔn / /
grammar (=a g. book)	das Grammatikbuch (–bücher)	das gramatikbōōkh (–bühkhər)
grammar (=language forms)	die Grammatik	dēē gramatik
grams	Gramm (s)	gram
grandchild	das Enkelkind (–er)	das engkəlkint (–kindər)
granddaughter	die Enkelin (–nen)	dēē engkəlin (–ən)
grandfather	der Großvater (–väter)	der grosfātər (–fēytər)
grandmother	die Großmutter (–mütter)	dēē grosmŭtər (–mütər)
grandson	der Enkel (–)	der engkəl
grant (for studies)	das Stipendium (–dien)	das shtipendyŭm (–dyən)
grapefruit (fresh)	die Grapefruit (–s)	dēē grāypfrōōt (–s)
tinned g.	die Grapefruit-konserve	dēē grāypfrōōt-kɔnservə
grapes	die Weintrauben (pl)	dēē vīntrowbən
a bunch of g.	eine Traube (–n)	īnə trowbə (–n)

grass	das Gras	das grās
grateful	dankbar	da͞ngkbār
gravy	die Soße (–n)	de͞e zosə (–n)
greasy (of food)	fett	fet
greasy (of hair)	fettig	fetih
green	grün	grühn
greengrocer's	der Gemüsehändler (–)	der gəmühzəhendlər
grey	grau	grow
grey (=g.-haired)	grau	grow
grill (vb)	grillen	grilən
groceries	die Lebensmittel (npl)	de͞e lāybənsmitəl
grocer's	der Lebensmittel-händler (–)	der lāybənsmitəl-hendlər
ground (=the g.)	der Boden	der bodən
group	die Gruppe (–n)	de͞e grǔpə
g. ticket	die Gruppenkarte (–n)	de͞e grǔpənkartə (–n)
grow (=cultivate)	anbauen ich baue / / an	anbowən ih bowə / / an
grow (of person)	wachsen	vaksən
guarantee (n)	die Garantie (–n)	de͞e garante͞e (–ən)
guarantee (vb)	garantieren	garante͞erən
guardian	der Vormund (–münde)	der formǔnt (–mündə)
guess	raten	rātən
guest	der Gast (¨e)	der gast (gestə)
guide (=person)	der Reiseführer (–)	der rīzəführər
guide (vb)	führen	führən
guide book	der Reiseführer (–)	der rīzəführər
guilty	schuldig	shǔldih
guitar	die Gitarre (–n)	de͞e gitarə (–n)
gum (of mouth)	das Zahnfleisch (no pl)	das tsānflīsh
chewing g.	der Kaugummi	der kowgǔmi
gun	das Gewehr (–e)	das gəvāyr (–ə)
gymnasium	die Turnhalle (–n)	de͞e tǔrnhalə (–n)

H

hair	das Haar (–e)	das hār (–ə)
hairbrush	die Haarbürste (–n)	de͞e hārbürstə (–n)
haircut	der Haarschnitt (–e)	der hārshnit (–ə)
hairdresser	der Friseur (–e) die Friseuse (–n)	der frizœr/de͞e frizœzə
hair dryer	der Fön (–e)	der fœn (–ə)

128

hairgrip	die Haarklammer (–n)	dee hārklamər
hair oil	das Haaröl (–e)	das hārœl (–ə)
a bottle of h. o.	eine Flasche H.	īnə flashə (n) hārœl
half	die Hälfte (–n)	dee helftə (–n)
h. a /litre/	ein halbes /Liter/	īn halbəs /leetər/
h. a /slice/	eine halbe /Scheibe/	īnə halbə /shībə/
ham	der Schinken (–)	der shingkən
h. /sandwich/	Schinken/brot/ (–e)	shingkən/brot/ (–ə)
/six/ slices of h.	/sechs/ Scheiben S.	/zeks/ shībən shingkən
hammer	der Hammer (–̈)	der hamər (hemər)
hand	die Hand (–̈e)	dee hant (hendə)
handbag	die Handtasche (–n)	dee hanttashə (–n)
handcream	die Handkreme (–s)	dee hantkrāym (–s)
handkerchief	das Taschentuch (–tücher)	das tashəntookh (–tühkhər)
handle (eg of a case)	der Henkel (–)	der hengkəl
hand luggage	das Handgepäck (no pl)	das hantgəpek
handmade	handgemacht	hantgəmākht
hang	hängen	hengən
hang gliding	das Drachenfliegen	das drākhənfleegən
happy	glücklich	glüklih
harbour	der Hafen (–̈)	der hāfən (heyfən)
h. master	der Hafenmeister	der hāfənmīstər
hard (=difficult)	schwer	shvāyr
hard (=not soft)	hart	hart
hare	der Hase (–n)	der hāzə (–n)
harpoon gun	die Harpune (–n)	dee harpoonə (–n)
harvest	die Ernte (–n)	dee erntə (–n)
hat	der Hut (–̈e)	der hoot (hühtə)
hate (vb)	hassen	hasən
have	haben	hābən
h. a rest	mich ausruhen	mih owsrooən
	ich ruhe mich aus	ih rooə mih ows
h. fun	mich amüsieren	mih amüzeerən
	ich amüsiere mich	ih amüzeerə mih
hay fever	der Heuschnupfen	der hoyshnŭpfən
he	er	āyr

	masculine	feminine	neuter
the/a (subject)	der/ein	die/eine	das/ein
the/a (object)	den/einen	die/eine	das/ein
the (plural, subject/object)	die	die	die

129

head (part of body)	der Kopf (ˉe)	der kɔpf (kœpfə)
headache	die Kopfschmerzen (mpl)	dēē kɔpfshmertsən
headphones	die Kopfhörer (mpl)	dēē kɔpfhœ̄rər
a pair of h.	ein Paar K.	īn pār kɔpfhœ̄rər
headwaiter	der Oberkellner (–)	der obərkelnər
health	die Gesundheit	dēē gəzünthīt
health certificate	der Gesundheitspaß (–pässe)	der gəzünthītspas (–pesə)
healthy	gesund	gəzünt
hear	hören	hœ̄rən
hearing aid	das Hörgerät (–e)	das hœ̄rgərēyt (–ə)
heart	das Herz (–en)	das herts (–ən)
h. attack	der Herzanfall (–fälle)	der hertsanfal (–felə)
h. trouble	die Herzbeschwerden (fpl)	dēē hertsbəshverdən
heat	die Hitze	dēē hitsə
heat wave	die Hitzewelle (–n)	dēē hitsəvelə (–n)
heater	der Heizofen (ˉ)	der hītsofən (–œ̄fən)
heating	die Heizung	dēē hītsüng
heavy	schwer	shvayr
heel (=part of body)	die Ferse (–n)	dēē ferzə (–n)
heel (=part of shoe)	der Absatz (ˉe)	der apzats (–zetsə)
high heeled	hochhackig	hokhhakih
low heeled	flach	flakh
height	die Höhe (–n)	dēē hœ̄ə (–n)
helicopter	der Hubschrauber (–)	der hoopshrowbər
help (n)	die Hilfe	dēē hilfə
help (vb)	helfen	helfən
helpful	hilfreich	hilfrīh
henna	die Henna	dēē hena
herbs	die Kräuter (pl)	dēē kroytər
here	hier	hēēr
hero	der Held (–en)	der helt (heldən)
heroine	die Heldin (–nen)	dēē heldin (–ən)
herring	der Hering (–e)	der hāyring (–ə)
high	hoch	hokh
h. chair	der Babystuhl (–stühle)	der bāybēēshtool (–shtühlə)
h. water	das Hochwasser	das hokhvasər
hijack (n)	die Entführung (–en)	dēē entführüng (–ən)
hill	der Hügel (–)	der hühgəl
hilly	hügelig	hühgəlih
hip	die Hüfte (–n)	dēē hüftə (–n)
hire (vb)	mieten	mēētən
history	die Geschichte (–n)	dēē gəshihtə (–n)

hit (vb)	treffen	**tref**ən
hitchhike	per Anhalter fahren	per **an**haltər **fā**rən
	ich fahre per A.	i<u>h</u> **fā**rə per **an**halter
hobby	das Hobby (–s)	das **ho**bi (–s)
hockey	das Hockey	das **ho**ke
play h.	H. spielen	**ho**ke sh**pēē**lən
	ich spiele H.	i<u>h</u> sh**pēē**lə **ho**ke
hole	das Loch (¨er)	das lo<u>kh</u> (**lœkh**ər)
holiday	die Ferien (pl)	dēē **fāy**ryən
h. camp	das Ferienlager (–)	das **fāy**ryən**lā**gər
package h.	die Pauschalreise (–n)	dēē **pow**shāl**rī**zə (–n)
public h.	der Feiertag (–e)	der **fī**ərtāk (–tāgə)
hollow (adj)	hohl	hol
home	die Heimat (–en)	dēē **hī**māt (–ən)
at h.	zu Hause	tsōō **how**zə
go h.	nach Hause gehen	nā<u>kh</u> **how**zə **gāy**ən
	ich gehe nach Hause	i<u>h</u> **gāy**ə nā<u>kh</u> **how**zə
homemade	selbstgemacht	**zelp**stgəma<u>kh</u>t
honest	ehrlich	**āyr**li<u>h</u>
honey	der Honig (–e)	der **ho**ni<u>h</u> (**ho**nigə)
a jar of h.	ein Glas (–) H.	īn glās (–) **ho**ni<u>h</u>
honeymoon	die Flitterwochen (pl)	dēē **flit**ərvo<u>kh</u>ən
hood (of a garment)	die Kapuze (–n)	dēē ka**pōō**tsə (–n)
hook	der Haken (–)	der **hā**kən
hoover (tdmk)	der Staubsauger (–)	der **shtowp**sowgər
hope (vb)	hoffen	**ho**fən
I h. not	hoffentlich nicht	**ho**fəntli<u>h</u> **ni<u>h</u>t**
I h. so	hoffentlich	**ho**fəntli<u>h</u>
horrific	schrecklich	**shrek**li<u>h</u>
hors d'oeuvres	die Vorspeise (–n)	dēē **for**shpīzə (–n)
horse	das Pferd (–e)	das pfāyrt (**pfāyr**də)
h. racing	das Pferderennen	das **pfāyr**dərenən
hose (=tube)	der Schlauch (¨e)	der shlow<u>kh</u> (**shloy<u>kh</u>**ə)
hospital	das Krankenhaus (–häuser)	das **krang**kənhows (–**hoy**zər)
hospitality	die Gastlichkeit	dēē **gast**li<u>h</u>kīt
host	der Gastgeber (–)	der **gast**gāybər
hostel (=youth h.)	die Herberge (–n)	dēē **her**bergə (–n)
hostess	die Gastgeberin (–nen)	dēē **gast**gāybərin (–ən)
hot	heiß	hīs
I'm h.	mir ist h.	mēēr ist hīs
it's h. (of things/food)	es ist h.	es ist hīs

it's h. (of the weather)	es ist h.	es ist **hīs**
hotel	das Hotel (–s)	das hotel (–s)
cheap h.	ein billiges H.	īn biligəs hotel
first class h.	ein erstklassiges H.	īn **āyrst**klasigəs hotel
medium-priced h.	ein H. mittlerer Preislage	īn hotel mitlərər **prīs**lāgə
hot-water bottle	die Wärmeflasche (–n)	dēē **verm**əflashə (–n)
hour	die Stunde (–n)	dēē **shtün**də (–n)
house	das Haus (¨-er)	das hows (**hoyz**ər)
housewife	die Hausfrau (–en)	dēē **hows**frow (–ən)
hovercraft	das Luftkissen- fahrzeug (–e)	das **lüft**kisənfārtsoyk (–tsoygə)
by h.	mit dem L.	mit dāym lüft - kisən**fārt**soyk
how?	wie?	vēē
humid	feucht	foyht
humour	der Humor	der **hōō**mor
he's got a sense of h.	er hat Sinn für H.	āyr hat zin führ **hōō**mor
hundred	das Hundert (–e)	das **hün**dərt (–ə)
hundreds of / /	Hunderte von / /	**hün**dərtə fon / /
hungry	hungrig	**hün**grih
be h.	h. sein	**hün**grih zīn
I'm h.	ich bin h.	ih bin **hün**grih
hunting	die Jagd	dēē yākt
go h.	auf die J. gehen	owf dēē **yā**kt gāyən
	ich gehe auf die J.	ih gāyə owf dēē **yā**kt
hurry	die Eile	dēē **ī**lə
I'm in a h.	ich bin in E.	ih bin in **ī**lə
hurry (vb)	eilen	**ī**lən
please h.!	machen Sie schnell bitte!	makhən zēē **shnel** bitə
hurt (adj)	verletzt	ferletst
husband	der Mann (¨-er)	der man (**men**ər)
hut	die Hütte (–n)	dēē **hüt**ə (–n)
hydrofoil	das Tragflügelboot (–e)	das **trāg**flühgəlbot (–ə)
by h.	mit dem T.	mit dāym **trāg**flügəlbot

Remember: [kh] as in acht (eight) [h] as in hungrig (hungry)
[œ] as in schön (beautiful) [üh] as in Tür (door)

I

ice	das Eis (no pl)	das īs
ice hockey	das Eishockey	das īshɔke
play i. h.	E. spielen	īshɔke shpeelən
	ich spiele E.	ih shpeelə īshɔke
ice skating	das Schlittschuhlaufen	das shlitshoolowfən
go i. s.	schlittschuhlaufen	shlitshoolowfən
	ich laufe schlittschuh	ih lowfə shlitshoo
ice cream	das (Speise)eis (no pl)	das (shpīzə)īs
iced (drink/water)	eisgekühltes	īsgəkühltəs
icy	eisig	īsih
idea	die Idee (–n)	dee idāy (–ən)
ideal (adj)	ideal	ideāl
identification	die Identifizierung (–en)	dee identifitseerüng (–ən)
identify	mich ausweisen	mih owsvīzən
	ich weise mich aus	ih vīzə mih ows
identity card	der Personalausweis (–e)	der perzonālowsvīs (–vīzə)
if	wenn	ven
i. you can	w. Sie können	ven zee kœnən
i. possible	w. möglich	ven mœklih
ill (=not well)	krank	krangk
he's i.	er ist k.	āyr ist krangk
illegal	illegal	ilegāl
illustration (in book)	die Abbildung (–en)	dee apbildüng (–ən)
immediate	sofortig	zofɔrtih
immediately	sofort	zofɔrt
immigration	die Einwanderung (–en)	dee īnvandərüng (–ən)
i. control	die Kontrolle (–n) bei der Einreise	dee kontrɔlə (–n) bī der īnrīzə
immune	immun	imoon
immunisation	die Impfung (–en)	dee impfüng (–ən)
immunise	impfen	impfən
immunity	die Immunität (no pl)	dee imüniteyt
diplomatic i.	die diplomatische I.	dee diplomātishə imüniteyt
impatient	ungeduldig	ŭngədŭldih
imperfect (goods)	fehlerhaft	faylərhaft
important	wichtig	vihtih
impossible	unmöglich	ŭnmœklih
improve	verbessern	ferbesərn

in	in	in
i. the morning	am Morgen	am mɔrgən
i./summer/	im /Sommer/	im /zɔmər/
i. /July/	im /Juli/	im /yōōli/
be i. (adv)	zu Hause sein	tsōō howzə zin
	ich bin zu Hause	ih bin tsōō howzə
in case of /fire/	bei /Feuer/	bī /foyər/
in front of	vor	fɔr
inch	der Zoll (–)	der tsɔl
include	einschließen	īnshlēēsən
	ich schließe ein	ih shlēēsə īn
including	einschließlich	īnshlēēslih
incredible	unglaublich	ŭnglowplih
independent	unabhängig	ŭnaphengih
indigestion	die Verdauungs-beschwerden (fpl)	dēē ferdowŭngs-bəshvāyrdən
i. tablet	eine Tablette (–n) gegen V.	īnə tabletə gāygən ferdowŭngs-bəshvāyrdən
individual (adj)	individuell	individŭel
indoors	innen	inən
indoor /swimming pool/	ein Hallenbad (–bäder)	īn halənbāt (–bēydər)
industry	die Industrie (–n)	dēē indŭstrēē (–ən)
inefficient	nicht tüchtig	niht tŭhtih
inexperienced	unerfahren	ŭnerfārən
infected	angesteckt	angəshtekt
infectious	ansteckend	anshtekənt
inflatable	aufblasbar	owfblāzbār
inflate	aufblasen	owfblāzən
	ich blase auf	ih blāzə owf
inform	benachrichtigen	bənākhrihtigən
i. /the police/ of / /	/die Polizei/ von / / b.	/dēē politsī/ fon / / bənākhrihtigən
	ich benachrichtige /die Polizei/ von / /	ih bənākhrihtigə /dēē politsī/ fon / /
informal	zwanglos	tsvanglos
information	die Auskunft (–künfte)	dēē owskŭnft- (–künftə)
i. desk	der Auskunftsschalter (–)	der owskŭnftsshaltər
i. office	das Informationsbüro (–s)	das informatsyons-büro (–s)
initials	die Initialen (fpl)	dēē initsyālən

134

injection	die Spritze (–n)	dēē **shprits**ə (–n)
I'd like a /tetanus/ i.	ich möchte eine /Tetanus/spritze	ih **mœht**ə īnə /**tāy**tanŭs/–shpritsə
injury	die Verletzung (–en)	dēē fer**lets**ŭng (–ən)
ink	die Tinte (–n)	dēē **tint**ə (–n)
a bottle of i.	eine Flasche (–n) T.	īnə flashə (–n) tintə
innocent (=not guilty)	unschuldig	**ŭn**shŭldih
inoculate	impfen	**impf**ən
inoculation	die Impfung (–en)	dēē **impf**ŭng (–ən)
inquiry	die Nachfrage (–n)	dēē **nākh**frāgə (–n)
make an i.	nachfragen	**nākh**frāgən
	ich frage nach	ih **frāg**ə nākh
insect	das Insekt (–en)	das in**zekt** (–ən)
i. bite	der Insektenstich (–e)	der in**zekt**ənshtih (–ə)
i. repellent	das Insektenspray (–s)	das in**zekt**ənsprāy (–s)
insecticide	das Insektizid (–e)	das inzektit**sēēt** (–ə)
a bottle of i.	eine Flasche (–n) I.	īnə flashə (–n) inzektit**sēēt**
inside (adv)	innen	**in**ən
inside (prep)	innerhalb	**in**ərhalp
i. /the house/	i. /des Hauses/	inərhalp /des **howz**əs/
insomnia	die Schlaflosigkeit	dēē **shlāf**lozihkīt
instead	anstatt	an**shtat**
i. of /coffee/	a. /Kaffee/	an**shtat** /ka**fāy**/
instructions	die Anweisungen (fpl)	dēē **an**vīzŭngən
i. for use	die Gebrauchs-anweisung (s)	dēē gə**browkhs**-anvīzŭng
instrument	das Instrument (–e)	das instrŭ**ment** (–ə)
musical i.	das Musik-instrument (–e)	das mŭ**zēēk**-instrŭment (–ə)
insulin	das Insulin	das intsŭ**lēēn**
insurance	die Versicherung (–en)	dēē fer**zih**ərŭng (–ən)
i. certificate	der Versicherungs-schein (–e)	der fer**zih**ərŭngsshīn (–ə)

---

	masculine	feminine	neuter
the/a (subject)	der/ein	die/eine	das/ein
the/a (object)	den/einen	die/eine	das/ein
the (plural, subject/object)	die	die	die

i. policy	die Versicherungs-police (–n)	dee ferzihərüngs-poleesə (–n)
insure /my life/	/mein Leben/ versichern	/mīn láybən/ ferzihərn
intelligent	klug	klook
intensive	intensiv	intenzeef
intercontinental (flight)	interkontinental	intərkontinentál
interested in / /	für / / interessiert	führ / / intəreseert
interesting	interessant	intəresant
internal	innerer	inərər
international	international	internatsyonál
interpret	dolmetschen	dolmetshən
interpreter	der Dolmetscher (–) die Dolmetscherin (–nen)	der dolmetshər/ dee dolmetshərin (–ən)
interval (= break)	die Pause (–n)	dee powzə (–n)
interval (in theatre)	der Zwischenakt (–e)	der tsvishənakt (–ə)
into	in	in
introduce	vorstellen	forshtelən
introduction	die Vorstellung (–en)	dee forshtelüng (–ən)
letter of i.	der Empfehlungsbrief (–e)	der empfáylüngsbreef (–ə)
invalid (n)	der Invalide (–n) die Invalide (–n)	der invaleedə (–n)/dee invaleedin (–ən)
invitation	die Einladung (–en)	dee īnlādüng (–ən)
invite	einladen	īnlādən
	ich lade ein	ih lādə īn
iodine	das Jod	das yot
a bottle of i.	eine Flasche (–n) J.	īnə flashə (–n) yot
iron (n) (object)	das Bügeleisen (–)	das bühgəlīzən
travelling i.	das Reisebügeleisen (–)	das rīzəbühgəlīzən
iron (vb) (clothing)	bügeln	bühgəln
ironmonger's	der Eisenwaren-händler (–)	der īzənvārənhendlər
irregular	unregelmäßig	ŭnráygəlmeysih
irritation (medical)	die Reizung (–en)	dee rītsüng (–ən)
island	die Insel (–n)	dee inzəl (–n)
itch	das Jucken (no pl)	das yŭkən

J

jacket	die Jacke (–n)	dee yakə (–n)
/tweed/ j.	die /Tweed/jacke (–n)	dee /tveet/yakə (–n)
jam	die Marmelade (–n)	dee marməlādə (–n)
January	der Januar	der yanūār
jar	das Glas (¨-er)	das glās (gleyzər)
a j. of /jam/	ein G. /Marmelade/	īn glās (–) /marməlādə/
jaw	der Kiefer (–)	der keefər
jazz	der Jazz	der djes
jealous	eifersüchtig	īfᵊrzühtih
he's j. of /me/	er ist e. auf /mich/	ayr ist īferzühtih owf /mih/
jeans	die Jeans (s)	dee djeens
a pair of j.	ein Paar J.	īn pār djeens
jelly (see under flavour)	das Gelee (–s)	das jelay
jellyfish	die Qualle (–n)	dee kvalə (–n)
Jew	der Jude (–n) die Jüdin (–nen)	der yoodə (–n)/dee yühdin (–ən)
jeweller's	der Juwelier (–e)	der yüveleer (–ə)
jewellery	der Schmuck	der shmŭk
jigsaw puzzle	das Puzzle (–s)	das pazəl (–s)
job	die Stelle (–n)	dee shtelə (–n)
jockey	der Jockey (–s)	der djoke (–s)
joke	der Spaß (¨-e)	der shpās (shpeysə)
journey	die Reise (–n)	dee rīzə (–n)
judo	das Judo	das yoodo
do some j.	J. treiben	yoodo trībən
jug	der Krug (¨-e)	der krook (krühgə)
a j. of / /	ein K. / /	īn krook / /
juice	der Saft (¨-e)	der zaft (zeftə)
grapefruit j.	der Grapefruitsaft (–säfte)	der graypfrootzaft (–zeftə)
lemon j.	der Zitronensaft (–säfte)	der tsitronənzaft (–zeftə)
orange j.	der Orangensaft (–säfte)	der oranjənzaft (–zeftə)
pineapple j.	der Ananassaft (–säfte)	der ananaszaft (–zeftə)
tomato j.	der Tomatensaft (–säfte)	der tomātənzaft (–zeftə)
juicy	saftig	zaftih
July	der Juli	der yooli
jump (vb)	springen	shpringən
junction	die Kreuzung (–en)	dee kroytsŭng (–ən)

| June | der Juni | der yōoni |
| junk shop | der Trödelladen (¨) | der trōedəllādən (–lāydən) |

K

keep (vb)	halten	haltən
kettle	der Kessel (–)	der kesəl
key	der Schlüssel (–)	der shlüsəl
key ring	der Schlüsselring (–e)	der shlüsəlring (–ə)
khaki (colour)	khaki	kāki
kick (vb)	stoßen	shtosən
kidneys	die Nieren (fpl)	dēē nēērən
kill (vb)	töten	tœtən
kilogramme/kilo	das Kilogramm/das Kilo	das kilogram/das kēēlo
kilometre	der Kilometer (–)	der kilomāytər
kind (adj) (=friendly)	nett	net
it's very k. of you	das ist sehr n. von Ihnen	das ist zāyr net fon ēēnən
kind (n) (=type)	die Art (–en)	dēē ārt (–ən)
a k. of /beer/	eine A. /Bier/	īnə ārt /bēēr/
kindness	die Güte (no pl)	dēē gühtə
king	der König (–e)	der kœnih (kœnigə)
kiss (n)	der Kuß (¨e)	der kŭs (küsə)
kiss (vb)	küssen	küsən
kit	die Ausrüstung (–en)	dēē owsrüstŭng (–ən)
first aid k.	der Verbandskasten (–kästen)	der ferbantskastən (–kestən)
kitchen	die Küche (–n)	dēē kühə
kite	der Drachen (–)	der drakhən
Kleenex (tissues) (tdmk)	die Kleenextaschentücher (npl) (tdmk)	dēē klēēnekstashəntükhər
a box of K.	eine Packung (–en) K.	īnə pakŭng klēēnekstashəntükhər
knee	das Knie (–)	das knēē (knēēə)
knife	das Messer (–)	das mesər
carving k.	das Vorlegemesser (–)	das forlāygəmesər
knit	stricken	shtrikən
knitting	das Stricken	das shtrikən
do some k.	stricken	shtrikən

Remember:[kh] as in acht (eight) [h] as in hungrig (hungry)
[œ] as in schön (beautiful) [üh] as in Tür (door)

k. needles	die Stricknadeln (fpl)	dēē **shtrik**nādəln
k. pattern	das Strickmuster (-)	das **shtrik**mŭstər
knitwear	die Strickwaren (pl)	dēē **shtrik**vārən
knob (door)	der Knauf (¨-e)	der knowf (**knoy**fə)
knob (radio)	der Knopf (¨-e)	der knɔpf (**knœp**fə)
know (a fact)	wissen	**vis**ən/
I k.	das weiß ich	das vīs i̱h
know (a person)	kennen	**ken**ən
I k. him	ich kenne ihn	i̱h **ken**ə ēen
Kosher	koscher	**kosh**ər

L

label (=luggage l.)	das Schildchen (-)	das **shilt**hən
stick-on l.	das Aufklebe-schildchen (-)	das **owf**klāybə-**shilt**hən
lace (=material)	die Spitze (-n)	dēē **shpits**ə (-n)
laces	die Schnürsenkel (pl)	dēē **shnühr**zen̄gkəl
ladder	die Leiter (-n)	dēē **līt**ər(-n)
Ladies' (=lavatory)	die Damentoilette (-n)	dēē **dā**məntwaletə (-n)
lady	die Dame (-n)	dēē **dā**mə (-n)
lake	der See (-n)	der zāy (-n)
lamb	das Lamm (¨-er)	das lam (**lem**ər)
a leg of l.	ein Lammkeule (-n)	īn **lam**koylə (-n)
l. chop	das Lammkotelett (-s)	das **lam**kotələt (-s)
lamp	die Lampe (-n)	dēē **lamp**ə (-n)
bicycle l.	die Fahrradlampe (-n)	dēē **fār**rātlampə (-n)
lampshade	der Lampenschirm (¨-e)	der **lamp**ənshirm (-ə)
land	das Land	das lant (**lend**ər)
landed (of a plane)	gelandet	gə**land**ət
landlady	die Vermieterin (-nen)	dēē fer**mēē**tərin (-ən)
landlord	der Vermieter (-)	der fer**mēē**tər
lane (=small road)	der Weg (¨-e)	der vek (**vāy**gə)
lane (=traffic l.)	die Fahrbahn (¨-en)	dēē **fār**bān (-ən)
language	die Sprache (-n)	dēē **shprā**khə (-n)
large (size)	groß	gros
last (= final)	letzter	**lets**tər

late	spät	shpeyt
he's l.	er kommt zu s.	ayr komt tsoo shpeyt
it's l. (= time of day)	es ist s.	es ist shpeyt
later (= at a l. time)	später	shpeytər
laugh (vb)	lachen	lakhən
launder	waschen	vashən
launderette	der Waschsalon (–s)	der vashzalon (–s)
laundry (place)	die Wäscherei (–en)	dee veshərī (–ən)
laundry (washing)	die Wäsche (no pl)	dee veshə
lavatory	die Toilette (–n)	dee twaletə (–n)
Gent's	die Herrentoilette (–n)	dee herəntwaletə (–n)
Ladies'	die Damentoilette (–n)	dee dāməntwaletə (–n)
law	das Gesetz (–e)	das gəzets (–ə)
lawyer	der Rechtsanwalt (–anwälte)	der rehtsanvalt (–veltə)
laxative	das Abführmittel (–)	das apführmitəl
mild l.	ein mildes A.	īn mildəs apführmitəl
strong l.	ein starkes A.	īn shtarkəs apführmitəl
suppository	das Zäpfchen (–)	das tsepfhən
lay-by	der Rastplatz (–plätze)	der rastplats (–pletsə)
lazy	faul	fowl
leaflet	der Prospekt (–e)	der prospekt (–ə)
leak (n)	das Loch (¨er)	das lokh (lœkhər)
leak (vb)	auslaufen	owslowfən
it's leaking	es läuft aus	es loyft ows
learner (driver)	der Fahrschüler (–)	der fārshülər
learn /German/	/Deutsch/ lernen ich lerne /Deutsch/	/doytsh/ lernən ih lernə /doytsh/
leather	das Leder (–)	das lāydər
l. goods shop	das Lederwarengeschäft (–e)	das lāydərvārəngəsheft (–ə)
leave	lassen	lasən
l. /my luggage/	/mein Gepäck/ zurücklassen ich lasse /mein Gepäck/ zurück	/mīn gəpek/ tsürüklasən ih lasə /mīn gəpek/ tsürük
l. me alone	l. Sie mich in Ruhe	lasən zee mih in rooə

I've left /my suitcase/ behind	ich habe /meinen Koffer/ zurückgelassen	ih habə /mīnən kɔfər/ tsŭrükgəlasən
leave (=depart)	abfahren	apfārən
l. at /4.30 p.m./	um /sechzehn Uhr dreißig/ a.	ŭm /zehtsayn ōor drīsih/ apfārən
l. in /July/	im /Juli/ a.	im /yōoli/ apfārən
l. on /Monday/	am /Montag/ a.	am /montāk/ apfārən
	ich fahre am Montag/ ab	ih fārə am /montāk/ ap
left (= not right)	links	lingks
left-handed	linkshändig	lingkshendih
left-luggage office	die Gepäck-aufbewahrung (–en)	dēē gəpek–owfbəvārŭng (–ən)
leg	das Bein (–e)	das bīn (–ə)
legal	gesetzlich	gəzetslih
lemon	die Zitrone (–n)	dēē tsitronə (–n)
a slice of l.	eine Scheibe (–n) Z.	īnə shībə (–n) tsitronə
l. juice	der Zitronensaft (–säfte)	der tsitronənzaft (–zeftə)
lemonade	die Limonade (–n)	dēē limonādə (–n)
a bottle of l.	eine Flasche (–n) L.	īnə flashə (–n) limonādə
a can of l.	eine Dose (–n) L.	īnə dozə (–n) limonādə
a glass of l.	ein Glas (–) L.	īn glās limonādə
lend	leihen	līən
could you l. me some /money/?	könnten Sie mir etwas /Geld/ l.?	kœntən zēē mēēr etvas /gelt/ līən
length	die Länge (–n)	dēē lengə (–n)
full l.	die volle L.	dēē fɔlə lengə
knee l.	die Knielänge	dēē knēēlengə
lengthen	verlängern	ferlengərn
lens (of camera)	die Linse (–n)	dēē linzə (–n)
l. cap	der Verschluß (–schlüsse)	der fershlŭs (–shlŭsə)
wide-angle l.	das Weitwinkel-objectiv (–e)	das vītvingkəl-ɔpyektēēf (–tēēvə)
zoom l.	die Gummilinse (–n)	dēē gŭmilinzə (–n)
less	weniger	vāynigər

	masculine	feminine	neuter
the/a (subject)	der/ein	die/eine	das/ein
the/a (object)	den/einen	die/eine	das/ein
the (plural, subject/object)	die	die	die

lesson	die Stunde (–n)	dēē **shtŭnd**ə (–n)
driving l.	die Fahrstunde (–n)	dēē **fār**shtŭndə (–n)
/German/ l.	die /Deutsch/–stunde (–n)	dēē /**doytsh**/shtŭndə (–n)
let (=allow)	lassen	**las**ən
let /me/ try	l. Sie /mich/ es versuchen	**las**ən zēē /mi_h_/ es ferz**ōō**khən
letter (correspondence)	der Brief (–e)	der brēēf (–ə)
air-l.	der Luftpostbrief (–e)	der **lŭft**pɔstbrēēf (–ə)
express l.	der Eilbrief (–e)	der **īl**brēēf (–ə)
l. box	der Briefkasten (–kästen)	der **brēēf**kastən (–kestən)
registered l.	der eingeschriebene Brief (–e)	der **īn**gəshrēēbənə brēēf (–ə)
letter (= of the alphabet)	der Buchstabe (–n)	der **bōŏkh**shtābə (–n)
lettuce	der grüne Salat (–e)	der **grüh**nə zalāt (–ə)
level (adj)	eben	**āy**bən
level (n) (=grade)	der Stand (ˑe)	der shtant (**shtend**ə)
level crossing	der Bahnübergang (–gänge)	der **bān**ühbərgang (–gengə)
library	die Bücherei (–en)	dēē **bükh**ərī (–ən)
licence	die Lizenz (–en)	dēē **lits**ents (–ən)
lid (of eye)	das Lid (–er)	das lēēt (**lēēd**ər)
lid (of pot)	der Deckel (–)	der **dek**əl
lie (n) (=untruth)	die Lüge (–n)	dēē **lüg**ə (–n)
lie (vb) (=l. down)	liegen	**lēēg**ən
lie (vb) (=tell an untruth)	lügen	**lühg**ən
lifebelt	der Rettungsgürtel (–)	der **retŭng̅s**gürtəl
lifeboat	das Rettungsboot (–e)	das **retŭng̅s**bot (–ə)
lifeguard	der Rettungsschwimmer (–)	der **retŭng̅s**shvimər
life jacket	die Schwimmweste (–n)	dēē **shvim**vestə (–n)
lift (n) (= elevator)	der Aufzug (–züge)	der **owfts**ōōk (–tsühgə)
lift (n) (=ride)		
could you give me a l. to / /?	könnten Sie mich nach / / mitnehmen?	**kœnt**ən zēē mi_h_ nākh / / **mit**nāymən

lift (vb)	aufheben	owfhāybən
	ich hebe auf	ih hāybə owf
light switch	der Lichtschalter (–)	der lihtshaltər
light (adj) (= not dark)	hell	hel
light (adj) (= not heavy)	leicht	līht
light (n) (electric l.)	das Licht (–er)	das liht (–ər)
can I have a l.?	haben Sie Feuer bitte?	hābən zēē foyər bitə
light /a fire/	/ein Feuer/ anzünden	/īn foyər/ antsündən
	ich zünde /ein Feuer/ an	ih tsündə /īn foyər/ an
light bulb	die Glühbirne (–n)	dēē glühbirnə (–n)
/40/ watt	/vierzig/ Watt	/fēērtsih/ vat
lighter (=cigarette l.)	das Feuerzeug (–e)	das foyərtsoyk (–tsoygə)
disposable l.	das Einwegfeuerzeug (–e)	das īnvek-foyərtsoyk (–tsoygə)
lighter fuel	das Feuerzeugbenzin	das foyərtsoykbentsēēn
like (prep)	so wie	zo vēē
what's it l.?	wie ist es?	vēē ist /es/
like (vb)	gern haben	gern hābən
do you l. /swimming/?	/schwimmen/ Sie gern?	/shvimən/ zēē gern
I l. it	ich habe es gern	ih hābə es gern
likely	wahrscheinlich	vārshīnlih
lime	die Limetta (Limetten)	dēē limeta (limetən)
l. juice	der Limettensaft (–säfte)	der limetənzaft (–zeftə)
limit (n)	die Grenze (–n)	dēē grentsə (–n)
height l.	die Maximalhöhe (–n)	dēē maksimālhœə (–n)
speed l.	Geschwindigkeits-begrenzung (–en)	dēē gəshvindihkīts-bəgrentsüng (–ən)
weight l.	das Höchstgewicht (–e)	das hœhstgəviht (–ə)
line	die Linie (–n)	dēē lēēnyə (–n)
outside l.	die Außenlinie (–n)	dēē owsənlēēnyə (–n)
telephone l.	die Leitung	dēē lītüng (–ən)
linen (bed)	die Bettwäsche (no pl)	dēē betveshə

linen (table)	die Tischwäsche (no pl)	dēē tishveshə
liner	der Passagierdampfer (–)	der pasajēērdampfər
lingerie department	die Damenwäsche-abteilung (–en)	dēē dāmənveshə aptīlūng (–ən)
lining	das Futter (no pl)	das fūtər
/fur/ l.	das /Pelz/futter (no pl)	das /pelts/fūtər
lip	die Lippe (–n)	dēē lipə (–n)
lower l.	die Unterlippe (–n)	dēē ŭntərlipə (–n)
upper l.	die Oberlippe (–n)	dēē obərlipə (–n)
lipstick	der Lippenstift (–e)	der lipənshtift (–ə)
liqueur	der Likör (–e)	der likœr (–ə)
liquid	die Flüssigkeit (–en)	dēē flüsihkīt (–ən)
list	die Liste (–n)	dēē listə (–n)
shopping l.	die Einkaufsliste (–n)	dēē īnkowfslistə (–n)
wine l.	die Weinkarte (–n)	dēē vīnkārtə (–n)
listen to /some music/	/Musik/ hören	/mŭzēēk/ hœrən
	ich höre /Musik/	ih hœrə /mŭzēēk/
litre	das Liter (–)	das lēētər
litter	der Abfall (–fälle)	der apfal (–felə)
little (adj)	klein	klīn
a l. boy	ein kleiner Junge	īn klīnər yŭngə
smaller	kleiner	klīnər
smallest	kleinste	klīnstə
little (n)	ein wenig	īn vāynih
a l. money	e. w. Geld	īn vāynih gelt
live (= be alive)	leben	lāybən
live (=reside)	wohnen	vonən
liver	die Leber (–n)	dēē lāybər (–n)
load	laden	lādən
loaf (of bread)	der Laib (–e)	der līp (lībə)
a large l.	ein großer L. Brot	īn grosər līp brot
a small l.	ein kleiner. L. Brot	īn klīnər līp brot
lobster	der Hummer (–)	der hŭmər
local (adj)	örtlich	œrtlih
l. crafts	das heimische Kunsthandwerk (s)	das hīmishə kŭnsthantverk
lock (n)	das Schloß (–er)	das shlɔs (shlœsər)
lock (vb)	zusperren	tsōōshperən
	ich sperre zu	ih shperə tsōō

Remember:[kh] as in acht (eight) [h] as in hungrig (hungry)
[œ] as in schön (beautiful) [üh] as in Tür (door)

144

locker	das Schließfach (¨-er)	das sh<u>lee</u>sfakh (–fehər)
left-luggage l.	das Gepäck-schließfach (–fächer)	das gəpeksh<u>lee</u>sfákh (–fehər)
logbook (car)	der Kraftfahrzeug-schein (–e)	der **kraft**fártsoygsh<u>ī</u>n (–ə)
lonely	einsam	<u>ī</u>nzām
long	lang	la<u>ng</u>
look after /the baby/	/das Baby/ betreuen	/das **b<u>ay</u>bee**/ bətroyən
	ich betreue /das Baby/	ih bətroyə /das **baybee**/
look at /this/	/das/ ansehen	/das/ **anz<u>ay</u>ən**
	ich sehe /das/ an	ih **z<u>ay</u>ə** /das/ an
look for /my passport/	/meinen Paß/ suchen	/m<u>ī</u>nən **pas**/ **z<u>oo</u>kh**ən
	ich suche /meinen Paß/	ih **z<u>oo</u>kh**ə /m<u>ī</u>nən **pas**/
look /smart/	/elegant/ aussehen	/elegant/ **ows<u>ay</u>ən**
	ich sehe /elegant/ aus	ih **z<u>ay</u>ə** /elegant/ ows
lorry	der Lastwagen (–)	der **last**v<u>ā</u>gən
lorry driver	der Lastwagenfahrer (–)	der **last**v<u>ā</u>gənfárər
lose	verlieren	ferl<u>ee</u>rən
I've lost /my wallet/	ich habe /meine Brieftasche/ verloren	ih habe /m<u>ī</u>nə **bree**ftashə/ ferlorən
lost	verloren	ferlorən
I'm l.	ich habe mich verirrt	ih h<u>ā</u>bə mih ferirt
lost property office	das Fundbüro	das **fŭnt**büro
lot	viel	f<u>ee</u>l
a l. of /money/	v. /Geld/	f<u>ee</u>l /gelt/
loud	laut	lowt
loudly	laut	lowt
lounge (in hotel)	der Aufenthaltsraum (–räume)	der **owfenthaltsrowm** (–roymə)
departure l.	die Abflughalle (–n)	d<u>ee</u> **apfl<u>oo</u>khalə** (–n)
TV l.	der Fernsehraum (–räume)	der **fern**z<u>ay</u>rowm (–roymə)
love (n)	die Liebe	d<u>ee</u> **l<u>ee</u>b**ə
make l.	mich lieben	mih **l<u>ee</u>b**ən
love (vb)	lieben	**l<u>ee</u>b**ən
low (=not high)	niedrig	n<u>ee</u>drih
l. water	das Niedrigwasser	das **n<u>ee</u>drih**vasər

145

low (=not loud)	leise	līzə
lower (vb)	herunterlassen	herŭntərlasən
LP (=long playing record)	die Langspielplatte (–n)	dēē langshpēēlplatə (–n)
lucky		
be l.	Glück haben	glük hābən
he's l.	er hat G.	āyr hat glük
luggage	das Gepäck (no pl)	das gəpek
cabin l.	das Handgepäck (no pl)	das hantgəpek
hand l.	das Handgepäck (no pl)	das hantgəpek
l. rack (in train)	das Gepäcknetz (–e)	das gəpeknets (–ə)
l. van (on train)	der Gepäckwagen	der gəpekvāgən
lump (body)	der Klumpen (–)	der klŭmpən
a l. of sugar	ein Stück Zucker	īn shtük tsükər
lunch	das Mittagessen (–)	das mitāgesən
have l.	zu Mittag essen	tsōō mitāk esən
packed l.	das Lunchpaket (–e)	das lanshpakət (–ə)
luxury	der Luxus (s)	der lŭksüs

M

machine	die Maschine (–n)	dēē mashēēnə (–n)
mad	verrückt	ferükt
made in / /	hergestellt in / /	hergəshtelt in / /
magazine	die Zeitschrift (–en)	dēē tsītshrift (–ən)
magnifying glass	das Vergrößerungsglas (–gläser)	das fergrœsərŭngsglās (–gleyzər)
mahogany (wood)	das Mahagoni (no pl)	das mahagoni
maid	das Dienstmädchen (–)	das dēēnstmeythən
m. service	der Zimmerservice	der tsimərservēēs
mail	die Post	dēē pɔst
by air-m.	die Luftpost	dēē lŭftpɔst
express m.	per Eilboten	per īlbotən
send it by / / m.	per / /post schicken	per / /pɔst shikən
surface m.	die Normalpost	dēē nɔrmālpɔst
main	Haupt/ /	howpt/ /
m. road	die Hauptstraße (–n)	dēē howptshtrāsə (–n)
make (n) (eg of a car)	die Marke (–n)	dēē markə (–n)

nake (vb)	machen	makhən
m. /a complaint/	mich beschweren	mih bəshvāyrən
	ich beschwere mich	ih bəshvāyrə mih
m. /money/	/Geld/ verdienen	/gelt/ ferdeenən
make-up (= face m.-u.)	das Make-up (s)	das māyk-ap
eye m.-u.	das Augen-make-up	das owgən-māyk-ap
male (adj)	männlich	menlih
mallet	der Holzhammer (–hämmer)	der hɔltshamər (–hemər)
man	der Mann (¨-er)	der man (menər)
young m.	der junge M.	der yüngə man
manager	der Direktor (–en)	der direktɔr (–ən)
manicure	die Maniküre (–n)	dee manikührə (–n)
m. set	das Maniküretui (–s)	das manikühretvee (–s)
man-made (adj)	künstlich	künstlih
m.-m. fibre	die Kunstfaser (–n)	dee künstfāzər (–n)
many	viele	feelə
map	die Landkarte (–n)	dee lantkārtə (–n)
large-scale m.	die L. in großem Maßstab	dee lantkārtə in grosəm masshtāp
m. of /Germany/	die L. von /Deutschland/	dee lantkārtə fɔn /doytshlant/
road m.	die Straßenkarte (–n)	dee shtrāsənkārtə (–n)
street m.	der Stadtplan (–pläne)	der shtatplān (–pleynə)
marble (material)	der Marmor (–e)	der marmɔr (–ə)
March	der März	der merts
margarine	die Margarine (s)	dee margareenə
mark (= spot/stain)	der Flecken (–)	der flekən
market	der Markt (¨-e)	der markt (merktə)
fish m.	der Fischmarkt (¨-e)	der fishmarkt (–merktə)
fruit & vegetable m.	der Obst– und Gemüsemarkt (¨-e)	der opst ünt gəmühzəmarkt (–merktə)
m. place	der Marktplatz (–plätze)	der marktplats (–pletsə)
meat m.	der Fleischmarkt (¨-e)	der flīshmarkt (–merktə)

	masculine	feminine	neuter
the/a (subject)	der/ein	die/eine	das/ein
the/a (object)	den/einen	die/eine	das/ein
the (plural, subject/object)	die	die	die

marmalade	die Orangenmarmelade (–n)	dee oranjenmārmelāde
a jar of m.	ein Glas (–) O.	īn glas oranjenmārmelāde
maroon (colour)	kastanienbraun	kastānyenbrown
married	verheiratet	ferhīrātet
mascara (for eyelashes)	die Wimperntusche	dee vimperntŭshe
masculine	männlich	menlih
mask	die Maske (–n)	dee maske (–n)
snorkel m.	der Schnorchel (–)	der shnorhel
mass (= Catholic service)	die heilige Messe	dee hīlige messe
massage	die Massage (–n)	dee masāje (–n)
mast	der Mast (–e)	der mast (–e)
mat	die Matte (–n)	dee matte (–n)
bath m.	die Badematte (–n)	dee bādematte (–n)
door m.	der Fußabstreifer	der foosapshtrīfer
match	das Streichholz (–er) (–)	das shtrīhholts (–hœltser)
a box of matches	eine Schachtel (–n) Streichhölzer	īne shakhtel (–n) strīhhœltser
match (= competition)	der Wettkampf (–̈e)	der vetkampf (–kempfe)
football m.	das Fußballspiel (–e)	das foosbalshpeel (–e)
material (= cloth)	der Stoff (–e)	der shtof (–e)
checked m.	der Karostoff	der kāroshtof
heavy m.	der schwere s.	der shvāyre shtof
lightweight m.	der leichte s.	der līhte shtof
plain m.	der einfarbige s.	der īnfarbige shtof
mattress	die Matratze (–n)	dee matrātse (–n)
mauve	hellviolett	helviolet
maximum (adj)	maximal	maksimāl
may	mögen	mœgen
May	der Mai	der mī
mayonnaise	die Mayonnaise	dee majonēyze
me	mich	mih
meal	die Mahlzeit (–en)	dee māltsīt (–en)
light m.	eine leichte M.	īne līhte māltsīt
mean (= not generous)	geizig	gītsih
mean (vb) (of a word)	heißen	hīsen
what does it m.?	was heißt das ?	vas hīst das
measles	die Masern (pl)	dee māzern
measure (vb)	messen	messen

148

meat	das Fleisch (s)	das flīsh
cold m.	der Aufschnitt	der owfshnit
beef	das Rindfleisch	das rintflīsh
lamb	das Lammfleisch	das lamflīsh
mutton	das Hammelfleisch	das haməflīsh
pork	das Schweinefleisch	das shvīnəflīsh
mechanic	der Mechaniker (–)	der mehānikər
mechanism	der Mechanismus (–nismen)	der mehanismŭs (– nismən)
medical	medizinisch	meditseenish
medicine	die Arznei (–en)	dee ārtsnī (–ən)
a bottle of m.	eine Flasche A.	īnə flashə ārtsnī
medium (size)	mittelgroß	mitəlgros
m.-dry (of sweetness)	herbsüß	herpzühs
m.-rare (eg of steak)	medium	māydyŭm
m.-sweet (of sweetness)	nicht zu süß	niht tsoo zühs
meet /your family/	/Ihre Familie/ kennenlernen	/eerə fameelyə/ kenənlernən
meeting (business)	die Versammlung (–en)	dee ferzamlŭng (–ən)
melon	die Melone (–n)	dee melonə (–n)
half a m.	eine halbe M.	īnə halbə melonə
a slice of m.	ein Stück M.	īn shtük melonə
member (of a group)	das Mitglied (–er)	das mitgleet (–gleedər)
memory	die Erinnerung (–en)	dee erinərŭng (–ən)
a good/bad m.	ein gutes/schlechtes Gedächtnis	īn gootəs/shlehtəs gədehtnis
happy memories	glückliche Erinnerungen (pl)	glüklihə erinərŭngən
mend	ausbessern	owsbesərn
men's outfitter's	das Herren-bekleidungsgeschäft (–e)	das herən-bəklīdŭngsgəsheft
menu	die Speisekarte (–n)	dee spīzəkartə (–n)
à la carte m.	die S.	dee spīzəkartə
set m.	die Tageskarte (–n)	dee tāgəskartə (–n)
mess	das Durcheinander (s)	das dürhīnandər
message	die Botschaft (–en)	dee botshaft (–ən)
metal	das Metall (–e)	das metal (–ə)
meter	der Zähler (–)	der tseylər
electricity m.	die Stromuhr (–en)	dee shtromoor (–ən)

gas m.	die Gasuhr (–en)	dēē gāsoor (–ən)
method	die Methode (–n)	dēē metodə (–n)
methylated spirit	der Spiritus (s)	der shpēēritŭs
a bottle of m. s.	eine Flasche (–n) S.	īnə flashə (–n) shpēēritŭs
metre (=length)	der/das Meter (–)	der/das māytər
microphone	das Mikrophon (–e)	das mikrofon (–ə)
midday	der Mittag (–e)	der mitāk (–tāgə)
middle	die Mitte (–n)	dēē mitə
in the m. of / /	in der M. von / /	in der mitə fon / /
middle-aged	in mittlerem Alter	in mitlərəm altər
midnight	die Mitternacht (–nächte)	dēē mitərnakht (–nehtə)
migraine	die Migräne (–n)	dēē migrēynə (–n)
mild (of antibiotic)	leicht	līht
mild (of tobacco)	mild	milt
mild (of weather)	mild	milt
mile	die Meile (–n)	dēē mīlə (–n)
milk	die Milch (s)	dēē milh
a bottle of m.	eine Flasche (–n) M.	īnə flashə (–n) milh
a glass of m.	ein Glas (–) M.	īn glās milh
powdered m.	das Milchpulver	das milhpŭlfər
tinned m.	die Kondensmilch	dēē kondensmilh
milk shake (see under flavour)	der Milkshake	der milhshāyk
million	die Million (–en)	dēē milyon (–ən)
millions of / /	Millionen von / /	milyonən fon / /
mince (vb)	hacken	hakən
minced meat	das Hackfleisch	das hakflīsh
mine (n)	das Bergwerk (–e)	das berkverk (–ə)
coal m.	das Kohlenbergwerk	das kolənberkverk
miner	der Bergmann (Bergleute)	der berkman (berkloytə)
mineral water	das Mineralwasser (–)	das minerālvasər
a bottle of m. w.	eine Flasche (–n) M.	īnə flashə (–n) minerālvasər
a glass of m. w.	ein Glas (–) M.	īn glas minerālvasər
fizzy m. w.	das M. mit Kohlensäure	das minerālvasər mit kolənzoyrə
plain m. w.	das M. ohne Kohlensäure	das minerālvasər onə kolənzoyrə

Remember:[kh] as in acht (eight) [h] as in hungrig (hungry)
[œ] as in schön (beautiful) [üh] as in Tür (door)

minibus	der Kleinbus (–se)	der **klīn**bŭs (–ə)
minimum (adj)	minimal	minim**āl**
mink	der Nerz (–e)	der **nerts** (–ə)
m. coat	der Nerzmantel (¨)	der **nerts**mantəl (–mentəl)
minus	minus	**mee**nŭs
minute (time)	die Minute (–n)	dee min**oo**tə (–n)
mirror	der Spiegel (–)	der **shpee**gəl
hand-m.	der Handspiegel (–)	der **hant**shpeegəl
Miss / /	Fräulein / /	**froy**līn / /
miss /the train/	/den Zug/ verpassen	/dayn ts**oo**k/ ferpasən
	ich verpasse /den Zug/	ih ferpasə /den ts**oo**k/
mist	der Nebel (–)	der **nay**bəl
mistake (n)	der Fehler (–)	der **fay**lər
mix (vb)	mischen	**mish**ən
mixer (of food)	der Mixer (–)	der **miks**ər
mixture	das Gemisch (–e)	das gə**mish** (–ə)
model (object)	das Modell (–e)	das mo**del** (–ə)
latest m.	das neueste M.	das **noy**əstə model
m. /aeroplane/	das Modell/flugzeug/	das mo**del**– /fl**oo**ktsoyk/
model (profession)	das Mannequin (–s)	das **man**əkin (–s)
modern	modern	mo**dern**
moment	der Moment (–e)	der mo**ment** (–ə)
Monday	der Montag (–e)	der **mon**tāk (–tāgə)
on Monday	am M.	am **mon**tāk
on Mondays	montags	**mon**tāks
money	das Geld (–er)	das **gelt** (geldər)
make m.	G. verdienen	gelt fer**dee**nən
	ich verdiene G.	ih fer**dee**nə gelt
mono (adj)	mono	**mo**no
month	der Monat (–e)	der **mo**nat (–ə)
last m.	letzten M.	**lets**tən monat
next m.	nächsten M.	**neyh**stən monat
this m.	diesen M.	**dee**zən monat
monthly	monatlich	**mo**natlih
monument	das Denkmal (¨er)	das **deng**kmāl (–meylər)
mood	die Laune (–n)	dee **low**nə (–n)
in a good/bad m.	in guter/schlechter L.	in **goo**tər/**shleh**tər **low**nə
moon	der Mond	der **mont** (**mon**də)
mop (n)	der Mop (–s)	der **mop** (–s)
moped	das Moped (–s)	das **mo**pet (mopeds)

151

more	mehr	māyr
m. /cake/ please	noch etwas /Kuchen/ bitte	nŏkh etvas /kōōkhən/ bitə
morning	der Morgen (–)	der mɔrgən
this m.	heute M.	hoytə mɔrgən
tomorrow m.	M. früh	mɔrgən früh
yesterday m.	gestern M.	gestərn mɔrgən
mortgage (n)	die Hypothek (–en)	dēē hüpotāyk (–ən)
mosque	die Moshee (–n)	dēē mɔshāy (–ən)
mosquito	der Moskito (–s)	der mɔskēēto (–s)
m. net	das Moskitonetz (–e)	das mɔskēētonets (–ə)
most	meist	mīst
m. /money/	das meiste /Geld/	das mīstə /gelt/
m. /people/	die meisten /Leute/	dēē mīstən /loytə/
motel	das Motel (–s)	das motel (–s)
mother	die Mutter (̈)	dēē mütər(mütər)
mother-in-law	die Schwiegermutter (̈)	dēē shvēēgərmütər (–mütər)
motor	der Motor (–en)	der motɔr (–ən)
outboard m.	der Außenbord- motor (–en)	der owsənbɔrtmotɔr (–ən)
motor racing	das Autorennen	das owtorenən
go m. r.	a. fahren	owtorenən fārən
	ich fahre a.	ih fārə owtorenən
motorail (ie car on a train)	der Autoreisezug	der owtorīzətsōōk
motorbike	das Motorrad (–räder)	das motɔrrāt (–reÿdər)
motorboat	das Motorboot (–e)	das motɔrbot (–ə)
motorist	der Fahrer (–)	der fārər
motorway	die Autobahn (–en)	dēē owtobān (–ən)
mouldy	schimmlig	shimlih
mountain	der Berg (–e)	der berk (bergə)
mountaineer	der Bergsteiger (–)	der berkshtīgər
mountaineering	das Bergsteigen	das berkshtīgən
go m.	b. gehen	berkshtīgən gāyən
	ich gehe b.	ih gāyə berkshtīgən
mountainous	bergig	bergih
mouse	die Maus (̈e)	dēē mows (moyzə)
mousetrap	die Mausefalle (–n)	dēē mowzəfalə (–n)
moustache	der Schnurrbart (̈e)	der shnōōrbārt (–bertə)
mouth	der Mund (̈er)	der münt (mündər)

mouthwash	das Mundwasser (–)	das **mŭnt**vasər
a bottle of m.	eine Flasche (–n) M.	**ī**nə flashə (–n) **mŭnt**vasər
move (vb)	bewegen	bə**vāy**gən
movement	die Bewegung (–en)	d**ēē** bə**vāy**gŭng (–ən)
Mr / /	Herr / /	her / /
Mrs / /	Frau / /	frow / /
much	viel	f**ēē**l
mud	der Schlamm	der shlam
muddy	schmutzig	**shmŭt**si̱h
mug	der Becher (–)	der **be**h̲ər
mumps	der Mumps	der mŭmps
murder (n)	der Mord (–e)	der mort (**mor**də)
murder (vb)	ermorden	er**mor**dən
muscle	der Muskel (–n)	der **mŭs**kəl (–n)
museum	das Museum (Museen)	das mŭ**zāy**ŭm (mŭ**zāy**ən)
mushrooms	die Champignons (mpl)	d**ēē** **sham**pinyo̱ns
mushroom /soup/	die Champignon-/suppe/	d**ēē** **sham**pinyo̱n-/**zŭ**pə/
music	die Musik	d**ēē** mŭ**zēē**k
classical m.	die klassische M.	d**ēē** **kla**sishə mŭ**zēē**k
folk m.	die Volksmusik	d**ēē** **fo̱lks**mŭz**ēē**k
light m.	die leichte M.	d**ēē** **līh̲**tə mŭz**ēē**k
pop m.	die Popmusik	d**ēē** **po̱p**mŭz**ēē**k
musical (=an entertainment)	das Musical (–s)	das **myōō**zikəl (–s)
musician	der Musiker (–) die Musikerin (–nen)	der **mōō**zikər/d**ēē** **mōō**zikərin (–ən)
Muslim	Moslem	**mo̱z**ləm
mussels	die Muscheln (fpl)	d**ēē** **mŭsh**əln
must	müssen	**mŭs**ən
mustard	der Senf (–e)	der zenf (–ə)

N

nail (finger/toe)	der Nagel (¨)	der **nā**gəl (**nēy**gəl)
nailbrush	die Nagelbürste (–n)	d**ēē** **nā**gəlbürstə (–n)
n. file	die Nagelfeile (–n)	d**ēē** **nā**gəlf**ī**lə (–n)

	masculine	feminine	neuter
the/a (subject)	der/ein	die/eine	das/ein
the/a (object)	den/einen	die/eine	das/ein
the (plural, subject/object)	die	die	die

n. scissors	die Nagelschere (–n)	dēē nāgəlshāyrə (–n)
n. varnish	der Nagellack (–e)	der nāgəllak
nail (metal)	der Nagel (–̈)	der nāgəl (nēygəl)
naked	nackt	nakt
name	der Name (–n)	der nāmə (–n)
first n.	der Vorname (–n)	der fornāmə (–n)
surname	der Familienname (–n)	der faméēlyənnāmə (–n)
napkin	die Serviette (–n)	dēē zervyetə (–n)
n. ring	der Serviettenring (–e)	der zervyetənring (–ə)
paper n.	die Papierserviette (–n)	dēē papēērzervyetə (–n)
nappy	die Windel (–n)	dēē vindəl (–n)
disposable nappies	die Wegwerf-windeln (fpl)	dēē vekverfvindəln
narrow	eng	eng
nasty (infml)	gemein	gəmīn
nation	die Nation (–en)	dēē natsyon (–ən)
national	national	natsyonāl
nationality	die Nationalität (–en)	natsyonalitēyt (–ən)
natural	natürlich	natührlih
nature	die Natur (–en)	dēē natōōr (–ən)
naughty (usually of young children)	ungezogen	ŭngətsogən
nausea	die Übelkeit	dēē ühbəlkīt
navigate	steuern	shtoyərn
navy	die Marine (–n)	dēē marēēnə (–n)
near (adv)	nahe	nāə
near (prep) /the station/	nahe /dem Bahnhof/	nāə /dāym bānhof/
neat (of a drink)	unverdünnt	ŭnferdünt
necessary	nötig	nœtih
necessity	die Notwendigkeit (–en)	dēē notvendihkīt (–ən)
neck	der Hals (–̈e)	der hals (helsə)
necklace	die Kette (–n)	dēē ketə (–n)
née	geborene	gəborənə
need (vb)	brauchen	browkhən
I n. /more money/	ich brauche /mehr Geld/	ih browkhə /māyr gelt/
needle	die Nadel (–n)	dēē nādəl (–n)
knitting needles	die Stricknadeln (pl)	dēē shtriknādəln
negative (=film n.)	das Filmnegativ (–e)	das filmnegatēēf (–tēēvə)
nephew	der Neffe (–n)	der nefə (–n)

nervous (=apprehensive)	nervös	nervōēs
nervous breakdown	der Nerven-zusammenbruch (–brüche)	der nervən-tsūzamənbrōōkh (–brükhə)
Nescafe (tdmk)	der Nescafé	der neskafay
net (=fishing n.)	das Netz (–e)	das nets (–ə)
hair net	das Haarnetz (–e)	das härnets (–ə)
net weight	das Nettogewicht	das netogəviht
never	niemals	neemāls
new (of things)	neu	noy
news	die Nachrichten (fpl)	dee näkhrihtən
newsagent's	der Zeitungshändler (–)	der tsītüngshendlər
newspaper	die Zeitung (–en)	dee tsītüng (–ən)
/English/ n.	die /englische/ Z.	dee /englishə/ tsītüng
evening p.	die Abendzeitung (–en)	dee ābənttsītüng (–ən)
local n.	die Lokalzeitung (–en)	dee lokaltsītüng (–ən)
morning p.	die Morgenzeitung (–en)	dee mɔrgəntsītüng (–ən)
next	nächster	neyhstər
next door	nebenan	nāybənan
n. d. /to the station/	neben /dem Bahnhof/	nāybən /dāym bānhof/
the house n. d.	das Haus n.	das hows nāybənan
next of kin	der Verwandte (–n)	der fervantə (–n)
next to / /	neben / /	nāybən / /
nib (of pen)	die Schreibfeder (–n)	dee shrīpfaydər (–n)
nice	nett	net
niece	die Nichte (–n)	dee nihtə (–n)
night	die Nacht (¨e)	dee nakht (nehtə)
last n.	gestern abend	gestərn ābənt
tomorrow n.	morgen abend	mɔrgən ābənt
tonight	heute abend	hoytə ābənt
nightclub	der Nachtklub (–s)	der nakhtklŭp (–s)
nightdress	das Nachthemd (–en)	das nakhthemt (–hemdən)
night life	das Nachtleben	das nakhtlāybən
no /money/	kein /Geld/	kīn /gelt/
no one	niemand	neemant
noisy	laut	lowt
nonsense	der Unsinn	der ŭnzin
nonstick	beschichtet	bəshikhtət
n. /frying-pan/	die beschichtete /Bratpfanne/	dee bəshikhtətə /brātpfanə/

155

nonstop	durchgehend	dŭrhgāyənt
normal	normal	nɔrmāl
north	der Norden	der nɔrdən
northeast	der Nordosten	der nɔrtɔstən
northwest	der Nordwesten	der nɔrtvestən
nose	die Nase (–n)	dee nāzə (–n)
nosebleed	der Nasenbluten (no pl)	das nāzənblootən
not	nicht	niht
note (=money)	der Schein (–e)	der shīn (–ə)
/10/ mark n.	der /Zehn/–markschein	der/tsāyn/– mārkshīn
note (written)	das Briefchen (–)	das breefhən
notebook	das Notizbuch (–bücher)	das notītsboòkh (–bühkhər)
nothing	nichts	nihts
notice	die Notiz (–en)	dee notīts (–ən)
n. board	die Anschlagtafel (–n)	dee anshlāktāfəl (–n)
November	der November	der novembər
now	jetzt	yetst
nowhere	nirgends	nirgənts
nude	nackt	nakt
n. show	die Nacktrevue (–n)	dee naktrəvüh (–ən)
number	die Zahl (–en)/die Nummer (–n)	dee tsāl (–ən)/dee nŭmər (–n)
n. /7/	Nummer /sieben/	nŭmər /zeebən/
telephone n.	die Telefonnummer (–n)	dee telefonnŭmər (–n)
wrong n.	die falsche Nummer	dee falshə nŭmər
nurse	die Krankenschwester (–n)	dee krangkənshvestər (–n)
nursery (=day n. for children)	der Kindergarten (¨)	der kindərgartən (–gertən)
nut	die Nuß (Nüsse)	dee nŭs (nüsə)
almonds	die Mandeln (fpl)	dee mandəln
peanuts	die Erdnüsse (fpl)	dee āyrtnüsə
nut (metal)	die Schraubenmutter (–n)	dee shrowbənmŭtər (–n)
a n. and bolt	eine Schraube (–n) mit Mutter	īnə shrowbə (–n) mit mŭtər
nutcrackers	der Nußknacker (–)	der nŭsknakər

Remember: [kh] as in acht (eight) [h] as in hungrig (hungry)
[œ] as in schön (beautiful) [üh] as in Tür (door)

| nylon | das Nylon (no pl) | das nīlɔn |
| a pair of nylons (stockings) | ein Paar Nylonstrümpfe | īn pār nīlɔnshtrümpfə |

O

oak (wood)	das Eichenholz	das īhənhɔlts
oar (for rowing)	das Ruder (–)	das rōōdər
October	der Oktober	der ɔktobər
of	von	fɔn
off (of light etc)	aus	ows
offence	das Vergehen (–)	das fergāyən
parking o.	das Parkvergehen (–)	das parkfergāyən
offer (n)	das Angebot (–e)	das angəbot (–ə)
make an o.	ein A. machen	īn angəbot makhən
office	das Büro (–s)	das büro (–s)
office worker	der Büroangestellte (–n) die Büroangestellte (–n)	der büroangəshteltə (–n)/dēē büroangəshteltə (–n)
official (adj)	offiziell	ɔfitsyel
official (n)	der Beamte (–n)	der bəamtə (–n)
often	oft	ɔft
oil (lubricating)	das Öl (–e)	das œl (–ə)
oil (salad)	das Salatöl	das zalātœl (–ə)
olive o.	das Olivenöl (–e)	das olēēvənœl (–ə)
vegetable o.	das Pflanzenöl (–e)	das pflantsənœl (–ə)
oil painting	das Ölgemälde (–)	das ēēlgəmēyldə
oily	ölig	ēēlih
ointment	die Salbe (–n)	dēē zalbə (–n)
a jar of o.	ein Dose (–n) S.	īnə dozə (–n) zalbə
a tube of o.	eine Tube (–n) S.	īnə tōōbə (–n) zalbə
old (of people and things)	alt	alt
he is /six/ years o.	er ist /sechs/ Jahre a.	āyr ist /zeks/ yārə
old-fashioned	altmodisch	altmodish
olives	die Oliven (pl)	dēē olēēvən
black o.	schwarze O.	shvartsə olēēvən
green o.	grüne O.	grühnə olēēvən
omelette	das Omelett (–s)	das ɔmlet (–s)
on	an/auf	an/owf
o. Monday	am Montag	am montāk
o. /the table/	auf /dem Tisch/	owf /dāym tish/

157

on (of light etc)	ein	īn
once (= one time)	einmal	īnmāl
one-way	einbahnig/die Einbahnstraße (–n)	īnbānih/dēē īnbānshtrāsə (–n)
onion	die Zwiebel (–n)	dēē tsvēēbəl (–n)
spring o.	die Frühjahrszwiebel (–n)	dēē frühyārstsvēēbəl (–n)
only	nur	nōōr
open (adj)	offen	ɔfən
open (vb)	öffnen	œfnən
open-air restaurant	das Gartenrestaurant (–s)	das gartənrestorant (–s)
o.-a. swimming pool	das Freibad (–̈er)	das frībāt (–bēȳdər)
opening times	die Öffnungszeiten (pl)	dēē œfnŭngstsītən
opera	die Oper (–n)	dēē opər (–n)
o. house	das Opernhaus (–häuser)	das opərnhows (–hoyzər)
operate (surgically)	operieren	operēērən
operation (surgical)	die Operation (–en)	dēē operatsyon (–ən)
opposite (adv)	gegenüber	gāȳgənühbər
o. /the station/	g. /dem Bahnhof/	gāȳgənühbər /dāym bānhof/
optician	der Optiker (–)	der optikər
or	oder	odər
orange (colour)	orangefarben	oranjənfarbən
orange (fruit)	die Orange (–n)	dēē oranjə (–n)
fizzy o.	der Sprudel mit Orangengeschmack (Fanta)	der shprōōdəl mit oranjəngəshmak (fanta)
o. juice	der Orangensaft (–säfte)	der oranjənzaft (–zeftə)
a bottle of o. juice	eine Flasche (–n) Orangensaft	īnə flashə (–n) oranjənzaft
a glass of o. juice	ein Glas (–) orangensaft	īn glās (–) oranjənzaft
orchestra	das Orchester (–)	das ɔrkestər
order /a steak/	/ein Steak/ bestellen	/īn stāyk/ bəshtelən
ordinary	gewöhnlich	gəvœnlih
organisation	die Organisation (–en)	dēē organizatsyon (–ən)
organise	organisieren	organizēērən
original	original	origināl
ornament	das Ornament (–e)	das ornament (–ə)

158

other	anderer	andərər
the o. /train/	der andere /Zug/	der andərə /tsōōk/
out	aus	ows
he's o.	er ist a.	āyr ist ows
out of date (eg clothes)	altmodisch	altmodish
out of date (eg passport)	abgelaufen	apgəlowfən
out of order	nicht in Ordnung	niht in ordnŭng
outside (adv)	draußen	drowsən
outside (prep)	außerhalb	owsərhalp
o. /the house/	a. /des Hauses/	owsərhalp /des howzəs/
oven	der Backofen (–öfen)	der bakofən (ōefən)
over (=above)	über	ühbər
overcoat	der Mantel (¨)	der mantəl (mentəl)
overcooked	verkocht	ferkokht
overland	über Land	ühbər lant
overseas	über See	ühbər zāy
overtake	überholen	ühbərholən
	ich überhole	ih ühbərholə
overweight (people)	dick	dik
be o.	dick sein	dik zīn
he's o.	er ist d.	āyr ist dik
be overweight (things)	überwiegen	ühbərvēēgən
owe	schulden	shŭldən
how much do I o. you?	was bin ich Ihnen schuldig?	vas bin ih ēēnən shŭldih
you o. me / /	sie sind mir / / schuldig	zēē zint mēēr / / shŭldih
owner	der Besitzer (–)	der bəzitsər
oxygen	der Sauerstoff	der zowərshtof
oysters	die Austern (fpl)	dēē owstərn
a dozen o.	ein Dutzend A.	īn dŭtsent owstərn

P

pack (vb)	packen	pakən
p. /my suitcase/	/meinen Koffer/ p.	/mīnən kofər/ pakən
package holiday	der Pauschalurlaub	der powsh**ā**lōōrlowp

	masculine	feminine	neuter
the/a (subject)	der/ein	die/eine	das/ein
the/a (object)	den/einen	die/eine	das/ein
the (plural, subject/object)	die	die	die

159

packet   die Schachtel (–n)   dēē **shakh**təl (–n)
  a p. of /cigarettes/   eine S.   īnə **shakh**təl
   (=20)   /Zigaretten/   /tsigaretən/
packing materials (to   das Packmaterial   das **pak**materīal
  prevent breakages)   (–ien)   (–yən)
pad (of writing   der Block (–̈e)   der blɔk (**blœk**ə)
  paper)
  sketch-p.   der Zeichenblock   der ts**ī**hənblɔk
    (–̈e)   (–blœkə)
paddle (for canoe)   das Paddel (–)   das **pad**əl
padlock (n)   der Vorhängeschloß   der **for**heñgəshlɔs
    (–schlösser)   (–shlœsər)
page (of a book)   die Seite (–n)   dēē z**ī**tə (–n)
pain   der Schmerz (–en)   der shmerts (–ən)
  I've got a   /mein Arm/ tut   /m**ī**n **arm**/ tōōt
  p. in /the arm/   weh   v**ā**y
painful   schmerzhaft   **shmerts**haft
painkiller   das schmerzstillende   das **shmerts**shtiləndə
    Medikament   medik**ament**
paint   die Farbe (–n)   dēē **fārb**ə (–n)
  a tin of p.   eine Dose (–n) F.   **ī**nə dozə (–n) **fārb**ə
paintbrush   der Pinsel (–)   der **pinz**əl
painting   das Gemälde (–)   das gəm**ēyld**ə
  oil p.   das Ölgemälde (–)   das ** œl**gəm**ēyld**ə
  watercolour   das Aquarell (–e)   das akvarel (–ə)
paints   die Farben (fpl)   dēē **fārb**ən
  a box of p.   ein Malkasten   **ī**n **māl**kastən
    (–kästen)   (–kestən)
pair   das Paar (–e)   das pār (–ə)
  a p. of / /   ein P. / /   **ī**n pār / /
palace   der Palast (Paläste)   der **pal**ast (palestə)
pale (of people &   blaß   blas
  things)
pants   die Unterhose (–n)   dēē **ŭnt**ərhozə (–n)
  a pair of p.   ein Paar U.   **ī**n pār **ŭnt**ərhozə
panty-girdle   das Miederhöschen   das **mēēd**ərhœshən
    (–)
paper   das Papier (–e)   das pap**ēēr** (–ə)
  airmail p.   das Luftpostpapier   das **lŭft**postpap**ēēr**
    (–e)   (–ə)
  a sheet of p.   ein Blatt (–) P.   **ī**n blat pap**ēēr**
  drawing p.   das Zeichenpapier   das ts**ī**hənpap**ēēr**
    (–e)   (–ə)
  wrapping p.   das Packpapier (–e)   das **pak**pap**ēēr** (–ə)
  writing p.   das Schreibpapier   das shr**ī**ppap**ēēr**
    (–e)   (–ə)
paperback   das Taschenbuch   das **tash**ənbōōkh
    (–̈er)   (–bühkhər)

paper clip	die Briefklammer (–n)	dēē brēēfklamər (–n)
parcel	das Paket (–e)	das pakāyt (–ə)
by p. post	die Paketpost	dēē pakāytpost
parent	der Elter (–n)	der eltər (–n)
park (n)	der Park (–s)	der park (–s)
park (vb)	parken	**park**ən
parking	das Parken	das **park**ən
no p.	P. verboten	parkən ferbotən
parliament	das Parlament (–e)	das parlament (–ə)
part	der Teil (–e)	der tīl (–ə)
p. of / /	T. von / /	tīl fon / /
partner (business)	der Partner (–) die Partnerin (–nen)	der **part**nər/dēē **part**nərin (–ən)
partridge	das Rebhuhn (¨er)	das **rāy**phōōn (–hühnər)
part-time work	die Teilzeitarbeit	dēē tīltsītārbīt
party	die Party (–s)	dēē **pār**ti (–s)
birthday p.	die Geburtstagsparty (–s)	dēē gəbōōrtstākspārti (–s)
party of /people/	die Gruppe (–n) von /Leuten/	dēē grüpə (–n) fon /loytən/
pass (n) (=p. to enter building)	der Paß (Pässe)	der pas (pesə)
mountain p.	der Gebirgspaß (¨pässe)	der gəbirgspas (–pesə)
passage (on a boat)	die Überfahrt (–en)	dēē ühbərfārt (–ən)
passenger (in boat)	der Passagier (–e)	der pasajēēr (–ə)
passenger (in train)	der Reisende (–n)	der rīzəndə (–n)
transit p.	der Durchreisende (–n)	der dürhrīzəndə (–n)
passport	der Paß (Pässe)	der pas (pesə)
past (prep)	vorbei	forbī
go p. /the station/	/am Bahnhof/ vorbeigehen	/am bānhof/ forbīgāyən
	ich gehe /am Bahnhof/ vorbei	ih gāyə /am bānhof/ forbī
pastilles	die Bonbons (mpl)	dēē bōbō
throat p.	die Hustenbonbons (mpl)	dēē hōōstənbōbō
pastries (=cakes)	die Törtchen (npl)	dēē tœrthən
patch (n)	der Flicken (–)	der flikən
patch (vb)	flicken	**flik**ən
pâté	die Pastete (–n)	dēē pastāytə (–n)
liver p.	die Leberpastete (–n)	dēē lāybərpastāytə (–n)
path	der Weg (–e)	der vāyg (vāygə)

patient (adj)	geduldig	gəd**ü**ldih
patient (n)	der Patient (–en)	der p**a**tsyent (–ən)
outp.	ambulanter P.	amb**ü**lantər p**a**tsyent
pattern	das Muster (–)	das m**ü**stər
dress p.	das Schnittmuster (–)	das shn**i**tmüstər
knitting p.	das Strickmuster (–)	das shtr**i**kmüstər
pavement	der Gehsteig (–e)	der g**ay**shtīk (–shtīgə)
pay	zahlen	ts**a**lən
by /credit card/	mit /Kreditkarte/	mit /kred**ee**tkartə/
in advance	vorauszahlen	for**ow**tsalən
in cash	bar	bār
in /pounds/	in /Pfund/	in /pf**u**nt/
the bill	die Rechnung	dēē reh**nü**ng
peach	der Pfirsich (–e)	der pf**i**rzih (–ə)
peanuts	die Erdnüsse (fpl)	dēē **ay**rtnüsə
a packet of p.	ein Paket E.	īn pak**ay**t **ay**rtnüsə
pear	die Birne (–n)	dēē b**i**rnə (–n)
pearl	die Perle (–n)	dēē p**e**rlə (–n)
peas	die Erbse (–n)	dēē **e**rpsə (–n)
pedestrian	der Fußgänger (–)	der f**oo**sgengər
p. crossing	der Fußgänger- überweg (–e)	der f**oo**sgengər- ü**ü**bərvek (–vāygə)
peel (vb)	schälen	sh**ay**lən
peg (=clothes p.)	die Wäscheklammer (–n)	dēē v**e**shəklamər (–n)
pen (=fountain p.)	der Füller (–)	der f**ü**lər
ballpoint p.	der Kugelschreiber (–)	der k**oo**gəlshrībər
pencil	der Bleistift (–e)	der bl**ī**shtift (–ə)
p. sharpener	der Bleistiftspitzer (–)	der bl**ī**shtiftshpitsər
pen friend	der Brieffreund (–e) die Brieffreundin (–nen)	der br**ee**ffroynt (–froyndə) dēē br**ee**ffroyndin (–ən)
penicillin	das Penizillin	das penitsil**ee**n
I'm allergic to p.	ich bin allergisch gegen P.	ih bin al**e**rgish g**ay**gən penitsil**ee**n
penknife	das Taschenmesser (–)	das t**a**shənmesər

Remember: [kh] as in acht (eight) [h] as in hungrig (hungry)
[œ] as in schön (beautiful) [üh] as in Tür (door)

people	die Leute (pl)	dēē loytə
pepper	der Pfeffer (–)	der pfefər
pepper (=vegetable)	die Paprikaschoten (fpl)	dēē paprikashotən
green p.	der grüne (–n) Paprika (–s)	der grünə (–n) paprika (–s)
red p.	der rote (–n) Paprika (–s)	der rotə (–n) paprika (–s)
peppermint (=flavour/drink)	der Pfefferminz (–e)	der pfefərmints (–ə)
p. (sweet)	der Pfefferminz- bonbon (–s)	der pfefərmintsbōbō
per annum	pro Jahr	pro yār
per cent	das Prozent (–e)	das protsent (–ə)
percolator	die Kaffeemaschine (–n)	dēē kafāymashēēnə (–n)
perfect (adj)	vollkommen	fɔlkɔmən
performance	die Aufführung (–en)	dēē owfführüng (–ən)
perfume	das Parfüm (–s)	das parfühm (–s)
a bottle of p.	eine Flasche P.	īnə flashə (–n) parfühm
period (=menstrual p.)	die Regeln (pl)	dēē rāygəln
period (of time)	die Periode (–n)	dēē periodə (–n)
perm (=permanent wave)	die Dauerwelle (–n)	dēē dowərvelə (–n)
permanent	ständig	shtendih
permission	die Erlaubnis (no pl)	dēē erlowpnis
p. to /enter/	die E. /einzutreten/	dēē erlowpnis /intsōōtrāytən/
permit (n)	der Ausweis (–e)	der owsvīs (–vīzə)
permit (vb)	erlauben	erlowbən
person	die Person (–en)	dēē perzon (–ən)
personal	persönlich	perzœnlih
pet	das Haustier (–e)	das howstēer (–ə)
petrol	das Benzin	das bentsēēn
petrol station	die Tankstelle (–n)	dēē tangkshtelə (–n)
petticoat	der Unterrock (–röcke)	der ŭntərɔk (–rœkə)
pheasant	der Fasan (–e)	der fazān (–ə)
photograph/photo	das Foto (–s)	das foto (–s)
black and white p.	das Schwarzweißfoto	das shvärtsvīsfoto (–s)
colour p.	das Farbfoto (–s)	das färbfoto (–s)
take a p.	fotografieren	fotografēērən
photographer	der Fotograf (–en)	der fotogrāf (–ən)
photographer's studio	das Fotoatelier (–e)	das fotoatelyāy (–s)

phrase	der Ausdruck (–drücke)	der owsdrük (–drükə)
phrase book	der Sprachführer (–)	der sprākhführər
piano	das Klavier (–e)	das klaveer (–ə)
pick (=gather flowers etc)	pflücken	pflükən
picnic	das Picknick (–e)	das piknik (–ə)
go on a p.	ein P. machen ich mache ein P.	īn piknik makhən ih makhə īn piknik
picture (drawing or painting)	das Bild (–er)	das bilt (bildər)
piece	das Stück (–e)	das shtük (–ə)
a p. of / /	ein S. / /	īn shtük / /
pig	das Schwein (–e)	das shvīn (–ə)
pigeon	die Taube (–n)	dee towbə (–n)
piles (illness)	die Hämorrhoiden (pl)	dee hemoroeedən
pill	die Tablette (–n)	dee tabletə (–n)
a bottle of pills	eine Flasche (–n) Tabletten	īnə flashə (–n) tabletən
sleeping pills	die Schlaftabletten (fpl)	dee shlāftabletən
the Pill	die Antibabypille (–n)	dee antibāybeepilə (–n)
pillow	das Kopfkissen (–)	das kopfkisən
p. case	der Kopfkissenbezug (–züge)	der kopfkisənbətsook (–tsühgə)
pilot	der Pilot (–en)	der pilot (–ən)
pin	die Nadel (–n)	dee nādəl (–n)
pine (wood)	das Kiefernholz	das keefərnholts
pineapple	die Ananas (–se)	dee ananas (–ə)
a slice of p.	eine Ananasscheibe (–n)	īnə ananasshībə (–n)
p. juice	der Ananassaft (–säfte)	der ananaszaft (–zeftə)
pink	rosa	roza
pint	das Pint (–s)	das pint (–s)
pip (=seed of citrus fruit)	der Kern (–e)	der kern (–ə)
pipe (smoker's)	die Pfeife (–n)	dee pfīfə (–n)
p. cleaner	der Pfeifenreiniger (–)	der pfīfənrīnigər
place (eg on a plane)	der Sitzplatz (¨e)	der zitsplats (–pletsə)
place (exact location)	der Ort (–e)	der ort (–ə)
p. of birth	der Geburtsort (–e)	der gəboortsort (–ə)
p. of work	der Arbeitsplatz (–plätze)	der ārbītsplats (–pletsə)

plaice	die Scholle (–n)	dēē shohlə (–n)
plain (adj) (=not coloured)	einfarbig	īnfarbih
plain (adj) (=not flavoured)	ungewürzt	ungəvürtst
plain (adj) (=simple)	einfach	īnfakh
plan (n)	der Plan (¨e)	der plān (plēynə)
plan (vb)	planen	plānən
planned (=already decided)	vorgesehen	forgəzāyən
plane (n) (infml)	das Flugzeug (–e)	das flōōktsoyk (–tsoygə)
by p.	mit dem F.	mit dāym flōōktsoyk
plant (n)	die Pflanze (–n)	dēē pflantsə (–n)
plant (vb)	pflanzen	pflantsən
plaster (for walls)	der Mörtel (–)	der mœrtəl
sticking p. (for cuts)	das Heftpflaster (–)	das heftpflastər
plastic	Plastik/ /	plastik/ /
plate (=dental p.)	die Gebißplatte (–n)	dēē gəbisplatə (–n)
plate (=dinner p.)	der Teller (–)	der telər
platform /8/	Bahnsteig /acht/	bānshtīk /akht/
platinum	das Platin	das plāteen
play (n) (at theatre)	das Schauspiel (–e)	das showshpēēl (–ə)
play (vb)	spielen	shpēēlən
p. a game of / /	/ / s.	/ / shpēēlən
play (vb) (an instrument)	spielen	shpēēlən
playground	der Spielplatz (–plätze)	der shpēēlplats (–pletsə)
playgroup	der Privat- kindergarten (–gärten)	der privāt – kindərgartən (–gertən)
pleasant	angenehm	angənāym
pleased	zufrieden	tsüfrēēdən
p. with / /	z. mit / /	tsüfrēēdən mit / /
plenty	viel	feel
p. of / /	v. / /	feel / /
pliers	die Zange (–n)	dēē tsangə (–n)
a pair of p.	eine Z.	īnə tsangə
plimsolls	die Turnschuhe (mpl)	dēē türnshōōə
a pair of p.	ein Paar T.	īn pār türnshōōə

	masculine	feminine	neuter
the/a (subject)	der/ein	die/eine	das/ein
the/a (object)	den/einen	die/eine	das/ein
the (plural, subject/object)	die	die	die

plug (electric)	der Stecker (–)	der **shtek**ər
adaptor p.	der Zwischenstecker (–)	der **tsvish**ənshtekər
/3/-pin p.	der /drei/poliger S.	der /drī/poligər shtekər
plug (for sink)	der Stopfen (–)	der **shtɔp**fən
plug in	anschießen	**an**shleesən
	ich schließe an	ih **shlees**ə an
plum	die Pflaume (–n)	dee **pflow**mə (–n)
plumber	der Installateur (–e)	der instalatœr (–ə)
plus	plus	plŭs
p.m.	nachmittags	**nākh**mitāks
pneumonia	die Lungenentzündung	dee **lŭng**ən-entsündŭng
poach	pochieren	pɔ**shee**rən
pocket	die Tasche (–n)	dee **tash**ə (–n)
pocket dictionary	das Taschenwörterbuch (–bücher)	das **tash**ənvœrtər-bookh (–bükhər)
pocketknife	das Taschenmesser (–)	das **tash**ənmesər
pocket money	das Taschengeld (–)	das **tash**əngelt
point (n) (= a sharpened p.)	die Spitze (–n)	dee **shpits**ə (–n)
point (vb) (= indicate)	zeigen	**tsī**gən
poison	das Gift (–e)	das gift (–ə)
poisoning	die Vergiftung	dee fer**gift**ŭng
food p.	die Lebensmittel-vergiftung	dee **layb**ənsmitəl-fergiftŭng
poisonous	giftig	**gift**ih
poker (= game)	das Poker	das **pok**ər
play p.	P. spielen	**pok**ər shpeelən
police	die Polizei (s)	dee poli**tsī**
police station	die Polizeiwache (–n)	dee poli**tsī**vakhə (–n)
policeman	der Polizist (–en)	der poli**tsist** (–ən)
polish (n)	das Poliermittel (–)	das po**lee**rmitəl
shoe p.	die Schuhcreme (–s)	dee **shoo**krāym (–s)
polish (vb)	polieren	po**lee**rən
polite	höflich	**hœf**lih
politician	der Politiker (–)	der po**lee**tikər
politics	die Politik (s)	dee poli**teek**
polo neck sweater	der Rollkragenpullover (–)	der **rɔl**krāgənpŭlovər
pond	der Teich (–e)	der tīh (–ə)

pony	das Pony (–s)	das pɔni (–s)
pony trekking	das Ponyreiten	das pɔnirītən
go p. t.	p. gehen	porirītən gāyən
	ich gehe p.	iḥ gāyə ponirītən
pool (=swimming pool)	das Schwimmbecken (–)	das **shvim**bekən
poor (=not rich)	arm	arm
poor (p. quality)	schlecht	shleḥt
pop (music)	die Popmusik	dēē **pɔp**müzēēk
popcorn	das Pop-corn	das **pɔp**kɔrn
popular	populär	popülēyr
population	die Bevölkerung (–en)	dēē bəfœlkərŭng (–ən)
pork	das Schweinefleisch	das **shvī**nəflīsh
pornographic	pornographisch	pornogräfish
port (=harbour)	der Hafen (–)	der **hā**fən (**hēy**fən)
portable	tragbar	**träg**bār
p. radio	das Transistorradio (–s)	das tranzistorrādyo (–s)
porter (hotel)	der Hotelportier (–s)	der hotelportyāy (–s)
porter (railway)	die Gepäckträger (–)	der gəpektrēygər
portion	die Portion (–en)	dēē portsyon (–ən)
a p. of / /	eine P. / /	īnə portsyon / /
portrait	das Porträt (–s)	das portrēyt (–s)
position	die Stellung (–en)	dēē **shtel**ŭng (–ən)
possible	möglich	mœkliḥ
post (vb)	schicken	shikən
p. this airmail	s. es als Luftpost	shikən es als **lŭft**post
as printed matter	als Drucksache	als **drŭk**zakhə
cheap rate	zu ermäßigter Gebühr	tsŭ ermēysigtər gəbühr
express	per Eilboten	per **īl**botən
parcel post	als Paket	als pakāyt
registered	als Einschreiben	als **īn**shrībən
surface mail	als Normalpost	als nɔr**māl**post
postage	das Porto	das **pɔr**to
postal order	die Postanweisung (–en)	dēē **pɔst**anvīzŭng (–ən)
postal rate for /England/	die Postgebühren für /England/	dēē **pɔst**gəbührən führ /**eng**lant/
postbox	der Briefkasten (–kästen)	der **brēēf**kastən (–kestən)
postcard	die Postkarte (–n)	dēē **pɔst**kartə (–n)
postcode	die Postleitzahl (–en)	dēē **pɔst**lītsāl (–ən)
poster	das Plakat (–e)	das plakāt (–ə)
post office	das Postamt (–ämter)	das **pɔst**amt (–emtər)

167

pot	die Kanne (–n)	dēē kanə (–n)
a p. of tea	eine K. (–n) Tee	īnə kanə (–n) tāy
potatoes	die Kartoffeln (fpl)	dēē kartəfəln
potato peeler	der Kartoffelschäler (–)	der kartəfəlshēylər
pottery (substance)	das Steingut (–)	das shtīngōōt
poultry	das Geflügel (no pl)	das gəflühgəl
chicken	das Huhn (-̈er)	das hōōn (hühnər)
duck	die Ente (–n)	dēē entə (–n)
turkey	der Truthahn (–hähne)	der trōōthān (–hēynə)
pound (money)	das Pfund (–e)	das pfünt (pfündə)
pound (weight)	das Pfund (–e)	das pfünt (pfündə)
pour	gießen	gēēsən
powder (face p.)	der Gesichtspuder(–)	der gəzihtspōōdər
baby p.	der Babypuder	der bābēēpōōdər
talcum p.	der Körperpuder	der kœrpərpōōdər
practice (=custom)	die Sitte (–n)	dēē zitə (–n)
practice (=training)	die Übung	dēē ühbüng
practise (=put into practice)	treiben	trībən
practise (=train)	üben	ühbən
pram	der Kinderwagen (–)	der kindərvāgən
prawns	die Garnelen (pl)	dēē garnāylən
precious	wertvoll	vertfol
p. stone	der Edelsteine (–e)	der āydəlshtīn (–ə)
prefer	vorziehen	fortseeən
	ich ziehe / / vor	ih tseeə / / for
pregnant	schwanger	shvangər
prepare	vorbereiten	forbərītən
	ich bereite / / vor	ih bərītə / / for
prescribe	vorschreiben	forshrībən
	ich schreibe / / vor	ih shrībə / / for
prescription	das Rezept (–e)	das rezept (–ə)
present (adj)	anwesend	anvāyzənt
present (n) (=gift)	das Geschenk (–e)	das gəshengk (–ə)
present (n) (time)	die Gegenwart	dēē gāygənvart
present (vb)	überreichen	ühbərrīhən
president (of company)	der Präsident (–en)	der prezident (–ən)
press (vb) (eg button)	drücken	drükən
press (vb) (ironing)	bügeln	bühgəln

Remember:[kh] as in acht (eight) [h] as in hungrig (hungry)
[œ] as in schön (beautiful) [üh] as in Tür (door)

pressure	der Druck (¨-e)	der drŭk
b. pressure	der Blutdruck	der blōōtdrŭk
pressure cooker	der Schnellkochtopf (–töpfe)	der shnelkɔkhtɔpf (–tœpfə)
pretty	hübsch	hüpsh
price	der Preis (–e)	der prīs (prīzə)
priest	der Priester (–)	der prēēstər
prince	der Prinz (–en)	der prints (–ən)
princess	die Prinzessin (–nen)	dēē printsesin (–ən)
print (n) (photographic)	der Abzug (–züge)	der aptsōōk (–tsühgə)
print (vb)	drücken	drükən
printer	der Drücker (–n)	der drükər
prison	das Gefängnis (–se)	das gəfengnis (–ə)
private	privat	privāt
p. /bath/	das eigene /Bad/	das īgənə /bāt/
prize	der Preis (–e)	der prīs (prīzə)
probable	wahrscheinlich	vārshīnlih
problem	das Problem (–e)	das problāym (–ə)
procession	die Prozession (–en)	dēē protsesyon (–ən)
produce (vb)	herstellen	hershtelən
product	das Produkt (–e)	das prodŭkt (–ə)
programme (of events)	das Programm (–e)	das program (–ə)
promise (n)	das Versprechen (–)	das fershprehən
promise (vb)	versprechen	fershprehən
pronounce	aussprechen	owsshprehən
	ich spreche aus	ih shprehə ows
proof	der Beweis (–e)	der bəvīs (–vīzə)
property (=belongings)	das Eigentum (¨-er)	das īgəntōōm (–tühmər)
prospectus	der Prospekt (–e)	der prospekt (–ə)
prostitute	die Prostituierte (–n)	dēē prostitüēērtə (–n)
protect	schützen	shütsən
p. me from / /	mich vor / / s.	mih for / / shütsən
protection	der Schutz	der shüts
protective	schützend	shütsənt
Protestant (adj)	evangelisch	evanggāylish
P. church	die evangelische Kirche	dēē evanggāylishə kirhə
prove	beweisen	bəvīzən
provisions	die Vorräte (pl)	dēē forrɛytə
prunes	die Dörrpflaumen (fpl)	dēē dœrpflowmən
pub	die Kneipe (–n)	dēē knīpə (–n)

public	öffentlich	œfəntlih
p. buildings	die öffentlichen Gebäude (npl)	dee œfəntlihən geboydə
p. convenience	die öffentlichen Toiletten (fpl)	dee œfəntlihən twaletən
p. /garden/	der Stadtpark (–s)	der shtatpärk
pull	ziehen	tseeən
pump	die Pumpe (–n)	dee pümpə (–n)
bicycle p.	die Fahrradpumpe (–n)	dee färrätpümpə (–n)
foot p.	die Fußpumpe (–n)	dee foospümpə (–n)
water p.	die Wasserpumpe (–n)	dee vasərpümpə (–n)
puncture	die Panne (–n)	dee panə (–n)
punish	bestrafen	bəshträfən
punishment	die Strafe (–n)	dee shträfə (–n)
pupil	der Schüler (–) die Schülerin (–nen)	der shühlər/dee shühlərin (–ən)
pure	rein	rin
purple	purpurrot	pürpürot
purse	der Beutel (–)	der boytəl
pus	der Eiter	der itər
push (vb)	schieben	sheebən
pushchair	der Kindershp"ort- wagen (–)	der kindərsport- vägən
put	legen/stellen	laygən/shtelən
p. on /my coat/	/den Mantel/ anziehen ich ziehe /den Mantel/ an	/dayn mantəl/ antseeən ih tseeə /dayn mantəl/ an
puzzle	das Rätsel (–)	das reytsəl
jigsaw p.	das Puzzle (–s)	das pazəl (–s)
pyjamas	der Schlafanzug (s)	der shläfantsook
a pair of p.	ein S.	in shläfantsook

Q

quail (=bird)	die Wachtel (–n)	dee vakhtəl (–n)
qualifications	die Qualifikationen (fpl)	dee kvalifikatsyonən
qualified	qualifiziert	kvalifitseert
quality	die Qualität (–en)	dee kvaliteyt (–ən)
quarrel (n)	der Streit (–e)	der shtrit (–ə)
quarter	das Viertel	das feertəl
a q. of an hour	eine Viertelstunde	inə feertəlshtündə

queen	die Königin (–nen)	dēē kœnigin (–ən)
query (vb)	beanstanden	bəanshtandən
I would like to q. /the bill/	ich möchte /die Rechnung/ b.	ih mœhtə /dēē rehnŭng/ bəanshtandən
question (n)	die Frage (–n)	dēē frāgə (–n)
question (vb)	fragen	frāgən
queue (n)	die Schlange (–n)	dēē shlāngə (–n)
queue (vb)	mich anstellen	mih anshtelən
	ich stelle mich an	ih shtelə mih an
quick	schnell	shnel
quickly	schnell	shnel
quiet (adj)	ruhig	rōōih
q. pleasel	ich bitte um Ruhe!	ih bitə ŭm rōōə
quinine	das Chinin	das hinēēn
quite	ganz	gants

R

rabbi	der Rabbi (Rabbinen)	der rabi (rabēēnən)
rabbit	das Kaninchen (–)	das kanēēnhən
rabies	die Tollwut	dēē tɔlvōōt
race (n) (=contest)	das Rennen	das renən
horse r.	das Pferderennen	das pfāyrdərenən
motor r.	das Autorennen	das owtorenən
race (vb)	rennen	renən
racecourse	die Rennbahn (–en)	dēē renbān (–ən)
racehorse	das Rennpferd (–e)	das renpfāyrt (–pfāyrdə)
races (=the r.)	das Pferderennen (–)	das pfāyrdərenən
racing	das Rennen	das renən
horse r.	der Pferderennensport	der pfāyrdərenshpɔrt
motor r.	das Autorennen	das owtorenən
racquet	der Schläger (–)	der shlēygər
tennis r.	der Tennisschläger (–)	der tenisshlēygər
squash r.	der Squashschläger (–)	der skŭɔshshlēygər
radio	das Radio (–s)	das rādyo (–s)
car r.	das Autoradio (–s)	das owtorādyo (–s)

	masculine	feminine	neuter
the/a (subject)	der/ein	die/eine	das/ein
the/a (object)	den/einen	die/eine	das/ein
the (plural, subject/object)	die	die	die

portable r.	das Transistorradio (–s)	das tranzistɔrrādyo (–s)
transistor r.	das Transistorradio (–s)	das tranzistɔrrādyo (–s)
radishes	die Radieschen (pl)	dēē radēēshən
raft	das Floß (ˑe)	das flos (flœsə)
life r.	das Rettungsfloß	das retūngzflos
rag (for cleaning)	das Wischtuch (ˑer)	das vishtōōkh (–tühkhər)
railway	die Eisenbahn (–en)	dēē īzənbān (–ən)
r. station	der Bahnhof (–höfe)	der bānhof (–hœfə)
underground r.	die Untergrundbahn	dēē ūntərgrüntbān
rain (n)	der Regen	der rāygən
rain (vb)	regnen	rāygnən
it's raining	es regnet	es rāygnət
raincoat	der Regenmantel (ˑˑ)	der rāygənmantəl (–mentəl)
raisins	die Rosinen (fpl)	dēē rozēēnən
rally	die Sternfahrt (–en)	dēē shternfārt (–ən)
motor r.	die Autosternfahrt (–en)	dēē owtoshternfārt (–ən)
range (=mountain r.)	die Bergkette (–n)	dēē berkketə (–n)
range (=r. of goods)	die Auswahl (no pl)	dēē owsvāl
rare (eg of steak)	englisch	ēnglish
medium-rare	medium	māydyüm
rare (=unusual)	selten	zeltən
rash	der Ausschlag (–schläge)	der owsshlāk (–shleygə)
rasher of bacon	die Speckschnitte (–n)	dēē shpekshnitə (–n)
raspberry	die Himbeere (–n)	dēē himbāyrə (–n)
a punnet of raspberries	ein Korb (–) Himbeeren	īn kɔrp himbāyrən
rat	die Ratte (–n)	dēē ratə (–n)
rate (n)	die Gebühr (–en)	dēē gəbühr (–ən)
cheap r. (mail, telephone)	die Normalgebühr	dēē nɔrmālgəbühr
exchange r.	der Wechselkurs	der veksəlkürs
postal r.	die Postgebühr	dēē pɔstgəbühr
r. per day	die Tagesgebühr	dēē tāgəsgəbühr
rates (charges)	die Gebühren (fpl)	dēē gəbührən
rattle (baby's r.)	die Rassel (–n)	dēē rasəl (–n)
rattle (noise)	das Rattern	das ratərn
raw	roh	ro

razor	der Rasierapparat (–e)	der razēēraparāt (–ə)
electric r.	der Elektrorasier (–)	der elektrorazēēr
r. blade	die Rasierklinge (–n)	dēē razēērklingə (–n)
a packet of r. blades	ein Päckchen Razierklingen	īn pekhən razēērklingən
reach (vb)	erreichen	erīhən
read /a magazine/	/eine Zeitschrift/ lesen	/īnə tsītshrift/ lāyzən
ready	fertig	fertih
real	wirklich	virklih
rear /coach/	der Hinter/wagen/	der hintər/vāgən/
reason (n)	der Grund (:e)	der grünt (gründə)
reasonable	vernünftig	fernünftih
receipt	die Quittung (–en)	dēē kvitüng (–ən)
receive	erhalten	erhaltən
recent	neu	noy
Reception (eg in a hotel)	der Empfang (:e)	der empfang (–fengə)
recharge (battery)	wiederaufladen ich lade wieder auf	vēēdərowflādən ih lādə vēēdər owf
recipe	das Rezept (–e)	das retsept (–ə)
recognise	erkennen	erkenən
recommend	empfehlen	empfāylən
record (n)	die Schallplatte (–n)	dēē shalplatə (–n)
33 r.p.m. r.	die Langspielplatte (–n)	dēē langshpēēlplatə (–n)
45 r.p.m. r.	die Single (–s)	dēē zingəl (–s)
classical r.	die klassische s..	dēē klasishə shalplatə
jazz r.	die Jazzplatte (–n)	dēē djesplatə (–n)
light music r.	die Platte (–n) mit Unterhaltungs- musik	dēē platə (–n) mit üntərhaltüngs- müzēēk
pop r.	die Schlägerplatte (–n)	dēē shlāgərplatə (–n)
record (vb)	aufnehmen ich nehme / / auf	owfnāymən ih nāymə / / owf
record player	der Plattenspieler (–)	der platənshpēēlər
record shop	das Schallplatten- geschäft (–e)	das shalplatəngəsheft (–ə)
rectangular	rechteckig	rehtekih
red	rot	rot
reduce	ermäßigen	ermēysigən
r. the price	den Preis e.	dayn prīs ermēysigən

173

reduction	die Ermäßigung (–en)	dēē ermēysigŭng (–ən)
reel (of cotton)	die Rolle (–n)	dēē rolə (–n)
reel (recording tape)	die Spule (–n)	dēē shpōōlə (–n)
refill (for a ballpoint)	die Mine (–n)	dēē mēēnə (–n)
refill (for a lighter)	die Nachfüllung (–en)	dēē nakhfülŭng (–ən)
refrigerator/fridge (infml)	der Kühlschrank (¨e)	der kühlshrangk (–shrengkə)
refund (n)	die Rückvergütung (–en)	dēē rükfergühtŭng (–ən)
refund (vb)	zurückzahlen ich zahle / / zurück	tsürüktsālən ih tsālə / / tsürük
registered (mail)	eingeschrieben	īngəshrēēbən
registration number	das Kennzeichen	das kentsīhən
regret (vb)	bedauern	bədowərn
regular /service/	der Normal/service/	der normāl/servēēs/
regulations	die Vorschriften (fpl)	dēē forshriftən
relations	die Verwandten (mpl)	dēē fervantən
relative (n)	der Verwandte (–n)	der fervantə (–n)
reliable	zuverlässig	tsüferlesih
religion	die Religion (–en)	dēē religyon (–ən)
religious	religiös	religyœs
remedy	das Heilmittel (–)	das hīlmitəl
remember	mich erinnern	mih erinərn
I don't r.	ich erinnere mich nicht	ih erinərə mih niht
I r. /the name/	ich erinnere mich an /den Namen/	ih erinərə mih an /dāyn nāmən/
remove	entfernen	entfernən
renew	erneuren	ernoyərn
rent (n) (payment)	die Miete (–n)	dēē mēētə (–n)
rent /a villa/	/eine Villa/ vermieten	/īnə vila/ fermēētən
repair (vb)	reparieren	reparēērən
repairs	die Reparatur (–en)	dēē reparatōōr (–ən)
do r.	reparieren	reparēērən
shoe r. (=shop)	die Schuhreparatur	dēē shōōreparatōōr
watch r. (=shop)	die Uhrenreparatur	dēē ōōrənreparatōōr
repay	zurückzahlen	tsürüktsālən
r. me	mir z.	mēēr tsürüktsālən
r. the money	das Geld z.	das gelt tsürüktsālən

Remember:[kh] as in acht (eight) [h] as in hungrig (hungry)
[œ] as in schön (beautiful) [üh] as in Tür (door)

	ich zahle das Geld zurück	ih tsālə das gelt tsŭrük
repeat	wiederholen	vēēdərholən
repellant	das Abwehrmittel (–)	das apvāyrmitəl
insect r.	das Insektenspray (–s)	das inzektənsprāy (–s)
replace	ersetzen	erzetsən
reply (n)	die Antwort (–en)	dēē antvort (–ən)
r.-paid	mit bezahlter Rückantwort	mit bətsāltər rükantvort
report (n)	der Bericht (–e)	der bəriht (–ə)
report (vb)	melden	meldən
r. a loss	/einen Verlust/ m.	/īnən ferlŭst/ meldən
	ich melde /einen Verlust/	ih meldə /īnən ferlŭst/
represent	vertreten	fertrāytən
reproduction (=painting)	die Reproduktion (–en)	dēē reprodŭktsyon (–ən)
request (n)	die Bitte (–n)	dēē bitə (–n)
make a r.	eine B. stellen	īnə bitə shtelən
reservation (hotel, restaurant, theatre)	die Reservierung (–en)	dēē rezervēērŭng (–ən)
make a r.	reservieren	rezervēērən
reserve (vb)	reservieren	rezervēērən
responsible	verantwortlich	ferantvortlih
r. for / /	v. für / /	ferantvortlih fŭhr /
rest (n)	die Ruhe	dēē rōōə
have a r.	mich ausruhen	mih owsrōōən
	ich ruhe mich aus	ih rōōə mih ows
rest (vb)	mich ausruhen	mih owsrōōən
restaurant	das Restaurant (–s)	das restorant (–s)
self-service r.	R. mit Selbstbedienung	restorant mit zelpstbədēēnŭng
restrictions	die Einschränkung (–en)	dēē īnshrengkŭng (–ən)
result	das Ergebnis (–se)	das ergāypnis (–ə)
retired (adj)	pensioniert	penzyonēērt
I'm r.	ich bin p.	ih bin penzyonēērt
return	die Rückfahrt (–en)	dēē rükfart (–ən)
day r.	die Tagesrückfahrkarte (–n)	dēē tāgəsrükfārkārtə (–n)
r. (ticket)	die Rückfahrkarte (–n)	dēē rükfārkārtə (–n)
return (=give back)	zurückgeben	tsŭrükgāybən
r. /this sweater/	/diesen Pullover/ z.	/dēēzən pŭlovər/ tsŭrükgāybən

	ich gebe /diesen Pullover/ zurück	iḫ gāybə /dēēzən pŭlovər/ tsŭrük
return (= go back)	zurückkehren	tsŭrükkāyrən
r. at /4.30/	um /sechzehn Uhr dreißig/ z.	ŭm /zehtsāyn ōor drīsiḫ/ tsŭrükkāyrən
r. in /July/	im /Juli/ z.	im /yōoli/ tsŭrükkāyrən
r. on /Monday/	am /Montag/ z.	am /montāk/ tsŭrükkāyrən
	ich kehre am /Montag/ zurück	iḫ kāyrə am /montāk/ tsŭrük
reverse the charges	ein R-Gespräch machen	īn er-gəshpreḫ makhən
I'd like to r. the c.	ich möchte ein R-Gespräch machen	iḫ mœhtə īn er-gəshpreḫ makhən
reward (n)	die Belohnung (–en)	dēē bəlonŭng (–ən)
reward (vb)	belohnen	bəlonən
rheumatism	der Rheumatismus	der roymatismŭs
rib (part of body)	die Rippe (–n)	dēē ripə (–n)
ribbon	das Band (–̈er)	das bant (bendər)
a piece of r.	ein Stück B.	īn shtük bant
typewriter r.	das Farbband	das fárbbant
rice	der Reis	der rīs
rich	reich	rīḫ
ride (vb)	fahren	fārən
r. a bicycle	radfahren	rātfārən
r. a horse	reiten	rītən
go for a r. (in a car)	herumfahren	herŭmfārən
	ich fahre herum	iḫ fārə herŭm
riding (=horse r.)	das Reiten	das rītən
go r.	r. gehen	rītən gāyən
	ich gehe r.	iḫ gāyə rītən
right (=correct)	richtig	rihtiḫ
right (=not left)	rechts	rehts
right-handed	rechtshändig	rehtshendiḫ
ring	der Ring (–e)	der ring (–ə)
/diamond/ r.	der /Diamant/ring (–e)	der /diamant/ring (–ə)
engagement r.	der Verlobungsring (–e)	der ferlobŭngsring (–ə)
wedding r.	der Ehering (–e)	der āyəring (–ə)
ring (vb) at the door	klingeln	klingəln
ring road	die Umgehungsstraße (–n)	dēē ŭmgāyŭngs-shtrāsə (–n)

rinse (n) (clothes)	die Spülung (–en)	dēē shpühlŭng (–ən)
colour r.	die Farbtönung (–en)	dēē färbtœnŭng (–ən)
rinse (vb)	spülen	shpühlən
ripe	reif	rīf
river (large)	der Fluß (–üsse)	der flŭs (flüsə)
river (small)	der Bach (–er)	der bakh (behər)
road	die Straße (–n)	dēē strāsə (–n)
main r.	die Hauptstraße (–n)	dēē howptshtrāsə (–n)
ring r.	die Umgehungs- straße (–n)	dēē ŭmgāyŭngs – shtrāsə (–n)
side r.	die Nebenstraße (–n)	dēē nāybənshtrāsə (–n)
roast (vb)	braten	brātən
r. beef	der Rinderbraten	der rindərbrātən
r. chicken	das Brathuhn	das brāthōōn
rock (n)	der Fels (–en)	der fels (felzən)
rod (=fishing r.)	die Rute (–n)	dēē rōōtə (–n)
roll (=bread r.)	das Brötchen (–)	das brœthən
a r. of /toilet paper/	eine Rolle (–n) /Toilettenpapier/	īnə rɔlə (–n) /twaletənpapēer/
roller skating	das Rollschuhlaufen	das rɔlshōōlowfən
go r. s.	Rollschuh laufen ich laufe Rollschuh	rɔlshōō lowfən ih lowfə rɔlshōō
roof	das Dach (–er)	das dakh (dehər)
roof rack	der Autogepäck- träger (–)	der owtogəpektrēygər
room	das Zimmer (–)	das tsimər
double r.	ein Doppelzimmer (–)	īn dɔpəltsimər
quiet r.	ein ruhiges Z.	īn rōōigəs tsimər
r. service	der Zimmerservice	der tsimərservēēs
r. with a view	ein Z. mit Aussicht	īn tsimər mit owsziht
single r.	ein Einzelzimmer (–)	īn īntsəltsimər
twin-bedded r.	ein Doppelzimmer	īn dɔpəltsimər
with /shower/	mit /Dusche/	mit /dŭshə/
without /bath/	ohne /Bad	onə /bat/
rope	das Seil (–e)	das zīl (–ə)
tow r.	das Abschleppseil (–e)	das apshlepzīl (–ə)

	masculine	feminine	neuter
the/a (subject)	der/ein	die/eine	das/ein
the/a (object)	den/einen	die/eine	das/ein
the (plural, subject/object)	die	die	die

rose	die Rose (–n)	dēē rozə (–n)
a bunch of roses	ein Strauß Rosen	īn shtrows rozən
rotten	verdorben	ferdorbən
rough (=not calm)	stürmisch	**shtür**mish
rough (=not smooth)	rauh	row
roughly (=approximately)	etwa	etva
round (adj)	rund	rŭnt
roundabout (n)	der Kreisverkehr	der **krīs**ferkāyr
route	die Route (–n)	dēē rōōtə (–n)
row (a boat)	rudern	**rōō**dərn
row (of seats)	die Reihe (–n)	dēē rīə (–n)
the /first/ r.	die /erste/ R.	dēē /āyrstə/ rīə
rowing boat	das Ruderboot (–e)	das **rōō**dərbot (–ə)
rub	reiben	**rī**bən
rubber (=eraser)	der Radiergummi	der ra**dēē**rgŭmi
rubber (substance)	der Gummi	der **gŭ**mi
r. boots	die Gummistiefel (mpl)	dēē **gŭ**mishtēēfəl
rubber band	das Gummiband (–bänder)	das **gŭ**mibant (–bendər)
rubbish (=litter)	der Abfall (–fälle)	der **ap**fal (–felə)
rucksack	der Rücksack (–säcke)	der **rük**zak (–zekə)
rude	unhöflich	**ŭn**hœflih
rug	der Vorleger (–)	der **for**lāygər
rugby	das Rugby	das **rak**bi
play r.	R. spielen	**rak**bi shpēēlən
	ich spiele R.	ih shpēēlə **rak**bi
rules	die Regeln (fpl)	dēē **rāy**gəln
rum	der Rum	der rŭm
run (vb)	rennen	**ren**ən
run (vb) (colour)	auslaufen	**ows**lowfən
does it r.?	läuft die Farbe beim Waschen aus?	loyft dēē **fär**bə bīm vashən ows
run over / /	/ / überfahren	/ / ühbər**fä**rən
run-resistant (tights etc)	laufmaschenfest	**lowf**mashənfest
rush hour	die Hauptverkehrszeit	dēē **howpt**ferkāyrstsīt

saccharine	der Saccharin	der zakhareen
s. tablet	die Saccharintablette (–n)	dee zakhareentabletə (–n)
sad	traurig	**trowrih**
saddle	der Sattel (¨)	der **za**təl (zetəl)
safe (adj)	sicher	**zi**hər
safe (n)	der Tresor (–e)	der trezor (–ə)
safety belt	der Sicherheitsgurt (–e)	der **zi**hərhītsgürt (–ə)
safety pin	die Sicherheitsnadel (–n)	dee **zi**hərhītsnādəl (–n)
sail (n)	das Segel (–)	das **zāy**gəl
sail (vb)	segeln	**zāy**gəln
sailing	das Segeln	das **zāy**gəln
go s.	s. gehen	**zāy**gəln **gāy**ən
	ich gehe s.	ih **gāy**ə **zāy**gəln
sailor	der Matrose (–n)	der matrozə (–n)
saint	der Heilige (–n) die Heilige (–n)	der **hī**ligə (–n)/dee **hī**ligə (–n)
salad	der Salat (–e)	der zal**āt** (–ə)
green s.	der grüne S.	der **grüh**nə zal**āt**
mixed s.	der gemischte S.	der gəmishtə zal**āt**
s. dressing	die Salatsoße (–n)	dee zal**āt**zosə (–n)
salary	das Gehalt (¨er)	das gə**halt** (–heltər)
sale	der Verkauf (¨e)	der fer**kowf** (–**koyf**ə)
sales manager	der Verkaufsleiter (–)	der fer**kowf**slītər
salmon	der Lachs (–e)	der laks (laksə)
smoked s.	geräucherter L.	gə**roy**hərtər laks
salt (n)	das Salz	das zalts
salted	gesalzen	gə**zalt**sən
same	gleich	**glīh**
the s. as / /	der gleiche wie / /	der **glīh**ə vee / /
sand	der Sand	der zant
sandals	die Sandalen (fpl)	dee zan**dāl**ən
a pair of s.	ein Paar S.	īn pār zan**dāl**ən
sandwich	das (belegte(–n)) Brot (–e)	das (bel**āyh**tə (–n)) brot (–ə)
a /cheese/ s.	ein /Käse/brot (–e)	īn /**kēy**zə/brot (–ə)
sandy	sandig	**zan**dih
sanitary towels	die Damenbinden (fpl)	dee **dā**mənbindən
sardines	die Sardinen (fpl)	dee zar**dee**nən
satin (adj)	Satin / /	za**tē** / /

satin (n)	der Satin	der zatĕ
satisfactory	befriedigend	bǝfreedigǝnt
Saturday	der Samstag (–e)/der Sonnabend (–e)	der **zamst**āk (–tāgǝ)/der **zon**abǝnt (–bǝndǝ)
on Saturday	am Samstag	am **zamst**āk
on Saturdays	samstags	**zamst**āks
sauce	die Soße (–n)	dee zosǝ (–n)
saucepan	der Topf (·̈e)	der tɔpf (**tœpf**ǝ)
saucer	die Untertasse (–n)	dee **ŭnt**ǝrtasǝ (–n)
a cup and s.	eine Tasse mit U.	īnǝ tasǝ mit **ŭnt**ǝrtasǝ
sauna	die Sauna	dee **zown**a
sausage	die Wurst (·̈e)	dee vŭrst (**vürst**ǝ)
save (money)	sparen	**shpār**ǝn
save (=rescue)	retten	**ret**ǝn
savoury (=not sweet)	pikant	pikant
say (something)	sagen	**zāg**ǝn
scale (on a map)	der Maßstab	der **māss**htāp
large s.	in grossem M.	in grosǝm **māss**htāp
small s.	in kleinem M.	in klīnǝm **māss**htāp
scales (=weighing machine)	die Waage (–n) (s)	dee **vāg**ǝ (–n)
scallops	die Kammuscheln (fpl)	dee **kamm**ŭshǝln
scar	die Narbe (–n)	dee **nārb**ǝ (–n)
scarf	der Schal (–s)	der shāl (–s)
/silk/ s.	/Seiden/schal	īn /**zīd**ǝn/shāl
scenery	die Landschaft	dee **lant**shaft
schedule	der Plan (·̈e)	der plān (**pleȳn**ǝ)
school	die Schule	dee **shōōl**ǝ (–n)
language s.	die Sprachschule (–n)	dee **shprākh**shōōlǝ (–n)
schoolboy	der Schüler (–)	der **shühl**ǝr
schoolgirl	die Schülerin (–nen)	dee **shühl**ǝrin (–ǝn)
science	die Wissenschaft (–en)	dee **vis**ǝnshaft (–ǝn)
scissors	die Schere (–n) (s)	dee **shāȳr**ǝ (–n)
a pair of s.	eine S.	īnǝ **shāȳr**ǝ
scooter (=child's s.)	der Roller (–)	der **rɔl**ǝr
motor s.	der Motorroller	der mo**tɔrrɔl**ǝr
score /a goal/	/ein Tor/ schießen ich schieße /ein Tor/	/īn tor/ **sheeȳs**ǝn ih sheeȳsǝ /īn tor/

Remember: [kh] as in acht (eight) [h] as in hungrig (hungry)
[œ] as in schön (beautiful) [üh] as in Tür (door)

180

scratch (n)	der Kratzer (–)	der **krats**ər
scratch (vb)	kratzen	**krats**ən
scream (n)	der Schrei (–e)	der shrī (–ə)
screen (=film s.)	die Leinwand (ˉe)	dēē **līn**vant (–vendə)
screen (=movable partition)	die Zwischenwand (ˉe)	dēē **tsvish**ənvant (–vendə)
screw	die Schraube (–n)	dēē **shrowb**ə (–n)
screwdriver	der Schraubenzieher (–)	der **shrowb**əntsēēər
sculpture	die Plastik	dēē **plastik**
sea	die See/das Meer	dēē zāy/das māyr
by s.	mit dem Schiff	mit dāym **shif**
seafood	die Meerestiere (npl)	dēē **māy**rəstēērə
search (n)	die Suche	dēē **zōōkh**ə
search (vb)	suchen	**zōōkh**ən
seasick		
be s.	seekrank sein	**zāy**krangk zīn
I feel s.	ich bin seekrank	ih bin **zāy**krangk
season	die Jahreszeit (–en)	dēē **yār**əstsīt (–ən)
season ticket	die Zeitkarte (–n)	dēē **tsīt**kartə (–n)
seasoning	das Gewürz (–e)	das gəvürts (–ə)
seat	der Platz (ˉe)	der plats (pletsə)
at a theatre	im Theater	im teātər
at the back	hinten	**hint**ən
at the front	vorn	fɔrn
by the exit	am Ausgang	am **owsgang**
by the window	am Fenster	am **fenst**ər
in a non-smoker (train)	in einem Nichtraucherabteil	in **īn**əm **nih**trowkhəraptīl
in a non-smoking section (aeroplane)	im Nichtraucherteil	im **nih**trowkhərtīl
in a smoker (train)	in einem Raucherabteil	in **īn**əm **rowkh**ər-aptīl
in the middle	in der Mitte	in der **mit**ə
in the smoking section (aeroplane)	im Raucherteil	im **rowkh**ərtīl
on a coach	im Bus	im **bŭs**
on a train	im Zug	im **tsōōk**
second (of time)	die Sekunde (–n)	dēē zekündə (–n)
second-hand	gebraucht	gə**browkht**
a s.-h. car	ein Gebrauchtwagen	īn gə**browkht**-vāgən
secret (adj)	geheim	gə**hīm**
secret (n)	das Geheimnis (–se)	das gə**hīm**nis (–ə)
secretary	die Sekretärin (–nen)	dēē sekretēyrin (–ən)

security	die Sicherheit	dēē **zih**ərhīt
s. check	die Sicherheits- überprüfung (–en)	dēē **zih**ərhīts- ühbər**prüh**füng (–ən)
s. control	die Sicherheits- kontrolle (–n)	dēē **zih**ərhīts- kɔntrɔlə (–n)
sedative	das Beruhigungs- mittel (–)	das bə**rōō**igüngsmitəl
see	sehen	**zāy**ən
see /the manager/	/den Geschäftsführer/ sprechen	/den gə**sheft**sfürər/ **shpre**hən
s. /the menu/	/die Speisekarte/ s.	/dēē **shpī**zəkärtə/ **zāy**ən
self-addressed envelope	der adressierte Briefumschlag	der adre**sēer**tə **brēē**fümshlāk
sell	verkaufen	fer**kowf**ən
Sellotape (tdmk)	der durchsichtige Klebestreifen	der **dürh**zihtigə **klāy**bəshtrīfən
send	schicken	**shik**ən
s. /a message/	etwas ausrichten lassen ich lasse etwas ausrichten	etvas **ows**rihtən lasən ih lasə etvas **ows**rihtən
s. / / to me	mir / / s.	mēer / / **shik**ən
separate (adj)	getrennt	gə**trent**
September	der September	der zep**tem**bər
septic	septisch	**zep**tish
serve	bedienen	bə**dēē**nən
service (car)	die Inspektion machen	dēē inspek**tsyon** makhən
service (church)	der Gottesdienst (–e)	der **gɔt**əsdēēnst (–ə)
service (=extra charge)	die Bedienung	dēē bə**dēē**nüng
room s.	der Zimmerdienst	der **tsim**ərdēēnst
24-hour s.	der 24-Stunden Dienst	der **fēer**ünttsvantsih- shtündəndēēnst
serviette	die Serviette (–n)	dēē zervyetə (–n)
set (n)	das Service (–s)	das zer**vēēs** (–əs)
dinner s.	das Eßservice (–s)	das es**zervēēs** (–əs)
tea s.	das Teeservice (–s)	das **tāy**zervēēs (–əs)
set (vb) (hair)	legen	**lāy**gən
shampoo and s. (n)	waschen und l.	vashən ünt **lāy**gən
several	mehrere	**māy**rərə
sew	nähen	**nāy**ən

182

sewing	die Näharbeit	dēē nēyarbīt
do some s.	nähen	nēyən
sex	das Geschlecht (–er)	das gəshlecht (–ər)
shade	der Schatten (–)	der shatən
in the s.	im S.	im shatən
shade (colour)	die Farbe (–n)	dēē farbə (–n)
shake (vb)	schütteln	shütəln
s. hands	die Hand geben	dēē hant gāybən
shampoo (n)	das Shampoo	das shampŭ
a bottle of s.	eine Flasche (–n) S.	īnə flashə (–n) shampŭ
a sachet of s.	ein Kissen (–) S.	īn kisən shampŭ
s. and blow dry	das Waschen und Fönen	das vashən ünt fœnən
s. and set	das Waschen und Legen	das vashən ünt lāygən
shampoo (vb)	waschen	vashən
shape (n)	die Form (–en)	dēē fɔrm (–ən)
share (vb)	teilen	tīlən
sharp (of things)	scharf	sharf
sharpen	schärfen	sherfən
shave (n)	das Rasieren	das razēērən
shave (vb)	mich rasieren	mih razēērən
	ich rasiere mich	ih razēērə mih
shaving brush	der Rasierpinsel (–)	der razēērpinzəl
shaving cream	die Rasiercreme (–s)	dēē razēērkrāym (–s)
a tube of s. c.	ein Tube (–n) R.	īnə tōōbə (–n) razēērkrāym
shaving soap	die Rasierseife	dēē razēērzīfə
a stick of s. s.	ein Stück R.	īn shtük razēērzīfə
shawl	der Schal (–s)	der shāl (–s)
she	sie	zēē
sheath (=Durex)	das Kondom (–e)	das kɔndom (–ə)
a packet of sheaths	ein Päckchen Kondome	īn pekhən kɔndomə
sheep	das Schaf (–e)	das shāf (–ə)
sheepskin	das Schaffell	das shaffel
s. /rug/	der Schaffell/teppich/	der shaffel/tepih/
sheet (bed linen)	das Laken (–)	das lākən
sheet (of paper)	das Blatt (¨-er)	das blat (bletər)

	masculine	feminine	neuter
the/a (subject)	der/ein	die/eine	das/ein
the/a (object)	den/einen	die/eine	das/ein
the (plural, subject/object)	die	die	die

shelf	das Brett (–er)	das bret (–ər)
book s.	das Bücherregal (–e)	das bükhərəgāl (–ə)
shell (sea-s.)	die Muschel (–n)	dēē müshəl (–n)
shellfish	das Muscheltier (–e)	das müshəlteer (–ə)
sheltered	geschützt	gəshütst
sherry	der Sherry	der sheri
a bottle of s.	eine Flasche (–n) S.	īnə flashə (–n) sheri
a s.	ein S.	īn sheri
shiny	glänzend	glentsənt
ship (n)	das Schiff (–e)	das shif (–ə)
ship (vb)	verschiffen	fershifən
shirt	das Hemd (–en)	das hemt (hemdən)
casual s.	das Freizeithemd (–en)	das frītsīthemt (–hemdən)
/cotton/ s.	das /Baumwolle/hemd	das /bowmvɔlə/hemt
formal s.	das Ausgehhemd (–en)	das owsgāyhemt (–hemdən)
short-sleeved s.	das H. mit kurzen Armeln	das hemt mit kürtsən ermɘln
shock (n)	der Schock (–s)	der shɔk (–s)
electric s.	der Schlag (–̈e)	der shlāk (–shlēygə)
state of s.	der S.	der shɔk
shockproof (eg of watch)	stoßfest	shtosfest
shoebrush	die Schuhbürste (–n)	dēē shōōbürstə (–n)
shoelaces	die Schnürsenkel (pl)	dēē shnührzengkəl
a pair of s.	ein Paar S.	īn par shnührzengkəl
shoepolish	die Schuhcreme (–s)	dēē shōōkrāym (–s)
shoes	die Schuhe (mpl)	dēē shōōə
a pair of s.	ein Paar S.	īn pār shōōə
boy's s.	die Jungenschuhe	dēē yüngənshōōə
girl's s.	die Mädchenschuhe	dēē mēythənshōōə
flat-heeled s.	die flachen S.	dēē flakhən shōōə
high-heeled s.	die hochhackigen S.	dēē hokhhakigən shōōə
ladies' s.	die Damenschuhe	dēē dāmənshōōə
men's s.	die Herrenschuhe	dēē herənshōōə
walking s.	die Sportschuhe	dēē shpɔrtshōōə
shoeshop	das Schuhgeschäft (–e)	das shōōgəsheft (–ə)
shoot (vb) (sport)	schießen	shēēsən
shop	das Geschäft (–e)/der Laden (–̈)	das gəsheft (–ə)/der lādən (lēydən)

shop assistant	der Verkäufer (–) die Verkäuferin (–nen)	der ferkoyfər/dēē ferkoyfərin (–ən)
shopping	das Einkaufen	das īnkowfən
go s.	e. gehen	īnkowfən gāyən
	ich gehe e.	ih gāyə īnkowfən
shopping bag	die Einkaufstasche (–n)	dēē īnkowfstashə (–n)
shopping centre	das Einkaufszentrum (–zentren)	das īnkowfstsentrüm (–tsentrən)
shore	der Strand (¨e)	der shtrant (shtrendə)
short (people)	klein	klīn
short (things)	kurz	kŭrts
short (time)	kurz	kŭrts
short circuit	der Kurzschluß (–schlüsse)	der kŭrtsshlŭs (–shlŭsə)
shorten	kürzen	kŭrtsən
shorts	die Shorts (pl)	dēē shorts
a pair of s.	ein Paar S.	īn pār shorts
shot (n)	der Schuß (¨sse)	der shus (shŭsə)
shoulder	die Schulter (–n)	dēē shŭltər (–n)
shout (n)	der Schrei (–e)	der shrī (–ə)
shout (vb)	schreien	shrīən
show	die Schau (–en)	dēē show (–ən)
fashion s.	die Modenschau	dēē modənshow
floor s.	die Revue	dēē rəvüh
strip s.	der Striptease	der shtriptēēs
variety s.	das Varieté	das varyetāy
show (vb)	zeigen	tsīgən
s. /it/ to me	mir /es/ z.	mēēr /es/ tsīgən
shower (=s. bath)	die Dusche (–n)	dēē dŭshə (–n)
shrimps	die Krabben (fpl)	dēē krabən
shutters	die Fensterläden (pl)	dēē fenstərlēydən
shy	schüchtern	shŭhtərn
sick	krank	krangk
I feel s.	mir ist schlecht	mēēr ist shleht
side (n) (in game)	die Mannschaft (–en)	dēē manshaft (–ən)
side (n) (of object)	die Seite (–n)	dēē zītə (–n)
sights (of a town)	die Sehenswürdigkeiten (fpl)	dēē zāyəns-vürdihkītən
sightseeing	die Besichtigung (–en)	dēē bəzihtigŭng (–ən)
go s.	die Sehenswürdigkeiten besichtigen	dēē zāyəns-vürdihkītən bəzihtigən

185

	ich besichtige die Sehenswürdigkeiten	ih bəzi**h**tigə dēē zā**y**əns-vürdih**k**ītən
sign (n)	das Zeichen (–)	das ts**ī**hən
sign /your name/	unterschreiben	ŭntərshr**ī**bən
s. here	bitte unterschreiben	bitə ŭntərshr**ī**bən
signal (n)	das Zeichen (–)	das ts**ī**hən
signal (vb)	winken	**vi**ŋgən
signature	die Unterschrift (–en)	dēē **ŭn**tərshrift (–ən)
signpost	der Wegweiser (–)	der **vek**v**ī**zər
silence	die Ruhe	dēē r**ōō**ə
silent	still	shtil
silk (adj)	seiden	z**ī**dən
silk (n)	die Seide	dēē z**ī**də
silver (adj)	silbern	**zi**lbərn
silver (n)	das Silber	das **zi**lbər
similar	ähnlich	**ēy**nli**h**
simple	einfach	**ī**nfa**kh**
sincere	aufrichtig	**ow**fri**h**ti**h**
sing	singen	**zi**ŋgən
singer	der Sänger (–) die Sängerin (–nen)	der ze**ŋ**gər/dēē ze**ŋ**gərin (–ən)
single (=not married)	unverheiratet	ŭnfer**h**ī**ī**rātət
s. bed	das Einzelbett (–en)	das **ī**ntsəlbet (–ən)
s. ticket	die einfache Fahrkarte	dēē **ī**nfa**kh**ə **fa**rkartə
sink (n)	die Spüle (–n)	dēē **shp**ühlə (–n)
sink (vb)	sinken	**zi**ŋgən
sister	die Schwester (–n)	dēē **shv**estər (–n)
sister-in-law	die Schwägerin (–nen)	dēē **shv**ē**y**gərin (–ən)
sit (see seat)	sitzen	**zi**tsən
please s. down	bitte Platz nehmen	bitə plats **nāy**mən
site	der Bauplatz (–plätze)	der **bow**plats (–pletsə)
camping s.	der Campingplatz (–plätze)	der **ke**mpi**ŋ**gplats (–pletsə)
caravan s.	der Karavanplatz (–plätze)	der **ka**ravanplats (–pletsə)
size	die Größe (–n)	dēē gr**ōē**se (–n)
large s.	groß	gros
medium s.	mittelgroß	**mi**təlgros
small s.	klein	kl**ī**n

Remember: [k̲h̲] as in acht (eight) [h̲] as in hungrig (hungry)
[ōē] as in schön (beautiful) [üh] as in Tür (door)

skating	das Schlittschuhlaufen	das **shlitsh**o͞olowfən
go s.	Schlittschuh laufen	**shlitsh**o͞o lowfən
	ich laufe Schlittschuh	ih̠ lowfə **shlitsh**o͞o
ice-s.	das Schlittschuh-laufen	das **shlitsh**o͞olowfən
roller-s.	das Rollschuh-laufen	der **rɔlsh**o͞olowfən
sketch (n)	die Skizze (–n)	de͞e **skits**ə (–n)
sketchpad	der Zeichenblock (–blöcke)	der **ts**i̠hənblɔk (–blœkə)
ski-boots	die Skistiefel (mpl)	de͞e **she͞e**shte͞efəl
a pair of s.-b.	ein Paar S.	i̠n pār **she͞e**shte͞efəl
skid (n)	das Rutschen	das **r**utshən
skid (vb) (car)	ausgleiten	**ows**gli̠tən
	ich gleite aus	ih̠ gli̠tə **ows**
skiing	das Skilaufen	das **she͞e**lowfən
go s.	s. gehen	**she͞e**lowfən gāyən
	ich gehe s.	ih̠ gāyə **she͞e**lowfən
water-s.	das Wasserskilaufen	das vasərs**he͞e**lowfən
ski lift	der Skilift (–e)	der **she͞e**lift (–ə)
skin	die Haut	de͞e howt
skin diving	das Sporttauchen	das **shpɔrt**towk̠hən
go s. d.	sporttauchen gehen	**shpɔrt**towk̠hən gāyən
	ich gehe sporttauchen	ih̠ gāyə **shpɔrt**towk̠hən
skirt	der Rock (-̈e)	der rɔk (rœkə)
long s.	ein langer R.	i̠n **lang**ər rɔk
short s.	ein kurzer R.	i̠n **kür**tsər rɔk
skis	die Skier (mpl)	de͞e **she͞e**ər
a pair of s.	ein Paar S.	i̠n pār **she͞e**ər
water s.	die Wasserskier (pl)	de͞e vasərs**he͞e**ər
sky	der Himmel	der **him**əl
sleep (n)	der Schlaf	der **shl**āf
sleep (vb)	schlafen	**shl**āfən
sleeper (on a train)	der Schlafwagen (–)	der **shl**āfvāgən
sleeping bag	der Schlafsack (–säcke)	der **shl**āfzak (–zekə)
sleeping berth	das Bett (–en)	das bet (–ən)
sleeping car	der Schlafwagen	der **shl**āfvāgən
sleeping pill	die Schlaftablette (–n)	de͞e **shl**āftabletə (–n)
sleepy	schläfrig	**shl**ēyfrih̠
be s.	s. sein	**shl**ēyfrih̠ zi̠n
I'm s.	ich bin s.	ih̠ bin **shl**ēyfrih̠

187

sleeves	die Ärmel (mpl)	dee ermǝl
long s.	lange Ä. (mpl)	langǝ ermǝl
short s.	kurze Ä. (mpl)	kürtsǝ ermǝl
sleeveless	ärmellos	ermǝllos
slice (n)	die Scheibe (–n)	dee shībǝ (–n)
a s. of / /	eine Scheibe / /	īnǝ shībǝ / /
slice (vb)	schneiden	shnīdǝn
slide viewer	der Gucki	der gǔki
slides	die Diapositiven (fpl)	dee diapoziteevǝn
colour s.	die Farbdiapositiven	dee farbdiapoziteevǝr.
slippers	die Hausschuhe (mpl)	dee howsshooǝ
a pair of s.	ein Paar H.	īn pār howsshooǝ
slippery	schlüpfrig	shlüpfrih
slope	der Abhang (–hänge)	der aphang (–hengǝ)
slot machine	der Automat (–en)	der owtomāt (–ǝn)
slow	langsam	langzām
slower	langsamer	langzāmǝr
slowly	langsam	langzām
small (size)	klein	klīn
smart (appearance)	schick	shik
smell (n)	der Geruch (¨e)	der gǝrükh (–rükhǝ)
smell (vb) (=have a certain smell)	riechen	reehǝn
smell (vb) (=perceive with nose)	riechen	reehǝn
smoke (n)	der Rauch	der rowkh
smoke /a cigarette/	/eine Zigarette/ rauchen	/īnǝ tsigaretǝ/ rowkhǝn
smoked (of fish & meat etc)	geräuchert	gǝroyhǝrt
s. /ham/	geräucherter /Schinken/	gǝroyhǝrtǝ /shingkǝn/
smoker	der Raucher (–)	der rowkhǝr
non-s.	der Nichtraucher (–)	der nihtrowkhǝr
smooth	glatt	glat
snack	der Imbiß (–isse)	der imbis (–ǝ)
snack-bar	die Imbißstube (–n)	dee imbisshtoobǝ (–n)
snake	die Schlange (–n)	dee shlangǝ (–n)
snakebite	der Schlangenbiß	der shlangǝnbis
sneeze (vb)	niesen	neezǝn

snorkel (n)	der Schnorchel (–)	der **shnɔrhəl**
s. mask	die Schnorchelmaske (–n)	dee **shnɔrhəlmaskə** (–n)
s. tube	der Schlauch (ˉe) des Schnorchels	der **shlowkh** (**shloyhə**) des **shnɔrhəls**
snorkel (vb)	schnorcheln	**shnɔrhəln**
snow (n)	der Schnee	der **shnāy**
snow (vb)	schneien	**shnīən**
it's snowing	es schneit	es schnīt
soak	einweichen	**īnvīhən**
	ich weiche / / ein	ih **vīhə** / / īn
soap	die Seife (–n)	dee **zīfə** (–n)
a bar of s.	ein Stück S.	īn stük **zīfə**
s. flakes	die Seifenflocken (pl)	dee **zīfənflɔkən**
shaving s.	die Rasierseife	dee razeer**zīfə**
soapy	seifig	**zīfih**
sober	nüchtern	**nühtərn**
socket	die Steckdose (–n)	dee **shtekdozə** (–n)
electric razor s.	die S. für Rasierapparate	dee **shtekdozə** führ razeeraparātə
light s.	die Glühbirnen-halterung (–en)	dee **glühbirnən**-haltərūng (–ən)
/3/–pin s.	die /drei/polige S.	dee /**drī**/poligər **shtekdozə**
socks	die Socken (fpl)	dee **zɔkən**
a pair of s.	ein Paar S.	īn pār **zɔkən**
long s.	die Kniestrümpfe (pl)	dee **kneeshtrümpfə**
short s.	die kurzen S.	dee **kŭrtsən zɔkən**
/woolen/ s.	die /Woll/socken	dee /**vɔl**/zɔkən
soda (water)	das Sodawasser	das zodavasər
a bottle of s. (w.)	eine Flasche (–n) S.	īnə flashə (–n) zodavasər
a glass of s. (w.)	ein Glas (–) S.	īn glās (–) zodavasər
soft (=not hard)	weich	**vīh**
sold	verkauft	ferkowft
soldier	der Soldat (–en)	der zɔl**dāt** (–ən)
sold out	ausverkauft	owsferkowft
sole (=fish)	die Seezunge (–n)	dee **zāytsŭngə** (–n)
sole (of shoe)	die Sohle (–n)	dee **zolə** (–n)

	masculine	feminine	neuter
the/a (subject)	der/ein	die/eine	das/ein
the/a (object)	den/einen	die/eine	das/ein
the (plural, subject/object)	die	die	die

solid	fest	fest
some		
s. /money/	etwas /Geld/	etvas /gelt/
someone	jemand	yāymant
something	etwas	etvas
somewhere	irgendwo	irgentvo
son	der Sohn (¨e)	der zon (zœnə)
song	das Lied (–er)	das lēēt (lēēdər)
folk s.	das Volkslied (–er)	das fɔlkslēēt (–lēēdər)
pop s.	der Schlager (–)	der shlāgər
son-in-law	der Schwiegersohn (¨e)	der shvēēgərzon (–zœnə)
soon	bald	balt
sore (adj)	wund	vŭnt
sore throat	die Halsschmerzen (mpl)	dēē halsshmertsən
sound (n)	das Geräusch (–e)	das gəroysh (–ə)
soup	die Suppe (–n)	dēē zŭpə (–n)
/chicken/ s.	die /Hühner/suppe	dēē /hühnər/zŭpə
sour	sauer	zowər
south	der Süden	der zühdən
s.east	der Südosten	der zühtɔstən
s.west	der Südwesten	der zühtvestən
souvenir	das Andenken (–)	das andengkən
souvenir shop	der Andenkenladen (¨)	der andengkənlādən (–lēydən)
space (room)	der Platz (¨e)	der plats (pletsə)
spade	der Spaten (–)	der shpātən
spanner	der Schrauben- schlüssel (–)	der shrowbənshlüsəl
adjustable s.	ein verstellbarer S.	īn fershtelbārər shrowbənshlüsəl
spare (adj)	übrig	ühbrih
s. parts	die Ersatzteile (npl)	dēē erzatstīlə
spare time	die Freizeit	dēē frītsīt
speak /English/	/englisch/ sprechen	/ēnglish/ shprehən
speak /to the manager/	/den Geschäftsführer/ sprechen	/dayn gəsheftsführər/ shprehən
special	besonders	bəzɔndərs
speed	die Geschwindigkeit (–en)	dēē gəshvindihkīt (–ən)
speedboat	das Schnellmotor- boot (–e)	das shnelmotɔrbot (–ə)
spell	buchstabieren	bookhshtabēērən
spend (money)	ausgeben	owsgāybən
	ich gebe / / aus	ih gāybə / / ows

spend (time)	verbringen	ferbrin͞gən
spice	das Gewürz (–e)	das gəvürts (–ə)
spicy	würzig	vürtsih̠
spider	die Spinne (–n)	de͞e shpinə (–n)
spilt	verschüttet	fershütət
spinach	der Spinat	der shpinät
spine (part of body)	das Rückgrat	das rükgrät
spirits (=alcohol)	die alkoholischen Getränke	de͞e alkoholishən gətren͞gkə
spit (vb)	spucken	shpŭkən
splendid	herrlich	herlih̠
spoil (vb)	verderben	ferderbən
sponge (bath s.)	der Schwamm (–̈e)	der shvam (shvemə)
spoon	der Löffel (–)	der lœfəl
spoonful	der Löffelvoll	der lœfəlfəl
a s. of / /	ein L. / /	īn lœfəlfəl / /
sport	der Sport	der shport
sports car	der Sportwagen (–)	der shportvägən
spot (=blemish)	der Pickel (–)	der pikəl
spot (=dot)	der Punkt (–e)	der pŭn͞gkt (–ə)
sprain (n)	die Verrenkung (–en)	de͞e feren͞gkŭn͞g (–ən)
sprained	verrenkt	feren͞gkt
spring (=season)	der Frühling	der frühlin͞g
in s.	im F.	im frühlin͞g
spring (=wire coil)	die Feder (–n)	de͞e fāydər (–n)
spring onion	der Frühjahrszwiebel (–n)	der frühyärstsve͞ebəl (–n)
sprouts (=Brussels s.)	der Rosenkohl (s)	der rozənkol
square (place)	der Platz (–̈e)	der plats (pletsə)
main s.	der Hauptplatz	der howptplats
square (=scarf)	das Tuch (–̈er)	das to͞okh (tühkhər)
a /silk/ s.	ein /Seiden/tuch	īn /zīdən/to͞okh
square (shape)	viereckig	fe͞erekih̠
squash	das Squash	das skŭosh
play s.	S. spielen	skŭosh shpe͞elən
squeeze (vb)	drücken	drükən
stable (for horses)	der Stall (–̈e)	der shtal (shtelə)
stadium	das Stadion (Stadien)	das shtädyən (shtädyən)
staff (=employees)	das Personal	das perzonäl
stage (in a theatre)	die Bühne (–n)	de͞e bühnə (–n)
stain	der Fleck (–en)	der flek (–ən)
s. remover	der Fleckenreiniger (–)	der flekənrīnigər
stained	fleckig	flekih̠

191

stainless steel	der rostfreie Stahl	der rɔstfrīə shtāl
s. s. /cutlery/	rostfreie /Bestecke/ (pl)	rɔstfrīə /bəshtekə/
staircase	das Treppenhaus (–häuser)	das trepənhows (–hoyzər)
stairs	die Treppe (–n)	dēē trepə (–n)
stale	altbacken	altbakən
stale (bread)	altbacken	altbakən
stamp (n)	die Briefmarke (–n)	dēē brēēfmarkə (–n)
a book of stamps	das Briefmarkenheft (–e)	das brēēfmarkənheft (–ə)
a /50/ pfennig s.	eine B. zu /50/ Pfennig	īnə brēēfmarkə tsōō /fünftsih/ pfenih
stand (vb)	stehen	shtāyən
standard (adj)	normal	nɔrmāl
star	der Stern (–e)	der shtern (–ə)
film s.	der Filmstar (–s)	der filmstār (–s)
starch (n)	die Stärke (–n)	dēē shterkə (–n)
starch (vb)	stärken	shterkən
start (n)	der Anfang (–fänge)	der anfang (–fengə)
start (vb)	anfangen	anfangən
s. /the journey/	/die Reise/ a.	/dēē rīzə/ anfangən
	ich fange /die Reise/ an	ih fangə /dēē rīzə/ an
starter (=hors d'oeuvre)	die Vorspeise (–n)	dēē forshpīzə (–n)
state (n)	der Zustand (–stände)	der tsŭshtant (–shtendə)
station (=railway s.)	der Bahnhof (–höfe)	der bānhof (–hœfə)
bus s.	die Bushaltestelle (–n)	dēē bŭshaltəshtelə (–n)
stationery	die Schreibwaren (pl)	dēē shrīpvārən
statue	die Statue (–n)	dēē shtātŭə (–n)
stay at / /	in / / bleiben	in / / blībən
for a night	eine Nacht	īnə nakht
for /two/ nights	/zwei/ Nächte	/tsvī/ nehtə
for a week	eine Woche	īnə vɔkhə
for /two/ weeks	/zwei/ Wochen	/tsvī/ vɔkhən
till / /	bis / /	bis / /
from / / till / /	von / / bis / /	fɔn / / bis / /

Remember: [kh] as in acht (eight) [h] as in hungrig (hungry)
[œ] as in schön (beautiful) [üh] as in Tür (door)

192

steak	das Steak (–s)	das stāyk (–s)
medium	medium	māydyŭm
rare	englisch	english
well-done	durchgebraten	dŭrhgəbrātən
steal	stehlen	shtāylən
steam (vb)	dämpfen	dempfən
steel	der Stahl	der shtāl
stainless s.	der rostfreie S.	der rɔstfrīə shtāl
steep	steil	shtīl
steer (vb) (boat)	steuern	shtoyərn
steer (vb) (car)	steuern	shtoyərn
step (n) (movement)	der Schritt (–e)	der shrit (–ə)
step (n) (part of staircase)	die Stufe (–n)	dēē shtŭfə (–n)
stereo (adj)	Stereo/ /	shtāyreo/ /
s. equipment	die Stereoanlage (–n)	dēē shtāyreoanlāgə (–n)
stereo (n)	die Stereoanlage (–n)	dēē shtāyreoanlāgə (–n)
stern (of boat)	das Heck (–s)	das hek (–s)
steward (plane or boat)	der Steward (–s)	der styōōərt (–s)
stewardess (plane or boat)	die Stewardeß (–ssen)	dēē styōōərdes (–ən)
stick (n)	der Stock (–̈e)	der shtɔk (shtœkə)
sticking plaster	das Pflaster (–)	das pflastər
sticky	klebrig	klāybrih
sticky tape (eg Sellotape (tdmk))	der Klebstreifen	der klāybshtrīfən
stiff	steif	shtīf
sting (n)	der Stich (–e)	der shtih (–ə)
/bee/ s.	der /Bienen/stich (–e)	der /bēēnən/shtih (–ə)
sting (vb)	stechen	shtehən
stir (vb)	rühren	rührən
stock (of things)	der Vorrat (–räte)	der forāt (–rēytə)
stockings	die Strümpfe (mpl)	dēē shtrümpfə
15/30 denier	fünfzehn/dreißig Denier	fünftsāyn/drīsih dənyāy
a pair of s.	ein Paar S.	īn pār shtrümpfə
/nylon/ s.	die /Nylon/–strümpfe	dēē /nīlɔn/–shtrümpfə
stolen	gestohlen	gəshtolən
stomach	der Magen (–̈)	der māgən (mēygən)
I've got a s. ache	ich habe Bauchschmerzen (pl)	ih hābə bowkhshmertsən

I've got a s. upset	ich habe einen verdorbenen M.	ih hābə īnən ferdɔrbənən māgən
stone (of fruit)	der Kern (–e)	der kern (–ə)
stone (substance)	der Stein	der shtīn
precious s.	der Edelstein (–e)	der āydəlshtīn (–ə)
stool	der Hocker (–)	der hɔkər
stop (n)	die Haltestelle (–n)	dēē haltəshtelə (–n)
bus s.	die Bushaltestelle (–n)	dēē büshaltəshtelə (–n)
tram s.	die Straßbahn-haltestelle (–n)	dēē shtrāsənbān-haltəshtelə (–n)
stop (vb)	halten	haltən
stop at / /	an / / halten	an / / haltən
store (=department s.)	das Kaufhaus (–häuser)	das kowfhows (–hoyzər)
storm	der Sturm (¨e)	der shtŭrm (shtürmə)
stormy	stürmisch	shtürmish
story	die Geschichte (–n)	dēē gəshihtə (–n)
straight	gerade	gərādə
stranger (n)	der Fremde (–n)	der fremdə (–n)
strap	das Band (¨er)	das bant (bendər)
watch-s.	das Uhrenarmband (–bänder)	das ōōrənarmbant (–bendər)
strapless	trägerlos	trēygərlos
straw (=drinking s.)	der Strohhalm (–e)	der shtrohalm (–ə)
strawberry	die Erdbeere (–n)	dēē āyrtbāyrə (–n)
a punnet of strawberries	ein Korb (–) Erdbeeren	īn kɔrp āyrtbāyrən
streak (n) (of hair)	die Strähne (–n)	dēē shtrāynə (–n)
I'd like my hair streaked	ich möchte mir die Haare strähnen lassen	ih mœhtə mēēr dēē hārə shtrāynən lasən
stream (n)	der Bach (¨e)	der bakh (behə)
street	die Straße (–n)	dēē shtrāsə (–n)
main s.	die Hauptstraße (–n)	dēē howptshtrāsə (–n)
stretcher	die Krankentrage (–n)	dēē krangkəntrāgə (–n)
strike (n)	der Streik (–s)	der shtrīk (–s)
be on s.	streiken	shtrīkən
strike (vb) (of clock)	schlagen	shlāgən
string	der Bindfaden (–fäden)	der bintfādən (–fēydən)
a ball of s.	eine Rolle (–n) B.	īnə rolə (–n) bintfādən
a piece of s.	ein Stück B.	īn shtük bintfādən
strip show	der Striptease	der shtriptēēs

striped	gestreift	gəshtrīft
strong (physically)	stark	shtark
s. /coffee/	starker /Kaffee/	shtārkər /kafāy/
stuck (eg a window)	klemmen	klemən
student	der Student (–en) die Studentin (–nen)	der shtŭdent (–ən)/dee shtŭdentin (–ən)
studio	das Studio (–s)	das shtōodyo (–s)
study	studieren	shtŭdeerən
s. at / /	in / / s.	in / / shtŭdeerən
s. /German/	/deutsch/ s.	/doytsh/ shtŭdeerən
stuffing (food)	die Füllung (–en)	dee fülŭng (–ən)
stuffing (material)	die Füllung (–en)	dee fülŭng (–ən)
stupid	dumm	dŭm
style	der Stil (–e)	der shteel (–ə)
stylus	die Schneidnadel (–n)	dee shnīdnādəl (–n)
ceramic	Keramik/ /	kerāmik/ /
diamond	Diamant/ /	diamant/ /
sapphire	Saphir/ /	zāfir/ /
subscribe to / /	/ / abonnieren ich abonniere / /	/ / abəneerən ih abɔneerə / /
subscription	das Abonnement (–s)	das abɔnəmā
substance	die Substanz (–en)	dee zŭpstants (–ən)
suburb	die Vorstadt (–städte)	dee forshtat (–shtetə)
subway	die Unterführung (–en)	dee ŭntərführŭng (–ən)
suede (n)	das Wildleder	das viltlāydər
s. /jacket/	eine Wildleder- /jacke/	īnə viltlāydər– /yakə/
suffer	leiden	līdən
s. from /headaches/	an /Kopf- schmerzen/ l. ich leide an /Kopfschmerzen/	an /kɔpfshmertsən/ līdən ih līdə an /kɔpfshmertsən/
sugar	der Zucker	der tsŭkər
a spoonful of s.	ein Löffel Z.	īn lœfəl tsŭkər
sugar lump	das Stück Zucker	das shtük tsŭkər
suggest	vorschlagen ich schlage / / vor	forshlāgən ih shlāgə / / for
suit (n)	der Anzug (–züge)	der antsook (–tsüghə)
suit (vb)	stehen	shtāyən

	masculine	feminine	neuter
the/a (subject)	der/ein	die/eine	das/ein
the/a (object)	den/einen	die/eine	das/ein
the (plural, subject/object)	die	die	die

suitable	passend	**pas**ənt
suitcase	der Koffer (–)	der **kɔf**ər
suite (= hotel s.)	die Suite (–n)	dēē **svēē**tə (–n)
summer	der Sommer	der **zɔm**ər
in s.	im S.	im **zɔm**ər
sun	die Sonne	dēē **zɔn**ə
in the s.	in der S.	in der **zɔn**ə
sunbathe	ein Sonnenbad nehmen	īn **zɔn**ənbāt **nāy**mən
	ich nehme ein S.	ih **nāy**mə īn **zɔn**ənbāt
sunbathing	das Sonnenbaden	das **zɔn**ənbādən
sunburn	der Sonnenbrand	der **zɔn**ənbrant
sunburnt	sonnenverbrannt	**zɔn**ənfer**brant**
Sunday	der Sonntag (–e)	der **zɔn**tāk (–tāgə)
on Sunday	am S.	am **zɔn**tāk
on Sundays	sonntags	**zɔn**tāks
sunglasses	die Sonnenbrille (–n) (s)	dēē **zɔn**ənbrilə (–n)
a pair of s.	eine S.	īnə **zɔn**ənbrilə
polaroid s.	die Polaroid-sonnenbrille	dēē **polaroyd**-**zɔn**ənbrilə
sunny	sonnig	**zɔn**ih
sunrise	der Sonnenaufgang (–gänge)	der **zɔn**ənowfgang (–gengə)
sunset	der Sonnenuntergang (–gänge)	der **zɔn**ənŭntərgang (–gengə)
sunshade	der Sonnenschirm (–e)	der **zɔn**ənshirm (–ə)
sunstroke	der Sonnenstich (–e)	der **zɔn**ənshtih (–ə)
suntan (n)	die Sonnenbräune	dēē **zɔn**ənbroynə
s. oil	das Sonnenöl (–e)	das **zɔn**ənœl (–ə)
suntanned	sonnengebräunt	**zɔn**əngəbroynt
supermarket	der Supermarkt (–märkte)	der **zōō**pərmarkt (–merktə)
supper	das Abendessen	das **āb**əntesən
have s.	zu Abend essen	tsōō **āb**ənt esən
supply (n)	die Versorgung	dēē fer**zɔr**güng
supply (vb)	versorgen	fer**zɔr**gən
suppository	das Zäpfchen (–)	das **tsepf**hən
sure	sicher	**zih**ər
he's s.	er ist s.	āyr ist **zih**ər
surface (n)	die Oberfläche (–n)	dēē **ob**ərflehə (–n)
s. mail	die Normalpost	dēē **nɔrmal**pɔst
surfboard	das Surfbrett (–er)	das **sürf**bret
surfing	das Wellenreiten	das **vel**ənrītən
go s.	w. gehen	**vel**ənrītən **gāy**ən
	ich gehe w.	ih **gāy**ə **vel**ənrītən

196

surgery (=place)	die Praxis (Praxen)	dēē **praksis** (**praks**ən)
doctor's s.	die Sprechstunde	dēē **shpreh**shtündə
surname	der Vorname (–n)	der **for**nāmə (–n)
surplus	der Überschuß (–schüsse)	der **üh**bərshŭs (–shüsə)
surprise (n)	die Überraschung (–en)	dēē ühbə**rash**ŭng (–ən)
surprised	überrascht	ühbə**rrasht**
s. at /the result/	über /das Ergebnis/ u.	ühbər /das er**gāy**pnis/ ühbə**rrasht**
surveyor	der Landmesser	der **lant**mesər
survive	überleben	ühbər**lāy**bən
suspect (vb)	verdächtigen	fer**deh**tigən
suspender belt	der Strumpfhalter (–)	der **shtrümpf**haltər
swallow (vb)	schlucken	**shlük**ən
sweat (n)	der Schweiß	der shvīs
sweat (vb)	schwitzen	**shvits**ən
sweater	der Pullover (–)	der **pŭl**ovər
/cashmere/ s.	der /Kaschmir/ pullover (–)	der /**kash**mir/ **pŭl**ovər
long-sleeved s.	der P. mit langen Ärmeln	der **pŭl**ovər mit **lang**ən erməln
short-sleeved s.	der P. mit kurzen Ärmeln	der **pŭl**ovər mit **kŭrts**ən erməln
sleeveless s.	der ärmellose P.	dēē **erm**əlozə **pŭl**ovər
sweep (vb)	fegen	**fāy**gən
sweet (=dessert)	der Nachtisch (–e)	der **nākh**tish (–ə)
sweet (n) (=confectionery)	der Bonbon (–s)	der **bō**bō (**bō**bō)
sweet (=not savoury)	süß	zühs
swelling	die Geschwulst	dēē gə**shvŭlst**
swim (n)	das Schwimmen	das **shvim**ən
have a s.	s. gehen	**shvim**ən **gāy**ən
	ich gehe s.	ih **gāy**ə **shvim**ən
swim (vb)	schwimmen	**shvim**ən
swimming	das Schwimmen	das **shvim**ən
go s.	s. gehen	**shvim**ən **gāy**ən
	ich gehe s.	ih **gāy**ə **shvim**ən
s. costume	der Badeanzug (–züge)	der **bād**əantsōōk (–tsühgə)
s. trunks	die Badehose (–n) (s)	dēē **bād**əhozə (–n)
swimming pool	das Schwimmbad (–̈er)	das **shvim**bāt (–bēydər)
heated s. p.	das geheizte Bad	das gə**hīts**tə bāt

197

indoor s. p.	das Hallenbad (–bäder)	das halənbāt (–bēydər)
open air s. p.	das Freibad (–bäder)	das frībāt (–bēydər)
public s. p.	das öffentliche Bad	das œfəntihə bāt
swing (n) (children's s.)	die Schaukel (–n)	dēē showkəl (–n)
switch (=light s.)	der Schalter (–) /der Lichtschalter (–)	der shaltər/der lihtshaltər
switch off	ausschalten	owsshaltən
	ich schalte aus	ih shaltə ows
switch on	einschalten	īnshaltən
	ich schalte ein	ih shaltə īn
swollen	geschwollen	gəshvolən
symptom	das Anzeichen (–)	das antsīhən
synagogue	die Synagoge (–n)	dēē zünagogə (–n)
synthetic	synthetisch	züntāytish

T

table	der Tisch (–e)	der tish (–ə)
table tennis	das Tischtennis	das tishtenis
play t. t.	T. spielen	tishtenis shpēēlən
	ich spiele T.	ih shpēēlə tishtenis
tablecloth	das Tischtuch (–̈er)	das tishtōōkh (–tühkhər)
tablemat	das Set (–s)	das zet (–s)
tablespoonful of / /	der Löffel / /	der lœfəl / /
tailor	der Schneider (–)	der shnīdər
take	nehmen	nāymən
take (time)	brauchen	browkhən
take away (vb)	mitnehmen	mitnāymən
take-away meal	das essen zum mitnehmen	das esən tsūm mitnāymən
take off /a coat/	/den Mantel/ ausziehen	/dāyn mantəl/ owstsēēən
	ich ziehe /den Mantel/ aus	ih tsēēə /dāyn mantəl/ ows
take out (tooth)	ziehen	tsēēən
talcum powder	der Körperpuder (–)	der kœrpərpōōdər
talk (n) (discussion, chat)	das Gespräch (–e)	das gəshpreyh (–ə)
talk (vb)	sprechen	shprehən
t. to me about / /	mit mir über / / s.	mit mēēr ühbər / / shprehən

---

Remember: [kh] as in acht (eight) [h] as in hungrig (hungry)
[œ] as in schön (beautiful) [üh] as in Tür (door)

tall	groß	gros
tame (adj)	zahm	tsām
tampons	die Tampons (mpl)	dēē tampɔns
a box of t. (eg Tampax (tdmk))	eine Schachtel (–n) T.	īnə **shakh**təl (–n) tampɔns
tank	der Tank (–s)	der ta͞ngk (–s)
water t.	der Wassertank (–s)	der **vas**ərta͞ngk (–s)
tap	der Wasserhahn (–hähne)	der **vas**ərhān (–he͞ynə)
cold t.	der Hahn für Kaltwasser	der hān führ **kalt**vasər
hot t.	der Hahn für Heißwasser	der hān führ **hī**svasər
tape	das Tonband (–bänder)	das **ton**bant (–bendər)
cassette	die Kassette (–n)	dēē kasetə (–n)
tape measure	das Meßband (–bänder)	das **mes**bant (–bendər)
tape recorder	der Tonbandapparat (–e)	der **ton**bantaparāt (–ə)
cassette recorder	der Kassetten- recorder (–)	der kasetənrekɔrdər
open reel recorder	das Tonbandgerät (–e)	das **ton**bantgəre͞yt (–ə)
tartan	das Schottenmuster (–)	das shɔtənmüstər
a t. skirt	ein Schottenrock (–röcke)	īn shɔtənrɔk (–rœkə)
taste (n)	der Geschmack (–̈e)	der gəshmak (geshmekə)
taste (vb) (=have a certain taste)	schmecken	shmekən
taste (vb) (perceive with tongue)	probieren	prɔbēērən
tasty	schmackhaft	shmakhaft
tax	die Steuer (–n)	dēē shtoyər (–n)
airport t.	die Flughafengebühr (–en)	dēē flo͞okhāfəngəbühr (–ən)
tax free	steuerfrei	shtoyərfrī
taxi	das Taxi (–s)	das taksi (–s)
by t.	mit dem T.	mit dа͞ym taksi
t. rank	der Taxistand	der taksishtant
taxi driver	der Taxifahrer (–)	der taksifārər
tea	der Tee	der tа͞y
a cup of t.	eine Tasse (–n) T.	īnə tasə (–n) tа͞y
a pot of t.	eine Kanne (–n) T.	īnə kanə (–n) tа͞y

199

China t.	der chinesische T.	der hināyzihə tāy
Indian t.	der indische t.	der īndishə tāy
tea towel	das Geschirrtuch (¨-er)	das gəshirtōōkh (-tühkhər)
tea (meal)	das Abendessen	das ābəntesən
have t.	zu Abend essen	tsōō ābənt esən
teabag	der Teebeutel (–)	der tāyboytəl
teach	lehren	lāyrən
t. (me) /German/	(mich) /Deutsch/ l.	(mih) /doytsh/ lāyrən
he teaches (me) /German/	er lehrt (mich) /Deutsch/	ayr layrt (mih) /doytsh/
teacher	der Lehrer (–) die Lehrerin (–nen)	der lāyrər/dēē lāyrərin (–ən)
team	die Mannschaft (–en)	dēē manshaft (–ən)
teapot	die Teekanne (–n)	dēē tāykanə (–n)
tear (n) (= hole in material)	der Riß (Risse)	der ris (–ə)
tear (vb) (material)	zerreißen	tserīsən
teaspoon	der Teelöffel (–)	der tāylœfəl
a teaspoonful of / /	ein T. / /	īn tāylœfəl / /
teat	der Sauger (–)	der zowgər
teenager	der Teenager (–)	der tēēnāydjər
teetotal	abstinent	apstinent
telegram	das Telegramm (–e)	das telegram (–ə)
t. form	das Telegramm-formular	das telegram - fərmŭlār
send a t.	ein T. schicken	īn telegram shikən
	ich schicke ein T.	ih shikə īn telegram
telephone /phone (n)	das Telefon (–e)	das telefon (–ə)
call box	die Telefonzelle (–n)	dēē telefontselə (–n)
t. call	der Anruf (–e)	der anrōōf (–ə)
t. directory	das Telefonbuch (–bücher)	das telefonbōōkh (–bühər)
on the phone	am T.	am telefon
telephone (vb)	anrufen	anrōōfən
t. Reception	den Empfang a.	dāyn empfang anrōōfən
	ich rufe an	ih rōōfə an
t. the exchange	das Fernsprechamt a.	das fernshprehamt anrōōfən
t. the operator	die Vermittlung a.	dēē fermitlŭng anrōōfən
t. this number	diese Nummer a.	dēēzə nŭmər anrōōfən

200

television/TV (infml)	das Fernsehen (–)	das **fern**zāyən
portable t.	der tragbare F.	der **trāg**bāre **fern**zāyən
t. aerial	die Fernsehantenne (–n)	dēē **fern**zāyantenə (–n)
t. channel	die Fernsehkanal (–kanäle)	der **fern**zāykanāl (–kanēylə)
t. programme	der Fernsehprogram (–e)	das **fern**zāyprogram (–ə)
t. set	der Fernsehaparat (–e)	der **fern**zāyaparāt (–ə)
on t./on TV	im F.	im **fern**zāyən
telex (vb)	fernschreiben	**fern**shrībən
tell me (something) about / /	mir (etwas) von / / erzählen	mēēr (etwas) fon / / ert**sēy**lən
he told /me/ about it	er hat es /mir/ gesagt	āyr hat es /mēēr/ gə**zāgt**
temperature (atmosphere, body)	die Temperatur (–en)	dēē temperatōōr (–ən)
temple	der Tempel (–)	der **tem**pəl
temporary	provisorisch	provi**zo**rish
tender (eg of meat)	zart	tsart
tennis	das Tennis	das **ten**is
play tenis	T. spielen	**ten**is **shpēē**lən
	ich spiele T.	ih **shpēē**lə **ten**is
tent	das Zelt (–e)	das tselt (–ə)
term (=expression)	der Ausdruck (–drücke)	der **ows**drük (–drükə)
term (=period of time)	das Semester (–)	das ze**mes**tər
terminus	die Endstation (–en)	dēē **ent**shtatsyon (–ən)
bus t.	die Busendstation (–en)	dēē **büs**entshtatsyon (–ən)
railway t.	der Kopfbahnhof (–höfe)	der **kopf**bānhof (–hœfə)
tram t.	die Straßenbahn-endstation (–en)	dēē **shtrā**sənbān-entshtatsyon (–ən)
terms	die Bedingungen (fpl)	dēē bə**din**güngən
terrace	die Terrasse (–n)	dēē te**ra**sə (–n)
terrible	furchtbar	**fürht**bār

	masculine	feminine	neuter
the/a (subject)	der/ein	die/eine	das/ein
the/a (object)	den/einen	die/eine	das/ein
the (plural, subject/object)	die	die	die

201

test (n)	die Prüfung (–en)	dee prühfūng (–ən)
test (vb)	prüfen	prühfən
textbook	das Lehrbuch (¨er)	das layrbookh (–bühkhər)
thank you for / / (vb)	Ihnen für / / danken	eenən führ / / dangkən
t. y. f. your hospitality	ich danke Ihnen für Ihre Gastlichkeit	ih dangkə eenən führ eerə gastlihkīt
theatre	das Theater (–)	das teātər
t. programme	das Theaterprogramm (–e)	das teāterprogram (–ə)
theft	der Diebstahl (¨e)	der deepshtāl (–shteylə)
then	dann	dan
there	da	dā
thermometer	das Thermometer (–)	das termomaytər
Centigrade t.	das Celsiusthermometer	das tselziüstermomaytər
Fahrenheit t.	das Fahrenheitthermometer	das fārənhīttermomaytər
clinical t.	das Fieberthermometer	das feebərtermomaytər
they	sie	zee
thick	dick	dik
thigh	der Schenkel (–)	der shengkəl
thin (coat etc)	dünn	dün
thin (of person)	schlank	schlangk
thing	das Ding (–e)	das ding (–ə)
things (=belongings)	die Sachen	dee zakhən
think about / /	über / / nachdenken ich denke über / / nach	ühbər / / nākhdengkən ih dengkə ühbər / / nākh
what do you t.?	woran denken Sie?	voran dengkən zee
thirsty	durstig	dürstih
be t.	d. sein	dürstih zīn
I'm t.	ich bin d.	ih bin dürstih
thousand	das Tausend (–e)	das towzənt (towzəndə)
thousands of / /	Tausende von / /	towzəndə fon / /
thread	der Faden (¨)	der fādən (feydən)
a reel of t.	eine Rolle (–n) F.	īnə rolə (–n) fādən
throat	der Hals (¨e)	der hals (helsə)
sore throat	die Halsschmerzen (mpl)	dee halsshmertsən

	ich habe Halsschmerzen	ih hābə halsshmertsən
t. pastilles	die Hustenbonbons (mpl)	dēē hŭstənbōbō
thumb	der Daumen (–)	der **dow**mən
thunderstorm	das Gewitter (–)	das gəvitər
Thursday	Donnerstag (–e)	**dɔ**nərstāk (–tāgə)
on Thursday	am D.	am **dɔ**nərstāk
on Thursdays	donnerstags	**dɔ**nərstāks
ticket	die Fahrkarte (–n)	dēē **fār**kārtə (–n)
child's t.	eine halbe F.	**ī**nə halbə **fār**kārtə
day return	eine Tagesrück- fahrkarte (–n)	eine **tā**gəs rük**fār**kārtə (–n)
first class t.	eine F. erster Klasse	**ī**nə **fār**kārtə **āy**rstər klasə
group t.	eine Gruppenfahrkarte (–n)	**ī**nə **grŭ**pən**fār**kartə (–n)
return t.	eine Rückfahrkarte (–n)	**ī**nə rük**fār**kārtə (–n)
season t.	eine Zeitkarte (–n)	**ī**nə **tsī**tkārtə (–n)
second class t.	eine F. zweiter Klasse	**ī**nə **fār**kārtə **tsvī**tər klasə
single	eine einfache F.	**ī**nə **ī**nfakhə **fār**kārtə
ticket office	der Fahrkartenschalter	der **fār**kārtənshaltər
tide	die Gezeiten (pl)	dēē gə**tsī**tən
high t.	die Flut	dēē flōōt
low t.	die Ebbe	dēē ebə
tidy (of people)	ordentlich	**ɔr**dəntlih
tidy (things)	ordentlich	**ɔr**dəntlih
tidy (vb)	aufräumen	**ow**froymən
	ich räume auf	ih roymə **owf**
tie (n)	die Krawatte (–n)	dēē kra**va**tə (–n)
tie (vb)	binden	**bin**dən
tiepin	die Krawattennadel (–n)	dēē kra**va**tən**nā**dəl (–n)
tight	eng	eng
tights	die Strumpfhose (–n)	dēē **shtrŭmpf**hozə (–n)
a pair of t.	eine S.	**ī**nə **shtrŭmpf**hozə
till (=until)	bis	bis
time	die Zeit (–en)	dēē tsīt (–ən)
the t. (clock)	die Uhr	dēē ōōr
/6/ times	/sechs/ Mal	/zeks/ māl
have a good t.	mich gut amüsieren	mih **gōōt** amü**zēē**rən

203

	ich amüsiere mich gut	ih amüzeerə mih goot
timetable	der Fahrplan (–pläne)	der fārplān (–pleynə)
bus t.	der Busfahrplan –pläne)	der busfārplān (–pleynə)
train t.	der Zugfahrplan (–pläne)	der tsookfārplān (–pleynə)
tin	die Dose (–n)	dee dozə (–n)
a t. of / /	eine D. / /	īnə dozə / /
tin opener	der Dosenöffner (–)	der dozənœfnər
tint (n) (=hair t.)	die Haarfarbe (–n)	dee hārfarbə (–n)
tint (vb)	färben	ferbən
tip (n) (money)	das Trinkgeld	das trinkgelt
tip (vb) (money)	ein T. geben	īn trinkgelt gāybən
t. /the waiter/	/dem Kellner/ ein T. geben	/dāym kelnər/ īn trinkgelt gāybən
	ich gebe /dem Kellner/ ein T.	ih gāybə /dāym kelnər/ īn trinkgelt
tired	müde	mühdə
tiring	ermüdend	ermühdənt
tissues/Kleenex (tdmk)	die Papiertücher (npl)	dee papeertühkhər
a box of t.	ein Paket Tempotaschentücher	īn pakāyt tempotashəntühkhər
title	der Titel (–)	der teetəl
to	zu	tsoo
toast (n)	der Toast	der tost
a slice of t.	eine Scheibe T.	īnə shībə tost
toast (vb)	toasten	tostən
tobacco	der Tabak	der tabak
tobacconist's	der Tabakwarenladen (–läden)	der tabakvārənlādən (–leydən)
today	heute	hoytə
toe	die Zehe (–n)	dee tsāyə (–n)
toenail	der Zehennagel (¨)	der tsayənāgəl (–neygəl)
together	zusammen	tsŭzamən
toilet	die Toilette (–n)	dee twaletə (–n)
toilet paper	das Toilettenpapier	das twaletənpapeer
a roll of t. p.	eine Rolle (–n) T.	īnə rolə (–n) twaletənpapeer
toilet water	das Toilettenwasser (–)	das twaletənvasər

Remember: [kh] as in acht (eight) [h] as in hungrig (hungry)
[œ] as in schön (beautiful) [üh] as in Tür (door)

tomato	die Tomate (–n)	dee tomātə (–n)
t. sauce	die Tomatensoße (–n)	dee tomātənzosə (–n)
tomato juice	der Tomatensaft (–säfte)	der tomātənzaft (–zeftə)
a bottle of t. j.	eine Flasche (–n) T.	īnə flashə (–n) tomātənzaft
a can of t. j.	eine Dose (–n) T.	īnə dozə (–n) tomātənzaft
a glass of t. j.	ein Glas (–) T.	īn glās (–) tomātənzaft
tomorrow	morgen	mɔrgən
ton	die Tonne (–n)	dee tɔnə (–n)
tongue (food)	die Zunge (–n)	dee tsŭngə (–n)
tongue (organ of mouth)	die Zunge (–n)	dee tsŭngə (–n)
tonic (water)	das Tonic	das tɔnik
tonight	heute abend	hoytə ābənt
tonsillitis	die Tonsillitis	dee tɔnzileetis
too (=more than can be endured)	zu	tsoo
t. /big/	z. /groß/	tsoo /gros/
tool	das Werkzeug (–e)	das verktsoyk (–tsoygə)
tooth	der Zahn (–̈e)	der tsān (tseȳnə)
wisdom t.	der Weisheitszahn (–̈e)	der vīshītstsān (–tseȳnə)
toothache	die Zahnschmerzen (mpl)	dee tsānshmertsən
toothbrush	die Zahnbürste (–n)	dee tsānbürstə (–n)
toothpaste	die Zahnpasta	dee tsānpasta
a tube of t.	eine Tube (–n) Z.	īnə toobə (–n) tsānpasta
toothpick	der Zahnstocher (–)	der tsānshtɔkhər
top	die Spitze (–n)	dee shpitsə (–n)
the t. of / /	die S. von / /	dee shpitsə fɔn / /
torch	die Taschenlampe (–n)	dee tashənlampə (–n)
tortoiseshell (adj)	aus Schildpatt	ows shiltpat
total (adj)	gesamt	gəzamt
total (n)	die Gesamtsumme (–n)	dee gəzamtzŭmə (–n)
touch (vb)	berühren	bərührən
tough (food)	zäh	tseȳ
tour	die Tour (–en)	dee toor (–ən)
conducted t.	die Führung (–en)	dee führŭng (–ən)

205

tourist	der Tourist (–en)	der tŭrist (–ən)
t. class	die Touristenklasse	dee tŭristənklasə
t. office	das Fremden-verkehrsbüro (–s)	das fremdən-ferkāyrzbüro (–s)
tow rope	das Abschleppseil (–e)	das apschlepzīl (–ə)
tow (vb)	schleppen	shlepən
towel (=bath t.)	das Badetuch (–tücher)	das bādətookh (–tühkhər)
towelling (material)	der Frotteestoff (–e)	der frotāyshtɔf (–ə)
tower	der Turm (¨e)	der tŭrm (türmə)
town	die Stadt (¨e)	dee shtat (shtetə)
t. centre	die Stadtmitte (–n)	dee shtatmitə (–n)
t. hall	das Rathaus (–häuser)	das räthows (–hoyzər)
toxic	giftig	giftih
toy	das Spielzeug (–e)	das shpeeltsoyk (–tsoygə)
t. shop	das spielwaren-geschäft (–e)	das shpeelvärən-gəsheft (–ə)
track (of animal)	die Spur (–en)	dee shpoor (–ən)
track (of tape)	die Spur (–en)	dee shpoor (–ən)
track (=race t.)	die Rennbahn (–)	dee renbān (–ən)
traditional	traditionell	traditsyonel
traffic	der Verkehr	der ferkāyr
traffic jam	der Verkehrsstau (–e)	der ferkāyrsshtow (–ə)
traffic lights	die Verkehrsampeln (fpl)	dee ferkāyrsampəln
trailer	der Anhänger (–)	der anhengər
train	der Zug (¨e)	der tsook (tsühgə)
boat t.	der Z. mit Schiffsanschluß	der tsook mit shifsanshlüs
express t.	der D-Zug (¨e)	der dāy-tsook (–tsühgə)
fast t.	der Eilzug (¨e)	der īltsook (–tsühgə)
slow t.	der Personenzug (¨e)	der perzonəntsook (–tsühgə)
train driver	der Führer	der führər
tram	die Straßenbahn (–en)	dee shtrāsənbān (–ən)
t. stop	die Straßenbahn-haltestelle (–n)	dee shtrāsənbān-haltəshtelə (–n)
t. terminus	die Endstation (–en)	dee entshtatsyon (–ən)
the t. for / /	die S. nach / /	dee shtrāsənbān nākh / /

by t.	mit dem S.	mit dāym shtrāsənbān
tranquiliser	das Beruhigungsmittel (–n)	das bərōōigüngsmitəl
transfer (vb)	transferieren	transfereēerən
transformer	der Transformator (–en)	der transfɔrmātɔr (transfɔrmātɔrən)
transistor (t. radio)	das Transistorradio (–s)	das tranzistɔrrādyo (–s)
transit passenger	der Durchreisende (–n)	der dúrhrīzəndə (–n)
in transit	im Transit	im tranzēet
translate	übersetzen	ühbərzetsən
translation	die Übersetzung (–en)	dēē ühbərzetsüng (–ən)
transparent	durchsichtig	dúrhzihtih
transport (n)	der Transport	der transpɔrt
public t.	die öffentlichen Verkehrsmittel (npl)	dēē œfəntlihən ferkāyrsmitəl
trap (n)	die Falle (–n)	dēē falə (–n)
trap (vb)	fangen	fangən
travel (vb)	reisen	rīzən
by air	mit dem Flugzeug	mit dāym flōōktsoyk
by boat, by bus	mit dem Boot, mit dem Bus	mit dāym bot mit dāym büs
by coach, by car	mit dem Reisebus, mit dem Auto	mit dāym rīzəbüs mit dāym owto
by hovercraft	mit dem Luftkissenfahrzeug	mit dāym lúftkisənfārtsoyk
by sea	mit dem Schiff	mit dāym shif
by train, by tram, by underground	mit dem Zug, mit der Straßenbahn, mit der U-Bahn	mit dāym tsōōk mit der shtrāsənbān mit der ōō-bān
on foot	zu Fuß	tsōō fōos
on the ferry	mit der Fähre	mit der fēyrə
overland	über Land	ühbər lant
to / /	nach / /	nākh / /
travel agent's	das Reisebüro (–s)	das rīzəbüro (–s)
traveller's cheque	der Reisecheck (–s)	der rīzəshek (–s)
tray	das Tablett (–s)	das tablet (–s)
treat (medically)	behandeln	bəhandəln

	masculine	feminine	neuter
the/a (subject)	der/ein	die/eine	das/ein
the/a (object)	den/einen	die/eine	das/ein
the (plural, subject/object)	die	die	die

207

treatment	die Behandlung (–en)	dēē bəhandlŭng (–ən)
tree	der Baum (⸚e)	der bowm (boymə)
triangular	dreieckig	drīekih
trim (haircut)	der Schnitt (–e)	der shnit (–ə)
trim (vb)	schneiden	shnīdən
trip (n)	der Ausflug (–flüge)	der owsflōōk (–flühgə)
coach t.	die Autobusreise (–n)	dēē owtobŭsrīzə (–n)
tripod	das Stativ (–e)	das shtatēēf (–tēēvə)
trolley (=luggage t.)	der Kofferkuli (–s)	der kɔfərkōōli (–s)
tropical	tropisch	tropish
trot (vb)	traben	trābən
trouble	das Problem (–e)	das problāym (–ə)
I'm in t.	ich bin in Schwierigkeiten (pl)	ih bin in shvēērihkītən
trousers	die Hose (–n) (s)	dēē hozə (–n)
a pair of t.	eine H.	īnə hozə
trout	die Forelle (–n)	dēē forelə (–n)
true	wahr	vār
trunk (for luggage)	der große Koffer	der grosə kɔfər
trunk (of tree)	der Stamm (⸚e)	der shtam (shtemə)
trust (vb)	vertrauen	fertrowən
I t. /her/	ich vertraue /ihr/	ih fertrowə /ēer/
truth	die Wahrheit (–en)	dēē vārhīt (–ən)
tell the t.	die W. sagen	dēē vārhīt zāgən
try on /this sweater/	/diesen Pullover/ anprobieren	/dēēzən pŭlovər/ anprobēērən
	ich probiere /diesen Pullover/ an	ih probēērə /dēēzən pŭlovər/ an
try /this ice-cream/	/dieses Eis/ probieren	/dēēzəs īs/ probēērən
	ich probiere /dieses Eis/	ih probēērə /dēēzəs īs/
T-shirt	das T-shirt (–s)	das tēē-shirt (–s)
tube	die Tube (–n)	dēē tōōbə (–n)
a t. of / /	eine T. / /	īnə tōōbə / /
tube (for a tyre)	der Schlauch (⸚e)	der shlowkh (shloyhə)
Tuesday	Dienstag (–e)	dēēnstāk (–tagə)
on Tuesday	am D.	am dēēnstāk
on Tuesdays	dienstags	dēēnstāks
tulip	die Tulpe (–n)	dēē tŭlpə (–n)
a bunch of tulips	ein Strauß (⸚) Tulpen	īn shtrows (⸚) tulpən

tunnel (n)	der Tunnel (–s)	der tŭnəl (–s)
turkey	der Truthahn (–hähne)	der trōōthān (–hēynə)
turn off (switch)	ausschalten ich schalte aus	owsshaltən ih shaltə ows
turn on (switch)	einschalten ich schalte ein	īnshaltən ih shaltə īn
turnip	die Rübe (–n)	dēē rühbə (–n)
turntable (on record player)	der Plattenteller (–)	der platəntelər
turpentine	das Terpentin	das terpentēēn
tweed	der Tweed	der tvēēt
tweezers	die Pinzette (–n)	dēē pintsetə (–n)
a pair of t.	eine P.	īnə pintsetə
twice	zweimal	tsvīmāl
twin	Zwillings/ /	tsvilings/ /
t. beds	die Einzelbetten (npl)	dēē īntsəlbetən
type (vb)	tippen	tipən
typewriter	die Schreibmaschine (–n)	dēē shrīpmashēēnə (–n)
typhoid	der Typhus	der tühfŭs
typical	typisch	tühpish
typist	die Stenotypistin (–nen)	dēē stenotüpistin (–ən)
tyre	der Reifen (–)	der rīfən

U

ugly	häßlich	heslih
ulcer	das Geschwühr (–e)	das gəshvühr (–ə)
umbrella	der Schirm (–e)	der shirm (–ə)
beach u.	der Sonnenschirm	der zɔnənshirm
umpire	der Schiedsrichter (–)	der shēētsrihtər
uncle	der Onkel (–)	der ɔngkəl
uncomfortable	unbequem	ŭnbəkvāym
unconscious	bewußtlos	bəvŭstlos
under	unter	ŭntər
undercooked	halbgar	halpgār
underground (u. railway train)	die Untergrundbahn (–en)	dēē ŭntərgrüntbān (–ən)
by u.	mit der U-bahn	mit der ōō-bān
underpants (for men)	die Unterhose (–n) (s)	dēē ŭntərhozə (–n)
a pair of u.	eine U.	īnə ŭntərhozə
understand	verstehen	fershtāyən
I don't u.	ich verstehe nicht	ih fershtāyə niht

209

underwear	die Unterwäsche (no pl)	dee ŭntərveshə
children's u.	die Kinderunterwäsche	dee kindərŭntərveshə
men's u.	die Herrenunterwäsche	dee herənŭntərveshə
women's u.	die Damenunterwäsche	dee dāmənŭntərveshə
unfashionable	unmodern	ŭnmodern
unfasten	losbinden	losbindən
	ich binde los	ih bində los
unfortunately	leider	līdər
unfriendly	unfreundlich	ŭnfroyntlih
uniform (n)	die Uniform (–en)	dee ŭnifɔrm (–ən)
in u.	in U.	in ŭnifɔrm
unique	einzig	īntsih
university	die Universität (–en)	dee univerziteyt (–ən)
unlocked	offen	ɔfən
unlucky		
be u.	Pech haben	peh hābən
he's u.	er hat P.	ayr hat peh
unpack	auspacken	owspakən
	ich packe aus	ih pakə ows
unpleasant	unangenehm	ŭnangənaym
unripe	unreif	ŭnrīf
untie	aufbinden	owfbindən
	ich binde auf	ih bində owf
until	bis	bis
unusual	ungewöhnlich	ŭngəvœnlih
up	auf	owf
are you going u.?	gehen Sie hinauf?	gayən zee hinowf
be u. (=out of bed)	auf sein	owf zīn
	ich bin auf	ih bin owf
upset (adj)	durcheinander	dŭrhīnandər
I've got a stomach u.	ich habe eine Magen-verstimmung	ih habə īnə māgənfershtimŭng
upside-down	umgekehrt	ŭmgəkayrt
upstairs	oben	obən
urgent	dringend	dringənt
urinate	Wasser lassen	vasər lasən
	ich lasse Wasser	ih lasə vasər
urine	der Urin	der ŭreen
us	uns	ŭnts
useful	nützlich	nütslih

Remember: [kh] as in acht (eight) [h] as in hungrig (hungry)
[œ] as in schön (beautiful) [üh] as in Tür (door)

use /your phone/	/Ihr Telefon/ benützen	/eer telefon/ bənütsən
usually	gewöhnlich	gəvöenliḥ
utensil	das Gerät (–e)	das gəreyt (–ə)

V

V -necked sweater	/ein Pullover/ mit V-Ausschnitt	/īn pŭlovər/ mit fow-owsshnit
vacancy (job)	die freie Stelle	dee frīə shtelə
vacancy (room)	Zimmer frei	tsimər frī
vacant	frei	frī
vaccinate	impfen	impfən
vaccination	die Impfung (–en)	dee impfŭng (–ən)
vaccine	der Impfstoff	der impfshtof (–ə)
vacuum cleaner	der Staubsauger (–)	der shtowpzowgər
vacuum flask	die Thermosflasche (–n)	dee termɔsflashə (–n)
valid /passport/	gültiger /Paß/	gültigər /pas/
valley	das Tal (¨er)	das tāl (teylər)
valuable	wertvoll	vertfɔl
valuables (pl)	die Wertsachen (pl)	dee vertzakhən
value (n)	der Wert (–e)	der vert (–ə)
value (vb)	schätzen	shetsən
van	der Lieferwagen (–)	der leefərvāgən
luggage v.	der Gepäckwagen	der gəpekvāgən
vanilla	die Vanille	dee vanilyə
variety	die Sorte (–n)	dee zɔrtə (–n)
various	verschieden	fersheedən
varnish (n)	der Lack (–e)	der lak (–ə)
nail v.	der Nagellack	der nāgəlak
varnish (vb) (eg boat)	firnissen	firnisən
vase (=flower v.)	die Vase (–n)	dee vāzə (–n)
vaseline	die Vaselincreme	dee vazeleenkrāym
a tube of v.	eine Tube V.	īnə toobə vazeleenkrāym
V.A.T.	die Mehrwertsteuer	dee māyrvertshtoyər
veal	das Kalbfleisch	das kalpflīsh
vegetables	das Gemüse (s)	das gəmühzə
fresh v.	frisches G.	frishəs gəmühzə
mixed v.	gemischtes G.	gəmishtəs gəmühzə
vegetarian	der Vegetarier (–)	der vegetāryər
vehicle	das Fahrzeug (–e)	das fārtsoyk (–tsoygə)
vein	die Vene (–n)	dee vāynə (–n)
velvet	der Samt	der zamt

venereal disease	die Geschlechtskrankheit (–en)	dēē gəshlehtskrangkhīt (–ən)
venison	der Rehbraten (–)	der rāybrātən
ventilator	der Ventilator (–en)	der ventilātor (ventilātorən)
very	sehr	zāyr
vest	das Unterhemd (–en)	das ŭntərhemt (–hemdən)
cotton v.	das Baumwoll-unterhemd	das bowmvɔl-ŭnterhemt (–hemdən)
woollen v.	das Wollunterhemd	das vɔlŭntərhemt (–hemdən)
via	über	ühbər
travel v. /Rome/	ü. /Rom/ reisen	ühbər /rom/ rīzən
	ich reise ü. /Rom/	ih rīzə ühbər /rom/
vicar	der Pastor (–en)	der pastor (pastorən)
view (n)	die Aussicht (–en)	dēē owsziht (–ən)
viewfinder	der Sucher (–)	der zookhər
villa (= holiday v.)	die Ferienvilla (–en)	dēē fāyryənvila (–vilən)
village	das Dorf (¨er)	das dɔrf (dœrfər)
vinegar	der Essig	der esih
a bottle of v.	eine Flasche (–n) E.	īnə flashə (–n) esih
oil and v.	E. und Öl	esih ŭnt ēl
violin	die Violine (–n)	dēē violēēnə (–n)
visa	das Visum (Visa)	das vēēzŭm (vīza)
visibility	die Sichtbarkeit	dēē zihtbārkīt
visit /a museum/	/ein Museum/ besichtigen	/īn mŭzāyŭm / bəzihtigən
vitamin pills	die Vitamintabletten (fpl)	dēē vitamēēntabletən
a bottle of v. p.	eine Flasche (–n) V.	īnə flashe (–n) vitamēēntabletən
vodka	der Wodka	der vɔtka
a bottle of v.	eine Flasche (–n) W.	īnə flashə (–n) vɔtka
a v.	ein W.	īn vɔtka
voice	die Stimme (–n)	dēē shtimə (–n)
volt	das Volt	das vɔlt
/110/ volts	/110/ V.	/hŭndərt tsāyn/ vɔlt
voltage	die Spannung (–en)	dēē shpanŭng (–ən)
high v.	die Hochspannung	dēē hokhshpanŭng

212

low v.	die Niedrigspannung	dee needrihshpanüng
volume (content)	der Inhalt	der inhalt
volume (noise)	die Lautstärke	dee lowtshterkə
vomit (n)	das Erbrochene	das erbrokhənə
vomit (vb)	mich erbrechen	mih erbrehən
	ich erbreche mich	ih erbrehə mih
voucher	der Gutschein (–e)	der gōōtshīn (–ə)
hotel v.	der Hotelgutschein (–e)	der hotelgōōtshīn (–ə)
voyage (n)	die Seereise (–n)	dee zāyrīzə (–n)

W

waist	die Taille (–n)	dee talyə (–n)
waistcoat	die Weste (–n)	dee vestə (–n)
wait /for me/	/auf mich/ warten	/owf mih/ vārtən
please wait /for me/	warten Sie bitte /auf mich/	vārtən zee bitə /owf mih/
waiter	der Kellner (–)	der kelnər
waiting room	das Wartezimmer (–)	das vārtətsimər
waitress	die Kellnerin (–nen)	dee kelnərin (–ən)
wake /me/ up	/mich/ aufwecken	/mih/ owfvekən
walk (n)	der Spaziergang (–̈e)	der shpatseergang (–gengə)
go for a w.	spazieren gehen	shpatseerən gāyən
	ich gehe spazieren	ih gāyə shpatseerən
walk (vb)	zu Fuß gehen	tsōō fōōs gāyən
	ich gehe zu Fuß	ih gāyə tsōō fōōs
walking	das Laufen	das lowfən
do some w.	laufen	lowfən
walking stick	der Spazierstock (–̈e)	der shpatseershtok (–shtœkə)
wall (=inside w.)	die Wand (–̈e)	dee vant (vendə)
wallet	die Brieftasche (–n)	dee breeftashə (–n)
walnut (nut)	der Walnuß (–nüsse)	der valnŭs (–nüsə)
walnut (wood)	das Nußbaumholz	das nŭsbowmholts
want	wollen	volən
w. /a room/	/ein Zimmer/ w.	/īn tsimər/ volən
	ich will /ein Zimmer/	ih vil /īn tsimər/
w. to /buy/ it	es /kaufen/ w.	es /kowfən/ volən

	masculine	feminine	neuter
the/a (subject)	der/ein	die/eine	das/ein
the/a (object)	den/einen	die/eine	das/ein
the (plural, subject/object)	die	die	die

	ich will es /kaufen/	ih vil es /kowfən/
war	der Krieg (–e)	der kreek (kreegə)
ward (in hospital)	die Station (–en)	dee shtatsyon (–ən)
wardrobe	der Schrank (–̈e)	der shrangk (shrengkə)
warm (adj)	warm	varm
warm (vb)	wärmen	vermən
warn	warnen	varnən
warning	die Warnung (–en)	dee varnüng (–ən)
wash (n)	das Waschen	das vashən
have a w.	mich w.	mih vashən
	ich wasche mich	ih vashə mih
wash (vb)	waschen	vashən
washbasin	das Waschbecken (–)	das vashbekən
washing machine	die Waschmaschine (–n)	dee vashmasheenə (–n)
washing powder	das Waschpulver (–)	das vashpülfər
wash up	abwaschen	apvashən
	ich wasche ab	ih vashə ap
wasp	die Wespe (–n)	dee vespə (–n)
w. sting	der Wespenstich (–e)	der vespənshtih (–ə)
waste (vb)	verschwenden	fershvendən
wastepaper basket	der Papierkorb (–̈e)	der papeerkorp (–koerbə)
watch (n)	die Uhr (–en)	dee oor (–ən)
w. strap	das Uhrenarmband	das oorənarmbant (–bendər)
face (of w.)	das Zifferblatt (–̈er)	das tsifərblat (–bletər)
hand (of w.)	der Uhrzeiger (–)	der oortsīgər
watchmaker's	der Uhrmacher (–)	der oormakhər
watch TV	fernsehen	fernzāyən
	ich sehe fern	ih zāyə fern
water	das Wasser (–)	das vasər
cold w.	kaltes W.	kaltəs vasər
drinking w.	das Trinkwasser	das tringkvasər
hot w.	heißes W.	hīsəs vasər
running w.	fließendes W.	fleesəndəs vasər
watercolour (=painting)	das Aquarell (–e)	das akvarel (–ə)
waterproof (adj)	wasserdicht	vasərdiht
water skiing	das Wasserskilaufen	das vasərsheelowfən
go w. s.	Wasserski laufen	vasərsheelowfən
	ich laufe Wasserski	ih lowfə vasərshee
watt	das Watt	das vat
/100/ watts	/100/ W.	/hündərt/ vat

wave (radio)	die Welle	dēē velə (–n)
medium w.	die Mittelwelle	dēē mitəlvelə
long w.	die Langwelle	dēē laṉgvelə
short w.	die Kurzwelle	dēē kŭrtsvelə
VHF	die Ultrakurzwelle	dēē ŭltrakŭrtsvelə
wave (sea)	die Welle (–n)	dēē velə (–n)
wax	das Wachs	das vaks
we	wir	vēēr
weak (physically)	schwach	shvakh
wear (vb) (clothes)	tragen	trāgən
weather	das Wetter	das vetər
w. conditions	die Wetter-bedingungen (fpl)	dēē vetər-bədiṉgŭṉgən
w. forecast	der Wetterbericht (–e)	der vetərbəriht (–ə)
wedding	die Hochzeit (–en)	dēē hokhtsīt (–ən)
Wednesday	der Mittwoch (–e)	mitvokh (–ə)
on Wednesday	am M.	am mitvokh
on Wednesdays	mittwochs	mitvokhs
week	die Woche (–n)	dēē vokhə (–n)
this w.	diese W.	dēēzə vokhə
last w.	letzte W.	letstə vokhə
next w.	nächste W.	nēyhstə vokhə
weekend	das Wochenende (–n)	das vokhənendə (–n)
weekly (adj)	wöchentlich	vœhəntlih
twice w.	zweimal in der Woche	tsvīmāl in der vokhə
weigh	wiegen	vēēgən
weight	das Gewicht	das gəviht
w. limit	die Gewichts-beschränkung	dēē gəvihts-bəshreṉgkŭṉg
welcome (vb)	willkommen heißen	vilkəmən hīsən
w. to / /	willkommen in / /	vilkəmən in / /
	ich heiße w.	ih hīsə vilkəmən
well (=all right)	wohl	vol
well-done (eg of steak)	durchgebraten	dŭrhgəbrātən
Wellingtons	die Gummistiefel (mpl)	dēē gŭmishtēēfəl
west	der Westen	der vestən
Western (=film)	der Wildwestfilm	der viltvestfilm
wet	naß	nas
I'm w.	ich bin durchnäßt	ih bin dŭrhnest
it's w.	es regnet	es rāygnət
/this towel/ is w.	/dieses Handtuch/ ist n.	/dēēzəs hanttōōkh/ ist nas

what?	was?	vas
at w. time?	um welche Uhr?	ŭm velhə ōōr
wheel	das Rad (-̈er)	das rāt (rēydər)
wheelchair	der Rollstuhl (–stühle)	der rɔlshtōōl (–shtühlə)
when?	wann?	van
where?	wo?	vo
which?	welcher (m)/welche (f)/welches (n)?	velhər/velhə/velhəs
w. /plane/?	welches /Flugzeug/?	velhəs /flōōktsoyk/
whisky	der Whisky (–s)	der viski (–s)
a bottle of w.	eine Flasche (–n) W.	īnə flashə (–n) viski
a w.	ein W.	īn viski
whistle (n)	die Pfeife (–n)	dēē pfīfə (–n)
white	weiß	vīs
w. coffee	Kaffee mit milch	kafāy mit milh
who?	wer?	vāyr
whole	ganz	gants
a w. /month/	ein ganzer /Monat/	īn gantsər /mōnāt/
the w. /month/	der ganze /Monat/	der gantsə /mōnāt/
whose?	wessen?	vesən
why?	warum?	varŭm
wick (lamp, lighter)	der Docht (–e)	der dɔkht (–ə)
wide	weit	vīt
widow	die Witwe (–n)	dēē vitvə (–n)
widower	der Witwer (–)	der vitvər
width	die Weite (–n)	dēē vītə (–n)
wife	die Frau (–en)	dēē frow (–ən)
wig	die Perücke (–n)	dēē perükə (–n)
wild (=not tame)	wild	vilt
w. animal	das wilde Tier	das vildə tēēr
win (vb)	gewinnen	gəvinən
wind (n)	der Wind	der vint
wind (vb) (clock)	aufziehen	owftsēēən
	ich ziehe auf	ih tsēēə owf
window	das Fenster (–)	das fenstər
french w.	die Balkontür (–en)	dēē balkontühr (–ən)
shop w.	das Schaufenster (–)	das showfenstər
windy	windig	vindih
it's w.	es ist w.	es ist vindih

Remember: [kh] as in acht (eight) [h] as in hungrig (hungry)
[œ] as in schön (beautiful) [üh] as in Tür (door)

wine	der Wein (–e)	der vīn (–ə)
a bottle of w.	eine Flasche (–n) W.	īnə flashə (–n) vīn
a carafe of w.	eine Karaffe (–n) W.	īnə karafə (–n) vīn
a glass of w.	ein Glas (–) W.	īn glās vīn
a half bottle of w.	eine halbe Flasche W.	īnə halbə flashə vīn
dry w.	herb	herp
red w.	rot	rot
rosé	rose	rozāy
sparkling w.	der Perlwein	der perlvīn
sweet w.	süß	zühs
white w.	weiß	vīs
wine glass	das Weinglas (¨er)	das vīnglās (–glēyzər)
wine list	die Weinkarte (–n)	dēē vīnkartə (–n)
wine merchant's	der Weinhändler (–)	der vīnhendlər
wing (bird or plane)	der Flügel (–)	der flühgəl
winter	der Winter (–)	der vintər
in w.	im W.	im vintər
wipe (vb)	wischen	vishən
wire	der Draht (¨e)	der drāt (drēytə)
a piece of w.	ein Stück D.	īn shtük drāt
with	mit	mit
without	ohne	ōnə
witness (n)	der Zeuge (–n) die Zeugin (–nen)	der tsoygə (–n)/dēē tsoygin (–ən)
woman	die Frau (–en)	dēē frow (–ən)
wonderful	wunderbar	vŭndərbār
wood (of trees)	der Wald (¨er)	der valt (veldər)
wood (substance)	das Holz (¨er)	das hɔlts (hœltsər)
wooden	hölzern	hœltsərn
wool	die Wolle	dēē vɔlə
woollen	woll/ /	vɔl/ /
word	das Wort (¨er)	das vɔrt (vœrtər)
work (n)	die Arbeit (–en)	dēē ārbīt (–ən)
do some w.	arbeiten	ārbītən
work (vb) (of machines)	in Betrieb sein	in bətrēēp zīn
	es ist in Betrieb	es ist in bətrēēp
work (vb) (of people)	arbeiten	ārbītən
world (the w.)	die Welt	dēē velt
worn-out	abgetragen	apgətrāgən
worried	besorgt	bəzɔrkt
worse (in health)	schlechter	shlehtər
he's w.	es geht ihm s.	es gāyt ēēm shlehtər

217

worse (things)	schlechter	shlehtər
w. than / /	s. als / /	**shleh**tər als / /
it's w.	es ist s.	es ist **shleh**tər
worst	schlechtest	**shleh**təst
the w. /hotel/	das schlechteste /Hotel/	das **shleh**təstə /hotel/
the w. /room/	das schlechteste /Zimmer/	das **shleh**təstə /tsimər/
worth		
be w.	wert sein	**vert** zīn
it's w. /5/ marks	es ist /fünf/ mark w.	es ist /**fünf**/ mārk **vert**
wound (=injury)	die Wunde (–n)	dēē vŭndə (–n)
wrap (vb)	einwickeln	**īn**vikəln
	ich wickle / / ein	ih viklə / / **īn**
gift-wrap (vb)	in Geschenkpapier e.	in gə**sheng**kpapēēr **īn**vikəln
wreath (funeral w.)	der Kranz (–e)	der krants (**krents**ə)
wreck (n)	das Wrack (–s)	das vrak (–s)
wrist	das Handgelenk (–e)	das **hant**gəleng̅k (–ə)
write	schreiben	**shrī**bən
writing paper	das Schreibpapier	das **shrī**ppapēēr
wrong	falsch	falsh
be w.	mich irren	mih irən
I'm w.	ich irre mich	ih irə mih
w. number	die falsche Nummer	dēē falshə nŭmər

X

x-ray	die Röntgenstrahlen (pl)	dēē **rœnt**gənshtrālən

Y

yacht	die Yacht (–en)	dēē yakht (–ən)
year	das Jahr (–e)	das yār (–ə)
last y.	letztes J.	**letst**əs yār
next y.	nächstes J.	**neks**təs yār
this y.	dieses J.	**dēēz**əs yār
yearly	jährlich	**yēyr**lih
yellow	gelb	gelp
yesterday	gestern	**gest**ərn
yoghurt	das/der Joghurt (–s)	das/der **yog**ŭrt (–s)
a carton of y.	ein Becher (–) J.	īn behər **yog**ŭrt
plain y.	ein einfacher J.	īn **īn**fakhər **yog**ŭrt
fruit y.	ein Fruchtjogurt	īn **früht**yogŭrt

young	jung	yŭng
young man	der junge Mann (junge Männer)	der **yŭng**ə man (**yŭng**ə menər)
young woman	die junge Frau (junge Frauen)	dēē **yŭng**ə frow (**yŭng**ə frowən)
youth hostel	die Jugendherberge (–n)	dēē **yōō**gəntherbergə (–n)

Z

zero (=nought)	die Null	dēē nŭl
zero (nought degrees)	der Gefrierpunkt	der gəfrēērpŭngkt
above z.	über dem G.	ühbər dāym gəfrēērpŭngkt
below z.	unter dem G.	ŭnter dāym gəfrēērpŭngkt
zip (n)	der Reißverschluß (–schlüsse)	der rīsfershlŭs (–shlüsə)
zoo	der Zoo (–s)	der tso (–s)
zoom lens	die Gummilinse (–n)	dēē gŭmilinzə (–n)

	masculine	feminine	neuter
the/a (subject)	der/ein	die/eine	das/ein
the/a (object)	den/einen	die/eine	das/ein
the (plural, subject/object)	die	die	die

Cooking methods

Remember: Ich möchte es /gut durchgebraten/, bitte (I'd like it /well done/ please)

als Püree (als pürāy)	mashed
frisch (frish)	fresh
garniert (garnēert)	dressed
gebacken (gəbakən)	baked
gebraten (gəbrātən)	fried
gedämpft (gədempft)	steamed
gefüllt (gəfült)	stuffed
gegrillt (gəgrilt)	grilled
gekocht (gəkokht)	boiled
geräuchert (gəroyhərt)	smoked
geröstet (gərœstət)	roasted
geschmort (gəshmort)	braised
gut durchgebraten (gōot dŭrhgəbrātən)	well done
in Essig (in esih)	in vinegar
mit Sahne (mit zānə)	creamed
nach Müllerin Art (nākh mülərin ārt)	meunière
pochiert (poshēert)	poached
roh (ro)	raw
verkocht (ferkokht)	overcooked

221

German foods

Remember: Ich möchte / /, bitte   I'd like / / please
        Haben Sie / /, bitte?   Have you got / / please?
Note: In Germany people tend to wish each other 'Guten Appetit'
(Enjoy your meal) before starting a meal.

Aal (m) (āl)	eel
Aal in Aspik (āl in aspēēk)	jellied eel
Abendbrot (n) (abəntbrot)	supper
Abendessen (n) (abəntesən)	dinner
Ananas (f) (ananas)	pineapple
Apfel (m) (apfəl)	apple
Apfelkuchen (m)	apple pie or tart
(apfəlkōōkhən)	
Apfelküchle (npl)	apple fritters
(apfəlkükhlə)	
Apfelsaft (m) (apfəlzaft)	apple juice
Apfelwein (m) (apfəlvīn)	apple wine
Apfelsine (f) (apfəlzēēnə)	orange
Appetit (apetēēt)	
etwas für den kleinen Appetit	for children (or for people who
(etvas führ den klīnən apetēēt)	only want a small portion)
Aprikosen (fpl) (aprikozən)	apricots
Artischocke (f) (artishokə)	artichoke
Aubergine (f) (oberjēēnə)	aubergine
Auster (f) (owstər)	oyster
Avokado (f) (avəkādo)	avocado pear
Banane (f) (bananə)	banana
Bedienung (f) (bədēēnŭng)	service
belegtes Brot (n) (bəlāyhtəs brot)	sandwich
Berliner Pfannkuchen (m)	doughnut
(berlēēnər pfankōōkhən)	

(m)	der (the)	(f)	die (the)	(n)	das (the)
	ein (a)		eine (a)		ein (a)
(mpl)	die (the, plural)	(fpl)	die (the, plural)	(npl)	die (the, plural)

Note: there is no need to translate 'some' eg Ich möchte /Kaffee/ (I'd like
/some coffee/).

Bier (n) (bēer)	beer
Bockbier (n) (bɔkbēer)	strong pale ale
dunkles Bier (n) (dùngkləs bēer)	brown ale
Export (n) (ekspɔrt)	lager
helles Bier (n) (heləs bēer)	pale ale
Pils (n) (pils)	pils beer
Starkbier (n) (shtarkbēer)	strong pale ale
Weizenbier (n) (vītsənbēer)	light beer made from wheat
ein Maß Bier (īn mäs bēer)	two pints of beer
Bierwurst (f) (bēervùrst)	garlic sausage
Birne (f) (birnə)	pear
Blätterteig (m) (bletərtīk)	flaky/puff pastry
Blumenkohl (m) (blōōmənkol)	cauliflower
Blutwurst (f) (blōōtvùrst)	black pudding
Bockwurst (f) (bɔkvùrst)	thick boiled sausage
Bohnen (fpl) (bonən)	beans
Brechbohnen (fpl) (brehbonən)	broad beans
Bowle (f) (bolə)	cold punch (often white wine and fresh fruit)
Brathähnchen (n) (brāthēynhən)	roast chicken
Bratkartoffeln (mpl) (brātkārtɔfəln)	roast potatoes
Bratwurst (f) (brātvùrst)	fried, spicy, pork sausages
Brechbohnen (fpl) (brehbonən)	broad beans
Breitlinge (npl) (brītlingə)	whitebait
Brezeln (fpl) (bretsəln)	Pretzels – a savoury biscuit baked in the form of a stick or loose knot, and eaten with butter
Brot (n) (brot)	bread
belegtes Brot (n) (bəlāyhtəs brot)	sandwich
Gewürzbrot (n) (gəvürtsbrot)	currant bread
Graubrot (n) (growbrot)	grey bread
Knäckebrot (n) (knekəbrot)	crispbread
Pumpernickel (m) (pùmpərnikəl)	pumpernickel (black rye bread)
Schwarzbrot (n) (shvärtsbrot)	black bread

223

Toastbrot (n) (**tost**brot)	white sliced loaf
Vollkornbrot (n) (**folk**ornbrot)	dark wholemeal bread
Weißbrot (n) (**vīs**brot)	crusty white bread
Brötchen (n) (**brēt**hən)	roll
Brunnenkresse (f) (**brü**nənkresə)	watercress
Bückling (m) (**bük**ling)	kipper
Butter (f) (**bü**tər)	butter
Champignons (mpl) (**sham**pinyōngs)	mushrooms
Chicorée Salat (m) (**shik**ərāy zalāt)	chicory salad
Chinesischer Tee (m) (**hin**āyzishər tāy)	china tea
Chips (ships)	crisps
Cordon bleu (**kor**dən blœ)	meat – usually veal, with ham and cheese, fried in breadcrumbs
Coupe Danmark (kōōp **dan**mārk)	ice cream, with cream and chocolate sauce
Cremesuppe (f) (**krāy**məzŭpə)	creamed soup
Dessert (n) (**desert**)	sundae
Dill (m) (dil)	dill
Ei (n) (ī)	egg
Eierspeisen (fpl) (**ī**ərshpīzən)	egg dishes
gekochtes Ei (n) (gə**kokh**təs ī)	boiled egg
pochiertes Ei (n) (po**shēēr**təs ī)	poached egg
Rührei (n) (**rühr**ī)	scrambled egg
Russische Eier (npl) (**rü**sishə īər)	egg mayonnaise with potato salad
Spiegeleier (npl) (**shpēē**gəlīər)	fried eggs
Eintopf (m) (**īn**topf)	hot pot, stew
Eis (n) (īs)	ice/ice cream
Eisbecher (m) (**īs**behər)	ice cream sundae
Eiskaffee (m) (**īs**kafāy)	ice cream and whipped cream in cold coffee
Portion gemischtes Eis (mit Sahne) (**portsion** gə**mish**təs īs (mit **zā**nə))	portion of ice cream of several flavours (with cream)

Eisbein (n) (īsbīn)	pork shank salted in jelly
Endiviensalat (m) (endeevyənzalāt)	a sliced green salad
Endpreis (m) (entprīs)	final price including service and VAT
Ente (f) (entə)	duck
Erbsen (fpl) (erpsən)	peas
Erdbeeren (fpl) (erdbāyrən)	strawberries
Essig (m) (esih)	vinegar
Fasan (n) (fazān)	pheasant
Filet (n) (filāy)	fillet
Kabeljaufilet (n) (kābəlyowfilāy)	cod fillet
Fisch (m) (fish)	fish
Fischgerichte (npl) (fishgərihtə)	fish dishes
Fleisch (n) (flīsh)	meat
Fleischgerichte (npl) (flīshgərihtə)	meat dishes
Hackfleisch (n) (hakflīsh)	minced meat
Fleischklops (m) (flīshklops)	meatball
Fleischküchle (n) (flīshkühhlə)	burger made of pork
Flußkrebs (m) (flüskrāyps)	crayfish
Forelle (f) (forelə)	trout
Frankfurter (f) (frangkfürtər)	hot-dog-like sausage
Frikadelle (f) (frikadelə)	rissole
Fruchteis (n) (frükhtīs)	sorbet
Frühstück (n) (frühshtük)	breakfast
Füllung (f) (fülüng)	filling/stuffing
Gang (m) (gang)	course
Mahlzeit mit 3 Gängen (māltsīt mit drī gengən)	3 course meal
Gans (f) (gans)	goose
Garnele (f) (gārnāylə)	prawn/shrimp
garniert mit (gārneert mit)	garnished with
Geflügel (n) (gəflühgəl)	poultry
Geflügelsalat (m) (gəflühgəlzalāt)	chicken salad
gemischter Salat (m) (gəmishtər zalāt)	mixed salad

225

Gemüse (ns) (gəmühzə)	vegetables
Gemüsesuppe (f) (gəmühzəzŭpə)	vegetable soup
Gerichte (npl) (gərihtə)	courses or dishes
Hauptgerichte (npl) (howptgərihtə)	main courses
Tagesgericht (tāgəsgəriht)	dish of the day
geschnetzeltes Kalbfleisch (n) (gəshnetsəltəs kalpflīsh)	chopped veal
Getränke (npl) (gətrenñgkə)	beverages
Gewürz (n) (gəvürts)	spice
Gewürzbrot (n) (gəvürtsbrot)	currant bread
Granatapfel (m) (granātapfəl)	pomegranate
Grapefruit (f) (grāÿpfrŏŏt)	grapefruit
Grapefruitkompott (n) (grāÿpfrŏŏtkəmpot)	grapefruit segments
Grapefruitsaft (m) (grāÿpfrŏŏtzaft)	grapefruit juice
Grillteller (m) (griltelər)	mixed grill
grüner Paprika (m) (grühnər paprika)	green pepper
grüner Salat (m) (grühnər zalāt)	green salad
Gulasch (n) (gŏŏlash)	goulash
Gulaschsuppe (f) (gŏŏlashzŭpə)	spicy meat soup
Gurke (f) (gừrkə)	cucumber
Gurkensalat (m) (gừrkənzalāt)	cucumber salad
Hackfleisch (n) (hakflīsh)	minced meat
Haferflocken (fpl) (hāfərflokən)	oats
Hähnchen (n) (heÿnhən)	chicken
Hammel (m) (haməl)	mutton

(m)	der (the)	(f)	die (the)	(n)	das (the)
	ein (a)		eine (a)		ein (a)
(mpl)	die (the, plural)	(fpl)	die (the, plural)	(npl)	die (the, plural)

Note: there is no need to translate 'some' eg Ich möchte /Kaffee/ (I'd like /some coffee/)

Hase (m) (**hā**zə)	hare
Hefe (f) (**hā**yfə)	yeast
Hefeteig (m) (**hā**yfətīk)	yeast dough
Heilbutt (m) (**hī**lbŭt)	halibut
Hering (m) (**hā**yriñg)	herring
Herz (n) (herts)	heart
Himbeeren (fpl) (**him**bāyrən)	raspberries
Hirschragout (n) (**hirsh**ragōō)	venison stew
Honig (m) (**honi**h)	honey
Huhn (n) (hōōn)	chicken
Hühnersuppe (f) (**hüh**nərzŭpə)	chicken soup
Hummer (m) (**hŭ**mər)	lobster
Hummersuppe (f) (**hŭ**mərzŭpə)	lobster soup
Imbiß (m) (**im**bis)	snacks
Schnellimbiß (m) (**shnel**imbis)	quick snacks
Indischer Tee (m) (**indi**shər tāy)	Indian tea
Ingwer (m) (**iñg**vər)	ginger
Italienischer Salat (m) (ital**yāy**nishər zalāt)	slices of cold meat in mayonnaise
Johannisbeeren (yo**ha**nisbāyrən)	redcurrants
Kabeljau (m) (**kā**bəlyow)	cod
Kabeljaufilet (n) (**kā**bəlyowfil**āy**)	cod fillet
Kaffee (m) (ka**fāy**)	coffee
Eiskaffee (m) (**īs**kafāy)	ice cream and whipped cream in cold coffee
Kalbfleisch (n) (**kalp**flīsh)	veal
Kalbshaxe (f) (**kalp**shaksə)	leg of veal
Kalbsleber (f) (**kalp**slāybər)	calf's liver
Kalbsschnitzel (n) (**kalp**sshnitsəl)	veal cutlet
Kammuschel (f) (ka**mŭ**shəl)	scallop
Kaninchen (n) (ka**nēēn**hən)	rabbit
Kännchen (n) (**ken**hən)	small pot (of tea or coffee)
Kanne (f) (**ka**nə)	pot
eine Kanne Tee (**ī**nə **ka**nə tāy)	a pot of tea

227

Karotten (fpl) (karɔtən)	carrots
Kartoffel (m) (kārtɔfəl)	potato
Kartoffelpüree (n) (kārtɔfəlpürāy)	mashed potato with cream and egg beaten in
Kartoffelsalat (m) (kārtɔfəlzalāt)	potato salad
Kroketten (fpl) (kroketən)	croquette potatoes
neue Kartoffeln (mpl) (noyə kārtɔfəln)	new potatoes
Pellkartoffeln (**pel**kārtɔfəln)	potatoes in their jackets
Salzkartoffeln (**zalt**skārtɔfəln)	boiled potatoes
Käse (m) (**kēy**zə)	cheese
Käsekuchen (m) (**kēy**zəkōōkhən)	cheesecake
Backsteinkäse (m) (**bak**shtīnkēyzə)	a strong, yellow cheese
Emmentaler (m) (eməntālər)	emmenthal
Hüttenkäse (m) (**hüt**ənkēyzə)	cottage cheese
Quark (m) (kvārk)	curd cheese
Räucherkäse (m) (**roy**hərkēyzə)	smoked cheese
Schafskäse (m) (**shāf**skēyzə)	sheep's cheese
Schimmelkäse (m) (**shim**əlkēyzə)	blue cheese
Streichkäse (m) (**shtrīh**kēyzə)	cream cheese
Tilsiter (m) (**til**zitər)	Tilsit (pale cheese with little holes, similar in texture to Edam)
Kasseler Rippchen (n) (**kas**ələr **rip**hən)	lightly smoked pork cutlet
Kastanien (fpl) (kastānyən)	chestnuts
Kekse (mpl) (**kāy**ksə)	biscuits
Kirschen (fpl) (**kir**shən)	cherries
Kleingebäck (ns) (**klīn**gəbek)	pastries
Knäckebrot (n) (**knek**əbrot)	crispbread
Knoblauch (m) (**knɔ**blowkh)	garlic
Kohl (m) (kol)	cabbage
Grünkohl (m) (**grühn**kol)	kale
Rotkohl (m) (**rot**kol)	red cabbage

Kokosnuß (f) (**ko**kosnŭs)	coconut
Kompott (m) (kɔm**pɔt**)	cold stewed fruit
Kopfsalat (m) (**kɔpf**zalāt)	lettuce
Kotelett (n) (kotəlet)	chop
Lammkotelett (n) (**lam**kotəlet)	lamb chop
Schweinskotelett (n) (**shvīns**kotəlet)	pork chop
Krabbe (f) (**krab**ə)	crab
Krabben (fpl) (**krab**ən)	shrimps/prawns

Krabbensalat (m)/Krabben-
  cocktail (m)
  (**krab**ənzalāt/**krab**ənkɔktāyl)
	shrimp cocktail/prawn cocktail

Kraftbrühe (f) (mit Ei (**kraft**brühə (mit ī))	beef tea (with egg)
Krapfen (m) (**krap**fən)	doughnut
Kräuter (npl) (**kroy**tər)	herbs
Krautsalat (m) (**krowt**zalāt)	cabbage salad
Kroketten (kroketən)	croquette potatoes
Kuchen (m) (**kōō**khən)	cake, tart, flan
Apfelkuchen (m) (**apf**əlkōōkhən)	apple tart
Käsekuchen (m) (**kēy**zəkōōkhən)	cheesecake
Marmorkuchen (m) (**mār**mɔrkōōkhən)	marble cake
Obstkuchen (m) (**opst**kōōkhən)	fruit tart
Pflaumenkuchen (m) (**pflow**mənkōōkhən)	plum tart

Streuselkuchen (m)
  (**shtroy**zəlkōōkhən)
	square piece of sponge cake
	  with a sprinkled topping of
	  crumble mix

Teekuchen (m) (**tāy**kōōkhən)	fruit cake
Kürbis (m) (**kür**bis)	marrow
Kutteln (**kŭt**əln)	tripe
Lachs (m) (laks)	salmon
Lamm (n) (lam)	lamb
Lammkeule (f) (**lam**koylə)	leg of lamb
Lammkotelett (n) (**lam**kotəlet)	lamb chop/cutlet

Lammragout (n) (**lam**ragōō)	ragout of lamb	
Lasagne (f) (lazanyə)	lasagne	
Lauch (m) (lowkh)	leek	
Leber (f) (**lāy**bər)	liver	
Leberkäs (m) (**lāy**bərkēys)	hot sliced meat loaf	
Leberknödel (m) (**lāy**bərknœdəl)	liver dumplings	
Leberpastete (f) (**lay**bərpastāytə)	liver pâté	
Leberwurst (f) (**lay**bərvŭrst)	liver sausage	
Lende (f) (**len**də)	loin	
Rinderlende (f) (**rin**dərlendə)	beef sirloin	
Schweinslende (f) (**shvīns**lendə)	loin of pork	
Limonade (f) (limon**ā**də)	lemonade	
Linsensuppe (f) (**lin**zənzŭpə)	lentil soup	
Mahlzeit (f) (**māl**tsīt)	meal	
Maiskolben am Spieß (m) (**mīs**kɔlbən am shp**ēē**s)	corn on the cob	
Makkaroni (mpl) (makaron**ēē**)	macaroni	
Makrele (f) (mak**rāy**lə)	mackerel	
Mandeln (fpl) (**man**dəln)	almonds	
Marmelade (f) (**mār**məl**ā**də)	jam/marmalade	
Marmorkuchen (m) (**mār**mɔrk**ōō**khən)	marble cake	
Matjesfilet (n) (**mat**yəsfil**āy**)	herring fillet	
Meeräsche (f) (**māy**reshə)	mullet	
Meerrettichsoße (f) (**māy**rretihzosə)	horseradish sauce	
Melone (f) (me**lo**nə)	melon	
Milch (f) (milh)	milk	
Milchshake (m) (**milh**shāyk)	milk shake	
Mineralwasser (n) (miner**āl**vasər)	mineral water	

(m)	der (the)	(f)	die (the)	(n)	das (the)
	ein (a)		eine (a)		ein (a)
(mpl)	die (the, plural)	(fpl)	die (the, plural)	(npl)	die (the, plural)

Note: there is no need to translate 'some', eg Ich möchte /Kaffee/ (I'd like /some coffee/)

Minze (f) (**mint**sə)	mint
Mittagessen (n) (**mit**āgesən)	lunch
Möhren (fpl) (**mē̃**rən)	carrots
Mohrenköpfe (**mor**ənkœpfə)	profiteroles
Mohrrüben (fpl) (**morr**ühbən)	carrots
Muschel (f) (**mū**shəl)	clam/mussel
Müsli (n) (**mūh**zli)	muesli
Nachspeise (f) (**nakh**shpīzə)	pudding/dessert/sweet
Nachtisch (m) (**nakh**tish)	pudding/dessert/sweet
Niere (f) (**nē̃**rə)	kidney
Nudeln (fpl) (**nōō**dəln)	noodles
Nüsse (fpl) (**nü**sə)	nuts
Obst (n) (opst)	fruit
Obstkuchen (m) (**opst**kōōkhən)	fruit tart
Obstsalat (m) (**opst**zalāt)	fruit cocktail/salad
Ochsenfleisch (n) (**oks**ənflīsh)	beef
Ol (n) (œl)	oil
Maisöl (n) (**mīs**œl)	corn oil
Olivenöl (n) (o**lēē**vənœl)	olive oil
Ölsardinen (n) (**œl**zārdēēnən)	sardines in oil
Pflanzenöl (n) (**pflan**tsənœl)	vegetable oil
Omelett (n) (**om**əlet)	omelette
Orange (f) (o**rä**jə)	orange
Orangensaft (m) (o**rä**jənzaft)	orange juice/orange squash
Pampelmuse (f) (pampəl**mōō**zə)	grapefruit
Paprika (m) (**pa**prika)	pepper (vegetable)
grüner Paprika (m) (**grüh**nər **pa**prika)	green pepper
roter Paprika (m) (**rot**ər **pa**prika)	red pepper
Paprikaschoten (fpl) gefüllt (**pa**prikashotən gəfült)	stuffed peppers
Pastete (f) (pas**tā**ytə)	pie (also pâté)
Wildpastete (f) (**vilt**pastāytə)	game pie
Petersilie (f) (**pāy**tərzēēlyə)	parsley
Pfannkuchen (m) (**pfan**kōōkhən)	pancake
Pfeffer (m) (**pfe**fər)	pepper

231

Pfeffersteak (n) (**pfef**ərstā**y**k)	steak spiced with pepper
Pfefferminze (f) (**pfef**ərmintsə)	peppermint
Pfifferlinge (mpl) (**pfif**ərli**n**gə)	chanterelles – type of mushroom
Pfirsich (m) (**pfir**zih)	peach
Pfirsich Melba (**pfir**zih **mel**ba)	peach melba
Pflaume (f) (**pflow**mə)	plum
Pflaumenkuchen (m) (**pflow**mənkoo**kh**ən)	plum tart
Pilze (mpl) (**pilt**sə)	mushrooms
Pommes frites (fpl) (pɔm**freet**s)	chips
Portion (f) (pɔrtsy**on**)	portion
Pudding (m) (**pŭ**di**n**g)	instant dessert
Pumpernickel (m) (**pŭm**pərnikəl)	Pumpernickel (black rye bread)
Quark (m) (kv**ark**)	curd cheese
Sahnequark (m) (**zān**əkvark)	creamed curd cheese
Radieschen (n) (ra**dēē**shən)	radish
Ragout (n) (ra**goo**)	ragout
Lammragout (n) (**lam**ragoo)	ragout of lamb
Rahm (m) (**rām**)	cream
Rehbraten (n) (**rāy**brātən)	venison steak
Rehrücken (m) (**rāy**rükən)	saddle of venison
Reis (m) (**rīs**)	rice
brauner Reis (m) (**brown**ər rīs)	brown rice
Rhabarber (m) (ra**bār**bər)	rhubarb
Rindfleisch (n) (**rint**flīsh)	beef
Rinds– (rints–)	beef (adj)
Rippchen (n) /Ripperl (n) (**rip**hən/**rip**ərl)	rib
Kasseler Rippchen (n) (**kas**ələr **rip**hən)	lightly smoked pork cutlet
Rollmops (m) (**rol**mɔps)	rollmop herring
Rosenkohl (ms) (**roz**ənkol)	brussels sprouts
Rotkohl (m) (**rot**kol)	red cabbage
Sachertorte (f) (**zakh**ərtɔrtə)	layered chocolate cake
Saft (m) (zaft)	juice
Apfelsaft (m) (**apf**əlzaft)	apple juice

232

Grapefruitsaft (m) (**grāȳpfrōōtzaft**)	grapefruit juice
Orangensaft (m) (**orāȷənzaft**)	orange juice
Tomatensaft (m) (**tomātənzaft**)	tomato juice
Traubensaft (m) (**trowb**ənzaft)	grape juice
Sahne (f) (**zān**ə)	cream (always double)
Sahnequark (m) (**zān**əkvärk)	creamed curd cheese
Sahnesteak (n) (**zān**əstāȳk)	steak prepared in cream
saure Sahne (f) (**zowr**ə **zān**ə)	sour cream
Schlagsahne (f) (**shlāk**zānə)	whipped cream
Salami (f) (zal**ām**i)	salami
Salat (m) (zal**āt**)	salad
Endiviensalat (m) (en**dēē**vȳənzalāt)	a sliced green salad
gemischter Salat (m) (gə**mish**tər zalāt)	mixed salad
grüner Salat (m) (**grüh**nər zalāt)	green salad
Italienischer Salat (m) (italy**āȳ**nishər zalāt)	slices of cold meat in mayonnaise
Kartoffelsalat (m) (k**ār**tɔfəlzalāt)	potato salad
Tomatensalat (m) (tom**āt**ənzalāt)	tomato salad
Salatsoße (f) (zal**āt**zosə)	vinaigrette
Salz (n) (zalts)	salt
Sardellen (fpl) (z**ār**delən)	anchovies
Sauerkraut (n) (**zow**ərkrowt)	sauerkraut (pickled cabbage often eaten hot)
saure Sahne (f) (**zowr**ə **zān**ə)	sour cream
Scheibe (f) (**shīb**ə)	slice
Schellfisch (m) (**shel**fish)	haddock
Schimmelkäse (m) (**shim**əlkēȳzə)	blue cheese
Schinken (m) (**shin͞g**kən)	ham
gekochter Schinken (m) (gə**kokh**tər **shin͞g**kən)	ham
roher Schinken (m) (**ro**ər **shin͞g**kən)	Parma ham

233

Schinkenwurst (f) (shin̄kənvŭrst)	hard, garlic sausage
Schlachtschüssel (f) (shlakhtshüsəl)	a selection of pork meats, sausage, and sauerkraut
Schlagsahne (f) (shlākzānə) Schlagrahm (m) (shlākrām)	whipped cream
Schnaps (m) (shnaps)	schnapps
Schnecken (fpl) (shnekən)	snails
Schnellimbiß (m) (shnelimbis)	quick snacks
Schnittlauch (m) (shnitlowkh)	chives
Schnitzel (n) (shnitsəl)	escalope
Jägerschnitzel (n) (yēygərshnitsəl)	veal escalope garnished with mushroom sauce
Kalbsschnitzel (n) (kalpsshnitsəl)	veal escalope
Wiener Schnitzel (n) (vēenər shnitsəl)	veal escalope with breadcrumbs
Zigeunerschnitzel (n) (tsigoynərshnitsəl)	veal escalope garnished with paprika sauce
Schokolade (f) (shokolādə)	chocolate
bittere Schokolade (f) (bitərə shokolādə)	plain chocolate
Milchschokolade (f) (milhshokolādə)	milk chocolate
Scholle (f) (shɔlə)	plaice
Schwarzwälderkirshtorte (f) (shvārtsveldərkirshtɔrtə)	Black Forest cherry cake
Schweinefleisch (n) (shvīnəflīsh)	pork
Schweinefilet (n) (shvīnəfilāy)	fillet of pork
Schweineleber (f) (shvīnəlāybər)	pig's liver

(m)	der (the)	(f)	die (the)	(n)	das (the)
	ein (a)		eine (a)		ein (a)
(mpl)	die (the, plural)	(fpl)	die (the, plural)	(npl)	die (the, plural)

Note: there is no need to translate 'some', eg Ich möchte /Kaffee/ (I'd like /some coffee/)

Schweineschnitzel (n) (**shvīn**əshnitsəl)	pork chop
Schweinshaxe (f) (**shvīns**haksə)	leg of pork
Schweinslende (f) (**shvīns**lendə)	loin of pork
Seehecht (m) (**zā**yheht)	hake
Seezunge (f) (**zā**ytsŭ̄ngə)	dover sole
Seezungenfilet (n) (**zā**ytsŭ̄ngənfilāy)	fillet of dover sole
Sekt (m) (zekt)	champagne (German variety)
Sellerie (f) (zelərē̄)	celery
Semmel (f) (**sem**əl)	roll
Senf (m) (zenf)	mustard
Sodawasser (n) (**zo**davasər)	soda water
Sortiment (n) (zərt**iment**)	assortment
Soße (f) (**zo**sə)	sauce
Bratensoße (f) (**brā**tənzosə)	gravy
Meerrettichsoße (f) (**mā**yrretihzosə)	horseradish sauce
Rahmsoße (**rām**zosə)	cream sauce
Salatsoße (f) (za**lāt**zosə)	vinaigrette
Soyasoße (f) (**zoy**azosə)	soya sauce
Tartarsoße (f) (tär**tār**zosə)	tartare sauce
Tomatensoße (f) (to**māt**ənzosə)	tomato sauce
weiße Soße (f) (**vīs**ə **zo**sə)	white sauce
Spätzle (npl) (**shpets**lə)	kind of pasta
Spargel (m) (**shpār**gəl)	asparagus
Spargelsalat (m) (**shpār**gəlzalāt)	asparagus tips
Speck (m) (shpek)	bacon
Speisekarte (f) (**shpīz**əkārtə)	menu
warme Speisen (fpl) (**vār**mə **shpīz**ən)	hot meals
kalte Speisen (fpl) (**kalt**ə **shpīz**ən)	cold meals
Spinat (m) (shpi**nāt**)	spinach
Stachelbeeren (fpl) (**shta**ẖəlbāyrən)	gooseberries

Stangenspargel (m) (**shtang**ənshpārgəl)	asparagus served whole
Steak (n) (stāyk)	steak
Pfeffersteak (n) (**pfef**ərstāyk)	steak spiced with pepper
Sahnesteak (n) (**zān**əstāyk)	steak prepared in cream
Steak Chateaubriand (n) (stāyk shatobrēēã)	Chateaubriand steak
St. Jakobs Muscheln (za**ng**kt **yak**ɔps **mū**shəln)	coquilles St. Jacques
Streichkäse (m) (**shtrīh**kēyzə)	cream cheese
Streuselkuchen (m) (**shtroy**zəlkōōkhən)	square piece of sponge cake with a sprinkled topping of crumble mix
Suppe (f) (**zŭp**ə)	soup
Gemüsesuppe (f) (gə**mūh**zəzŭpə)	vegetable soup
Gulaschsuppe (f) (**gōō**lashzŭpə)	spicy meat soup
Tagessuppe (f) (**tāg**əszŭpə)	soup of the day
Zwiebelsuppe (f) (**tsvēē**bəlzŭpə)	onion soup
Suppenbrühe (f) (**zŭp**ənbrühə)	broth
Süßstoff (m) (**sühs**shtɔf)	saccharin, sweetener
Tafelspitz (**tāf**əlshpits)	boiled fillet of beef
Tagesgericht (n) (**tāg**əsgəriht)	dish of the day
Tagessuppe (f) (**tāg**əszŭpə)	soup of the day
Tee (m) (tāy)	tea
Chinesischer Tee (m) (**hināy**zishər tāy)	China tea
Indischer Tee (m) (**in**dishər tāy)	Indian tea
eine Tasse (f) Tee (**īn**ə **tas**ə tāy)	a cup of tea
ein Kännchen (n) Tee (**īn kenh**ən tāy)	a pot of tea
Teig (m) (tīk)	pastry
Blätterteig (m) (**blet**ərtīk)	flaky/puff pastry
Hefeteig (m) (**hāy**fətīk)	yeast dough
Mürbeteig (m) (**mürb**ətīk)	short crust pastry
Teigwaren (fpl) (**tīk**vārən)	pasta
Terrine (f) (te**rēē**nə)	pâté (usually home-made)

236

Thunfisch (m) (**tōōn**fish)	tuna
Toast (m) (tost)	toast
Tomate (f) (to**māt**ə)	tomato
Tomatensaft (m) (to**māt**ənzaft)	tomato juice
Tomatensalat (m) (to**māt**ənzal**āt**)	tomato salad
Torte (f) (**tort**ə)	gateau
Sachertorte (f) (**zakh**ərt**ort**ə)	layered chocolate cake
Schwarzwälderkirschtorte (f) (shvärtsveldər**kirsh**tortə)	Black Forest cherry cake
Trauben (fpl) (**trowb**ən)	grapes
Traubensaft (m) (**trowb**ənzaft)	grape juice
Truthahn (m) (**trōōt**hān)	turkey
Vanille (f) (va**nily**ə)	vanilla
Viertel (n) (**fēērt**əl)	quarter (of a litre)
Vorspeisen (fpl) (**for**shpīzən)	hors d'oeuvres/starters
Wackelpeter (m) (vakəlp**āyt**ər)	jelly
Waffel (f) (**vaf**əl)	waffle
Walnüsse (fpl) (**val**nüsə)	walnuts
Wasser (n) (**vas**ər)	water
Mineralwasser (n) (mine**rāl**vasər)	mineral water
Wassermelone (f) (**vas**ərmelonə)	water melon
Wein (m) (vīn)	wine
Moselwein (m) (**moz**əlvīn)	Moselle wine
Rheinwein (m) (**rīn**vīn)	Rhine wine
Rotwein (m) (**rot**vīn)	red wine
Weißwein (m) (**vīs**vīn)	white wine
Weinbrand (m) (**vīn**brant)	brandy
Weinkarte (f) (**vīn**kārtə)	wine list
Weintrauben (fpl) (**vīn**trowbən)	grapes
Weißkraut (n) (**vīs**krowt)	white cabbage
Wermut (m) (**vayr**mōōt)	vermouth
Wiener (f) (**vēēn**ər)	hot-dog-like sausage
Wiener Schnitzel (n) (**vēēn**ər **shnit**səl)	veal escalope with breadcrumbs
Wild (n) (vilt)	game

237

Wodka (m) (vŏtka)	vodka	
Wurst (f) (vŭrst)	sausage (sliced meat)	
Frankfurter (f) (**fraṉg**kfŭrtər)	hot-dog-like sausage	
Wiener (f) (**vēē**nər)	hot-dog-like sausage	
Blutwurst (f) (**blōōt**vŭrst)	black pudding	
Bockwurst (f) (**bok**vŭrst)	thick, large sausage like large frankfurter	
Bratwurst (f) (**brāt**vŭrst)	fried, spicy pork sausage	
Leberwurst (f) (**lāy**bərvŭrst)	liver sausage	
Salami (f) (zalāmi)	salami	
Schinkenwurst (f) (**shiṉg**kənvŭrst)	hard garlic sausage	
Würstchen (npl)/Würste (fpl) (**vŭrst**hən/**vŭrst**ə)	sausages (eg hot-dog sausages)	
Wurstsalat (m) (**vŭrst**zalāt)	salad made with sliced sausage, tomato and onion	
Zitrone (f) (tsitronə)	lemon	
Zitronensaft (m) (tsi**tron**ənzaft)	lemon juice	
Zucchini (mpl) (tsŭ**kēē**nēē)	courgettes	
Zucker (m) (**tsŭ**kər)	sugar	
Zuckerglasur (f) (**tsŭ**kərglazōōr)	icing	
Zunge (f) (tsŭṉgə)	tongue	
Zwieback (ms) (**tsvēē**bak)	rusks, French toasts	
Zwiebel (f) (**tsvēē**bəl)	onion	
Zwiebelsuppe (f) (**tsvēē**bəlzŭpə)	onion soup	

(m)	der (the)	(f)	die (the)	(n)	das (the)
	ein (a)		eine (a)		ein (a)
(mpl)	die (the, plural)	(fpl)	die (the, plural)	(npl)	die (the, plural)

Note: there is no need to translate 'some' eg Ich möchte /Kaffee/ (I'd like /some coffee/).

238

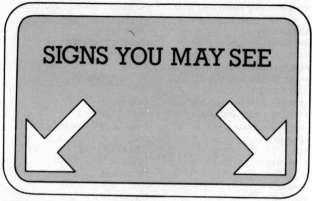

SIGNS YOU MAY SEE

The vowel sounds 'ä', 'ö' and 'ü' may sometimes be written as 'ae', 'oe' and 'ue'.

eg Eichstaett (Eichstätt)
  Koeln   (Köln)
  Muenchen (München)

AB 1300 UHR GEÖFFNET	Doors open 1.00 p.m.
ABENDVORSTELLUNG	Evening performance
ABFAHRT	Departures
ABFAHRTSZEITEN	Departure times
ABFÄLLE	Litter
ABFLUGHALLE	Departure lounge
ABHOLLAGER	Cash and carry
ABSATZBAR	Heel bar
ABSENDERANGABE	Sender's address
ABSTAND HALTEN	Keep your distance
ABTEILUNG	Department
ACHTUNG	Take care
ACHTUNG VOR DEM HUND	Beware of the dog
ADAC	German equivalent of AA/RAC
AGENTUR	Agency
ALARMZEICHEN	Alarm signal
AN	On (switches etc)
ANKUNFT	Admissions/arrivals
ANLIEGER FREI	Access only
ANSCHNALLEN	Fasten seat belts

239

AN SONN- UND FEIERTAGEN FREI	No charge Sundays and Bank Holidays
ANZAHLUNG	Deposits
APOTHEKE	Dispensing chemist
ARZT	Doctor
AUFENTHALTSRAUM	Lounge
AUFENTHALTSRAUM FÜR HOTELGÄSTE	Residents' lounge
AUFENTHALTSRAUM MIT BAR	Lounge bar
AUFPASSEN BEIM AUFSTEHEN	Mind your head
AUF- UND ABLADEN	Loading and unloading only
AUFZUG	Lift
AUS	Off (switches etc)
AUSFAHRT	Exit
AUSFLÜGE	Excursions
AUSGANG	Exit
AUSKUNFT	Enquiries
AUSPUFFSCHNELLDIENST	Fast fit exhaust service
AUSSER BETRIEB	Not in use
AUSSTIEG IN DER MITTE	Leave by centre doors
AUSVERKAUF	Sale
AUSVERKAUFSPREISE	Reduced
AUSVERKAUFT	Sold out
AUTOBAHN	Motorway
AUTOBAHNKREUZ	Motorways merge
AUTOMATISCHE SCHRANKEN	Automatic barriers
AUTOMATISCHE TÜR	Automatic doors
AUTOMIETE	Car hire
AUTORÜCKGABE	Return cars only (car hire)
AUTOWÄSCHE	Car wash
AUTOZUBEHÖR	Car accessories
BADEN VERBOTEN	No bathing
BAHNSTEIG	Platform
BAHNÜBERGANG	Level crossing
BAUSTELLE	Building site/road works ahead
BAUSTELLENVERKEHR	Construction traffic
BEGEBEN SIE SICH WIEDER ZU IHREM PLATZ	Return to seat
BEILAGEN	Portions of vegetables
BEI NÄSSE	In wet weather
BEI VERSAGEN KNOPF DRÜCKEN	Press button to get money back

BEKANNTMACHUNG	Notice
BENÜTZUNG AUF EIGENE GEFAHR	Use at your own risk
BENZIN	Petrol
BERGBAHN	Mountain railway
BESCHEIDE	Messages
BESETZT	Engaged/no vacancies/occupied
BESTECK	Cutlery (in self-service restaurant)
BESUCHER	Visitors
BETRETEN AUF EIGENE GEFAHR	Enter at your own risk
BETRETEN VERBOTEN	Keep out/no trespassing
BETRETEN VERBOTEN (AUßER FÜR SONDERBERECHTIGTE)	No admittance (except on business)
BETRIEBSFERIEN	Holidays
BIBLIOTHEK	Public library
BITTE IN ZIMMER 00 ANMELDEN	Please report to room number 00
BITTE LÄUTEN	Please ring
BITTE MOTOR ABSCHALTEN	Please switch engine off
BITTE NACHSENDEN	Please forward
BLUMENHÄNDLER	Florist
BOOTSVERLEIH	Boats for hire
BRIEFE	Letters
BRIEFKASTEN	Posting box
BRIEFMARKEN	Stamps
BUCHFÜHRUNG	Accounts
BUSABFAHRT	Coach departures
BUSHALTESTELLE	Bus stop/coach station
BUSRUNDFAHRTEN MIT FÜHRUNG	Conducted coach tours
CAMPINGWAGEN NICHT ZUGELASSEN	No caravans
DAMEN	Ladies/Ladies' room
DAMENFRISÖR	Ladies' hairdressing
DIENSTFAHRZEUGE	Official cars
DJH	Youth hostel
DROGERIE	Chemist (no prescriptions)
DRÜCKEN	Push
DURCHGEHEND	Continuously
EIN	In
EINBAHNSTRAßE	One way street
EINFAHRT	Way in

EINFAHRT FREIHALTEN	Do not obstruct entrance
EINGANG	Entrance
EINGESCHRIEBEN	Recorded delivery
EINGESCHRIEBENE BRIEFE	Registered letters
EINGESCHRIEBENES GEPÄCK	Registered luggage
EINORDNEN	Get in lane
EINSCHIFFUNG	Embarkation
EINSPURIGER VERKEHR	Single file traffic
EINSPURIG MIT AUSWEICHSTELLEN	Single track with passing places
EINSTIEG NUR VORN	Entrance at front
EINTRITT (FREI)	Admission (Free)
EINTRITT VERBOTEN	Do not enter
EINZAHLUNGEN	Deposits, payments
EIS	Ices
ELEKTROARTIKEL	Electrical goods
ELTERN HAFTEN FÜR IHRE KINDER	Parents are responsible for their children
EMPFANG	Reception
ENDE	End
ENTWERTEN	Cancel (a pre-paid ticket)
ENTWICKELN VON FARBFILMEN	Colour processing
ERDGESCHOß	Ground floor
ERFRISCHUNGEN	Refreshments
ERMÄßIGUNGEN	Reductions
ERSATZTEILE	Spare parts
ERWACHSENE	Adults
EVANGELISCHER GOTTESDIENST	Protestant Service
FAHRAUSWEIS	Ticket
FÄHRE	Ferry
FAHRGELD BEREITHALTEN	Exact fare
FAHRGELDZUSCHLAG	Excess fares
FAHRKARTE LÖSEN – BITTE BEHALTEN	Take ticket – keep it please
FAHRKARTENAUSGABE	Ticket office
FAHRPLAN	Timetable
FAHRPREIS	Fare
FAHRRADVERLEIH	Bicycle hire
FAHRSPUR GESPERRT	Lane closed
FAHRSTUHL	Lift
FAMILIENNAME	Last name
FEIERTAG	(Public) Holiday

242

FERNSCHREIBERDIENST	Telex service
FERNSEHEN	Television
FERNWAHLMÜNZFERNSPRECHER	STD coin box phone
FESTHALTEN	Hold tight
FEUERGEFÄHRLICH	Highly inflammable
FEUERLEITER	Fire escape
FLUG	Flight
FLUGHAFENBUS	Airport bus
FLUGLINIENINFORMATION	Airline information
FRAUEN	Women
FREI	Vacant
FREIGEGEBEN AB 16 JAHREN	No children under 16
FREI HALTEN	Keep clear
FREMDENZIMMER	Room to let
FRISCH GESTRICHEN	Wet paint
FRISÖR	Hairdressing salon
FÜHRER	Guide
FUNDBÜRO	Lost property office
FUßGÄNGERÜBERGANG	Pedestrian crossing
FUßWEG	Footpath
GARAGE (EINFAHRT FREIHALTEN)	Garage (in constant use)
GARDEROBE	Cloakroom
GASTHAUS	Inn/Pub
GASTHOF	Inn/Pub
GEBRAUCHTWAGEN	Second-hand cars
GEBÜHREN	Charges
GEFAHR	Danger
GEFÄHRLICHE STRÖMUNGEN	Dangerous currents
GEGENVERKEHR	Two-way traffic
GEHILFE	Attendant
GELANDET	Landed
GELDANWEISUNGEN	Money orders
GELDEINWURF	Insert coin
GELDSTRAFE	Fine
GENAUEN BETRAG BEREITHALTEN	Have exact money ready
GEPÄCK	Luggage
GEPÄCKABGABE	Left luggage
GERICHTSGEBÄUDE	Court house
GESCHÄFTSZEITEN	Hours of business
GESCHLOSSEN (MITTAGSPAUSE)	Closed (for lunch)
GETRÄNKEAUTOMAT	Drinks vending machine

243

GIFT	Poison
GLEICHSTROM	DC (direct current)
GLEISE NICHT BETRETEN	Don't cross the lines
GMBH.	Co. Ltd.
GRENZÜBERGANG	Frontier
GRIFF	Hold
GRIFF DREHEN	Turn handle
GRÜNANLAGEN NICHT BETRETEN	Please do not walk on the grass
GRUPPENERMÄßIGUNG	Reduction for groups
HABEN SIE IHREN SCHLÜSSEL ABGEGEBEN?	Have you left your key?
HAFEN	Port
HAFENANLAGEN	Docks
HANDGEPÄCK	Hand luggage
HAUPTBAHNHOF	Main station (in a city)
HAUSHALTSWARENABTEILUNG	Household department
HAUSIEREN VERBOTEN	No hawking
HEILIGE MESSE	Mass (in church)
HEIß	Hot (on taps)
HEIßE GETRÄNKE	Hot drinks
HERREN	Gentlemen/Gents
HERRENBEKLEIDUNG	Menswear
HEUTIGE VORSTELLUNG(EN)	Today's performance(s)
HIER KEIN ÜBERGANG	Do not cross here
HIER SPRECHEN	Speak here
HIER WARTEN	Wait here
HIER ZAHLEN	Pay here
HINTEN EINSTEIGEN	Entrance at rear
HOCHSPANNUNG	High voltage
HÖCHSTBELASTUNG	Maximum load
HÖCHSTPARKDAUER	Maximum stay (parking place)
HÖHE	Headroom
HOTELDIREKTION	Hotel management
HOTELEINGANG	Hotel entrance
HOTELRESERVIERUNGEN	Hotel reservations
HUNDE BITTE AN DIE LEINE	Please keep dogs on a lead
HUNDE NICHT ZUGELASSEN	No dogs
HUPEN VERBOTEN	Do not sound your horn
ILLUSTRIERTE	Magazines
IM AUSLAND	Abroad
IMBIß	Light refreshments

IMBIßSTUBE	Cafeteria/snack bar
IMPFUNG	Immunisation
INFORMATIONSSCHALTER	Information desk
INTERNATIONALE REISEHILFE	International travellers' aid
KAFFEESTUBE	Coffee bar
KALT	Cold (on taps)
KALTE GETRÄNKE	Cold drinks
KALTWASSER	Cold water
KARTEN	Tickets
KASSE	Cash desk/till
KASSE GESCHLOSSEN	Till closed
KASSIERER	Cashier
KEHRE	Hairpin bend
KEIN ABFALL	Dumping prohibited
KEINE ANHÄNGER	No trailers
KEIN AUSGANG	No way out
KEINE DURCHFAHRT	No thoroughfare
KEINE EINFAHRT	No access
KEIN EINGANG	Exit only/no entry
KEINE FUßGÄNGER	No pedestrians
KEIN TRINKWASSER	Not drinking water
KELLER	Basement
KIND(ER)	Child(ren)
KINDERABTEILUNG	Children's department
KIRCHE	Church
KLINGELN	Ring
KONTROLLZONE	Controlled zone
KOPIERDIENST	Copying service
KOSTENPFLICHTIG	At owner's expense
KRAFTFAHRZEUGE NICHT ZUGELASSEN	Motor vehicles prohibited
KRANKENHAUS	Hospital
KRANKENWAGEN	Ambulance
KURVENREICHE STRECKE	Bends
LADENDIEBSTAHL WIRD GEAHNDET	Shoplifters will be prosecuted
LANDWIRTSCHAFTLICHER VERKEHR FREI	Access for farm traffic
LANGSAM	Slow
LANGSAM FAHREN	Reduce speed now
LEBENSGEFAHR	Danger

245

LEER	Empty
LINKS FAHREN/GEHEN	Keep left
LKW	Lorries
LUFT	Air
LUFTPOST	Airmail
MÄNNER	Men
MEHRWERTSTEUER	VAT
MESSE	Mass (in church)
METALLWAREN	Hardware
MITTAGSTISCH	Lunch menu
MÖBELABTEILUNG	Furniture department
MODE	Fashions
MOTOR ABSTELLEN	Switch off engine
MÜNZEINWURF	Insert coin
MÜNZEN	Coins
MÜNZRÜCKGABE	Reject coins
MÜNZWECHSLER	Coin change
NÄCHSTE LEERUNG	Next collection (letter box)
NACHTGLOCKE	Night bell
NÄHERE EINZELHEITEN AUF ANFRAGE	Details available on request
NAHRUNGSMITTELABTEILUNG	Food hall
NEBENGEBÄUDE	Annexe
NICHT ANGREIFEN	Do not touch
NICHT BERÜHREN	Do not touch
NICHT FÜTTERN	Do not feed (animals)
NICHT MIT DEM FAHRER SPRECHEN	Do not speak to the driver
NICHT RAUCHEN	Do not smoke
NICHTRAUCHER	Non-smoker
NICHT RESERVIERT	Unreserved
NICHT STÖREN	Do not disturb
NICHT ÜBERHOLEN	No overtaking
NICHT VOR DER TREPPE STEHEN	Do not stand near the stairs
NICHTS ZU VERZOLLEN	Nothing to declare
NOTAUSGANG	Emergency exit/fire exit
NOTBEHANDLUNG	Emergency treatment
NOTFALL	Emergency
NOTSCHALTER	Emergency switch
NUR ABENDS	Evening(s) only
NUR FAHRRÄDER	Cyclists only
NUR FÜR ANLIEGER	Except for access

246

NUR FÜR BÜSSE	Buses only
NUR FÜR DAMEN	Ladies only
NUR FÜR FUßGÄNGER	Pedestrians only
NUR FÜR HOTELGÄSTE	Residents only
NUR FÜR PERSONAL	Staff only
NUR FÜR RASIERAPPARATE	Shavers only
NUR KRAFTFAHRRÄDER	Motor cycles only
NUR MÄNNER	Men only
NUR MIT SONDERGENEHMIGUNG	Permit holders only
NUR STEHPLÄTZE	Standing room only
OBEN/UNTEN	(This side) up/down
OBERDECK	Upper deck
OFFEN (TÄGLICH)/(BIS)	Open (daily)/(till)
ÖFFNUNGSZEITEN	Opening hours
ÖL	Oil
OPTIKER	(Ophthalmic) optician
PAKETE	Packets
PARFÜMERIE	Perfumery
PARKEN VERBOTEN	No parking
PARKPLATZ	Parking
PARKPLATZ (VOLL)	Car park (full)
PARKZEIT 30 MINUTEN	Waiting limited to 30 minutes
PARKZEIT MAXIMUM 2 STUNDEN	Maximum 2 hours (parking)
PARTNERSTADT	Twin town
PAUSE	Intermission
PKW	Cars
PLATZ	Seat
PLATZRESERVIERUNG	Seat reservations
POLIZEI	Police
POLIZEIMELDUNG	Police notice
PORTIER	Porter
POST	Mail
POSTAMT	Post Office
POSTLAGERND	Poste Restante
POSTLEITZAHL	Postal code
PRAKT. ARZT	Doctor
PREISE	Prices/tariff
PRIVAT	Private
PRIVATGRUNDSTÜCK	Private property
PRIVATPARKPLATZ	Private parking only
RADFAHREN VERBOTEN	No cycling

RASTPLATZ	Lay-by
RASTSTÄTTE	Services
RAUCHEN VERBOTEN	No smoking
RAUCHER	Smoker
RÄUMUNGSVERKAUF	Closing down sale
RECHTS FAHREN/GEHEN	Keep right
RECHTS STEHEN, BITTE	Please stand on the right
REIHE	Row
REINIGUNG	Cleaners
REISEBÜRO	Travel office
REISEFÜHRER	Guide
REISEGEPÄCK	Luggage
REISEGESELLSCHAFT	Travel agency
REISEZIEL	Destination
REPARATUREN	Repairs
RESERVIERT	Reserved
RESERVIERUNGEN	Reservations
RESTBETRAG	Change (money)
RETTUNGSRINGE	Lifebelts
ROLLSPLITT	Loose chippings
ROLLTREPPE	Escalator
ROTES KREUZ	Red Cross
RÜCKGABEKNOPF	Press to reject
RUHE	Quiet
RUHETAG	Rest day
RUNDFAHRT	Tour
SACKGASSE	Cul-de-sac/No through road
SB-TANKSTELLE	Self service petrol station
SCHALLPLATTEN	Records
SCHALTER GESCHLOSSEN	Position closed
SCHLÜSSELANFERTIGUNG	Keys cut here
SCHLÜSSELFÄCHER	Left luggage lockers
SCHNELLDIENST	While you wait
SCHNELLGERICHTE	Snacks
SCHNELLIEFERUNG	Express delivery
SCHRITT FAHREN	Dead slow
SCHUHABTEILUNG	Shoe department
SCHUHE	Footwear
SCHUHREPARATUREN	Shoe repairs
SCHULE	School
SCHWIMMBAD	Swimming pool

SCHWIMMEN UND BADEN VERBOTEN	No bathing/swimming
SEHR LANGSAM	Dead slow
SELBSTBEDIENUNG	Self-service
SELBST TANKEN	Self-service (petrol)
SESSELLIFT	Chair lift
SICHERHEITSUNTERSUCHUNG	Security checks in operation
SOMMERSCHLUßVERKAUF	Summer sale
SONDERANGEBOTE	Bargains/special offers
SONDERMARKEN	Special issue (stamps)
SOUVENIRLADEN	Gift shop
SPARKASSE	Bank
SPÄTVORSTELLUNG	Late performance/show
SPEISEKARTE	Menu
SPEISEWAGEN	Restaurant car
SPIELWARENABTEILUNG	Toy department
SPORTKLEIDUNG	Casual wear
SPRECHSTUNDEN	Surgery hours
SPRECHZEITEN	Surgery hours
SPRECHZIMMER	Surgery
2-SPURIGER VERKEHR	2-lane traffic
STADTAUTOBAHN	Urban clearway
STADTMITTE	Town centre
STATION	Ward/Underground station
STEIGUNG 11%	Hill 11%/1 in 10
STRAßE FREI	Road clear
STRICKWAREN	Knitwear
24 STUNDEN	24 hours
SÜßWAREN UND ZIGARETTEN	Sweets and cigarettes
TABAKWARENHÄNDLER	Tobacconist
TAGESAUSFLÜGE	Day excursions
TAGESTOUREN	Day tours
TANKSTELLE	Petrol station/service area
TELEFONBUCH	Telephone directory
THEATERKASSE	Box office
TOILETTENARTIKEL	Toiletries
TOURISTENKARTEN	Tourist tickets
TREFFPUNKT	Arrivals
TREPPE	Stairs
TRINKWASSER	Drinking water
TROCKENREINIGUNG	Dry cleaning

TÜRE SCHLIEßEN	Close door (firmly)
TÜR OFFEN/ZU	Door open/shut
ÜBERGEWICHTESZUSCHLAG	Excess baggage charge
ÜBERNACHTUNG UND FRÜHSTÜCK	Bed and breakfast
UMGEHUNGSSTRAßE	Ring road
UMKLEIDERAUM	Changing room
UMLEITUNG	Diversion
UMWEG	Detour
UNFALL	Accident
UNFÄLLE	Casualties
UNSICHTBARE EINFAHRT	Concealed entrance
UNTEN	Down
UNTERFÜHRUNG	Subway
UNTERGRUND	Underground
UNTERGRUNDBAHN	Underground station
UNTERKUNFT	Accommodation
UNTERWÄSCHE	Underwear
UNUNTERBROCHENE VORFÜHRUNG	Continuous performances
VERBOTEN	Prohibited
VERKAUFS- UND KUNDENDIENST	Sales and service
VERKEHRSAMT	Tourist office
VERKEHRSAMPELN	Traffic signals ahead
VERLÄNGERTE ÖFFNUNGSZEITEN (DONNERSTAG BIS 7 UHR)	Late shopping (Thursdays 7 p.m.)
VERSPÄTET	Delayed
VOLL	Full
VON KINDERN FERNHALTEN	Keep away from children
VORAUSBESTELLUNG	Advance booking
VORFAHRT BEACHTEN	Give way major road ahead
VORHANGSTOFFE	Furnishing fabrics
VORSICHT	Caution
VORSICHT RAMPE	Ramp ahead
VORSICHT! STUFE!	Mind the step
VORSICHTIG FAHREN	Please drive carefully
VORSTELLUNG ENDET	Performance ends
VORVERKAUFSSTELLE	Booking office
WACHHUND	Guard dog
WARME KÜCHE (DURCHGEHEND)	Hot meals served all day
WARMWASSER	Warm water
WARNUNG	Warning

250

WARTEN BIS MÜNZE FÄLLT	Allow time for coin to drop
WARTERAUM	Waiting area
WARTEZIMMER	Waiting room
WASCHSALON	Launderette
WASCHSTRAßE	Car wash
WECHSEL	Exchange
WECHSELGELD	Change (money)
WECHSELKURSE	Rates of exchange
WECHSELSTROM	AC (alternating current)
WECHSELSTUBE	Bureau de Change
WEINE UND SPIRITUOSEN	Wines and spirits
WEINSTUBE	Wine bar
WILLKOMMEN IN ...	Welcome to ...
WINTERSCHLUßVERKAUF	Winter sale
ZAHNARZT	Dentist
ZEITUNGEN	Newspapers
ZELTEN	Camping
ZELTEN VERBOTEN	No camping
ZENTRUM	Town centre
ZERBRECHLICH	Fragile, with care
ZIEHEN	Pull
ZIMMER FREI	Room to let
ZIMMERMÄDCHEN	Chambermaid
ZIMMERNACHWEIS	Accommodation bureau
ZIMMERSERVICE	Room service
ZIMMER ZU VERMIETEN	Rooms to let
ZIRKUS	Circus
ZOLL	Customs
ZOLLFREIES GESCHÄFT	Duty free shop
ZOLLPFLICHTIGE WAREN	Goods to declare
ZONE	Fare stage
ZU ALLEN ZEITEN	At any time
ZUBEHÖR	Accessories
ZU DEN BOOTEN	To the boats
ZU DEN BUSSEN	To the coaches
ZU DEN GLEISEN	To the platforms (train)
ZU DEN ZÜGEN	To the trains
ZUFAHRT	Access
ZU MIETEN	To let
ZUSCHLAG	Additional charge

Countries, currencies, nationalities and languages

Country, area or continent		Main unit of currency	Description & nationality (feminine form given in brackets)	Main language(s)
Africa	Afrika	—	Afrikaner(-in)	—
Albania	Albanien	Lek	Albaner(-in)	Albanisch
Algeria	Algerien	Dinar	Algerier(-in)	Arabisch/ Französisch
Argentina	Argentinien	Peso	Argentinier(-in)	Spanisch
Asia	Asien	—	Asiate (Asiatin)	—
Australia	Australien	Dollar	Australier(-in)	Englisch
Austria	Österreich	Schilling	Österreicher(-in)	Deutsch
Bahrain	Bahrain	Dinar	Bahrainer(-in)	Arabisch
Belgium	Belgien	Franc	Belgier(-in)	Flämisch/ Französisch
Bolivia	Bolivien	Peso	Bolivianer(-in)	Spanisch
Brazil	Brasilien	Cruzeiro	Brasilianer(-in)	Portugiesisch
Bulgaria	Bulgarien	Lev	Bulgare (Bulgarin)	Bulgarisch
Burma	Birma	Kyat	Birmane (Birmanin)	Birmanisch
Canada	Kanada	Dollar	Kanadier(-in)	Englisch/ Französisch
Chile	Chile	Peso	Chilene (Chilenin)	Spanisch
China	China	Yuan	Chinese (Chinesin)	Chinesisch

English	German	Currency	Nationality	Language
Colombia	Kolumbien	Peso	Kolumbianer(-in)	Spanisch
Costa Rica	Costa Rica	Colon	Costaricaner(-in)	Spanisch
Cuba	Kuba	Peso	Kubaner(-in)	Spanisch
Cyprus	Zypern	Pound	Zypriote (Zypriotin)	Griechisch/Türkisch
Czechoslovakia	Tschechoslowakei	Koruna	Tschechoslowake (Tschechoslowakin)	Tschechisch/Slowakisch
Denmark	Dänemark	Krone	Däne (Dänin)	Dänisch
Ecuador	Ekuador	Sucre	Ekuadoreaner(-in)	Spanisch
Egypt	Ägypten	Pound	Ägypter(-in)	Arabisch
Eire	Irland	Punt	Ire (Irin)	Englisch/Gälisch
England	England	Pound	Engländer(-in)	Englisch
Ethiopia	Äthiopien	Dollar	Äthiopier(-in)	Amharisch
Europe	Europa	—	Europäer(-in)	—
Finland	Finnland	Markka	Finne (Finnin)	Finnisch
France	Frankreich	Franc	Franzose(Französin)	Französisch
Germany	Deutschland			
West G.	Bundesrepublik Deutschland (BRD)	Deutschmark	Deutscher (Deutsche)	Deutsch
East G.	Deutsche Demokratische Republik (DDR)	Mark	Deutscher (Deutsche)	Deutsch
Ghana	Ghana	New Cedi	Ghanaer(-in)	Akan/Englisch
Greece	Griechenland	Drachma	Grieche (Griechin)	Griechisch
Guatemala	Guatemala	Quetzal	Guatemalteke (Guatemaltekin)	Spanisch

Country, area or continent	Main unit of currency	Description & nationality (feminine form given in brackets)	Main language(s)
Guyana	Dollar	Guyaner(-in)	Englisch
Holland (The Netherlands)	Guilder	Holländer(-in)	Holländisch
Holland (Die Niederlande)			
Hong Kong	Dollar	Hongkongchinese (Hongkong-chinesin)	Chinesisch/Englisch
Hongkong			
Hungary	Forint	Ungar(-in)	Ungarisch
Ungarn			
Iceland	Krona	Isländer(-in)	Isländisch
Island			
India	Rupee	Inder(-in)	Hindi/Englisch
Indien			
Indonesia	Rupiah	Indonesier(-in)	Bahasa Indonesisch
Indonesien			
Iran	Rial	Perser(-in)	Farsi
Iran			
Iraq	Dinar	Iraker(-in)	Arabisch
Irak			
Israel	Pound	Israeli(-n)	Hebräisch
Israel			
Italy	Lira	Italiener(-in)	Italienisch
Italien			
Jamaica	Dollar	Jamaiker(-in)	Englisch
Jamaika			
Japan	Yen	Japaner(-in)	Japanisch
Japan			
Jordan	Dinar	Jordanier(-in)	Arabisch
Jordanien			
Kenya	Shilling	Kenianer(-in)	Suaheli
Kenia			
Kuwait	Dinar	Kuwaiter(-in)	Arabisch
Kuwait			
Lebanon	Pound	Libanese (Libanesin)	Arabisch
Libanon			
Libya	Dinar	Libyer(-in)	Arabisch
Libyen			
Luxembourg	Franc	Luxemburger(-in)	Französisch/Deutsch
Luxemburg			

Malaysia	Malaysia	Dollar	Malaysier(–in)	Malaiisch/ Chinesisch
Malta	Malta	Pound	Malteser(–in)	Maltesisch/Englisch
Mexico	Mexiko	Peso	Mexikaner(–in)	Spanisch
Morocco	Marokko	Dirham	Marokkaner(–in)	Arabisch/ Französisch
New Zealand	Neuseeland	Dollar	Neuseeländer(–in)	Englisch
Nicaragua	Nicaragua	Cordoba	Nikaraguaner(–in)	Spanisch
Nigeria	Nigeria	Naira	Nigerianer(–in)	Hausa/Ibo/Yoruba/ Englisch
Northern Ireland	Nordirland	Pound	Nordire (Nordirin)	Englisch
Norway	Norwegen	Krone	Norweger(–in)	Norwegisch
Pakistan	Pakistan	Rupee	Pakistani (Pakistanerin)	Urdu
Paraguay	Paraguay	Guarani	Paraguayer(–in)	Spanisch
Peru	Peru	Sol	Peruaner(–in)	Spanisch
Poland	Polen	Zloty	Pole (Polin)	Polnisch
Portugal	Portugal	Escudo	Portugiese (Portugiesin)	Portugiesisch
Romania	Rumänien	Leu	Rumäne (Rumänin)	Rumänisch
Saudi Arabia	Saudi Arabien	Riyal	Saudiaraber(–in)	Arabisch
Scotland	Schottland	Pound	Schotte (Schottin)	Englisch/Gälisch
Singapore	Singapur	Dollar	Singapurer(–in)	Malaiisch/ Chinesisch/ Englisch/Tamil
South Africa	Südafrika	Rand	Südafrikaner (–in)	Afrikaans/Englisch
Spain	Spanien	Peseta	Spanier(–in)	Spanisch

Country, area or continent	Main unit of currency	Description & nationality (feminine form given in brackets)	Main language(s)
Sudan — Sudan	Pound	Sudanese (Sudanesin)	Arabisch
Sweden — Schweden	Krona	Schwede (Schwedin)	Schwedisch
Switzerland — Schweiz	Franc	Schweizer(-in)	Französisch/ Deutsch/ Italienisch/ Rätoromanisch
Syria — Syrien	Pound	Syrier(-in)	Arabisch
Tanzania — Tansania	Shilling	Tansanier(-in)	Suaheli
Thailand — Thailand	Baht	Thailänder(-in)	Thai
Tunisia — Tunesien	Dinar	Tunesier(-in)	Arabisch/ Französisch
Turkey — Türkei	Lira	Türke (Türkin)	Türkisch
Union of Soviet Socialist Republics (USSR)/Russia — Union der Sozialistischen Sowjetrepubliken (UdSSR)/Rußland	Rubel	Russe (Russin)	Russisch
United Kingdom (UK) (England, Northern Ireland, Scotland, Wales, Channel Islands) — das Vereinigte Königreich (England, Nordirland, Schottland, Wales, die Kanalinseln)	Pound (Sterling)	Brite (Britin)	Englisch

United States of America (USA)	die Vereinigten Staaten von Amerika (USA)	Dollar	Amerikaner(–in)	Englisch
Uruguay	Uruguay	Peso	Uruguayer(–in)	Spanisch
Venezuela	Venezuela	Bolivar	Venezolaner(–in)	Spanisch
Vietnam	Vietnam	Dong	Vietnamese (Vietnamesin)	Vietnamesisch
Wales	Wales	Pound	Waliser(-in)	Walisisch/Englisch
Yugoslavia	Jugoslawien	Dinar	Jugoslawe (Jugoslawin)	Serbokroatisch
Zaire	Zaire	Zaire	Zairer(–in)	Französisch
Zimbabwe	Zimbabwe	Dollar	Zimbabwier (–in)	Englisch

The motorist abroad

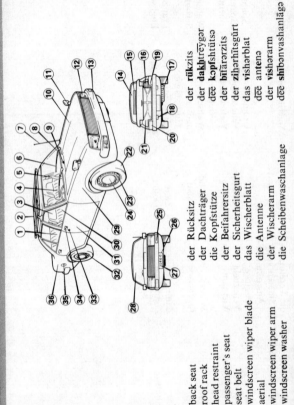

1 back seat — der Rücksitz — der rükzits
2 roof rack — der Dachträger — der dakhtrēyger
3 head restraint — die Kopfstütze — dēē kopfshtütse
4 passenger's seat — der Beifahrersitz — der bīfārarzits
5 seat belt — der Sicherheitsgurt — der zihərhītsgürt
6 windscreen wiper blade — das Wischerblatt — das visherblat
7 aerial — die Antenne — dēē antene
8 windscreen wiper arm — der Wischerarm — der visherarm
9 windscreen washer — die Scheibenwaschanlage — dēē shībenvashanläge

10 bonnet	die Motorhaube	dē **motorhowbə**
11 exterior mirror	der Seitenspiegel	der zītənshpēgəl
12 headlight	der Scheinwerfer	der shīnverfər
13 bumper	die Stoßstange	dē shtosshtangə
14 rear window	die Heckscheibe	dē hekshībə
15 rear window heater	die Heckscheibenheizung	dē hekshībənhītsūng
16 spare wheel	das Reserverad	das rezervərāt
17 fuel tank	der Kraftstoffbehälter	der **kraftshtəfbehelter**
18 hazard warning light	das Warmblinklicht	das **vārnblingkliht**
19 brake light	das Bremslicht	das **bremzliht**
20 rear light	das Rücklicht	das **rükliht**
21 boot	der Kofferraum	der **kofərowm**
22 tyre	der Reifen	der rīfən
23 front wheel	das Vorderrad	das **fordərāt**
24 hubcap	die Radkappe	dē **rātkapə**
25 sidelight	das Seitenlicht	das zītenliht
26 number plate	das Nummernschild	das **nümərnshilt**
27 registration number	die Autonummer	dē **owtonūmər**
28 windscreen	die Windschutzscheibe	dē **vintshütsshībə**
29 front wing	der Vorderflügel	der **fordərflügel**
30 driver's seat	der Fahrersitz	der **fārerzits**
31 door	die Tür	dē tühr
32 rear wheel	das Hinterrad	das **hintərāt**
33 lock	das Schloß	das shlos
34 door handle	der Türgriff	der **tührgrif**
35 petrol filler cap	der Tankverschluß	der **tangkfərshlüs**
36 rear wing	der Rückflügel	der **rükflügel**

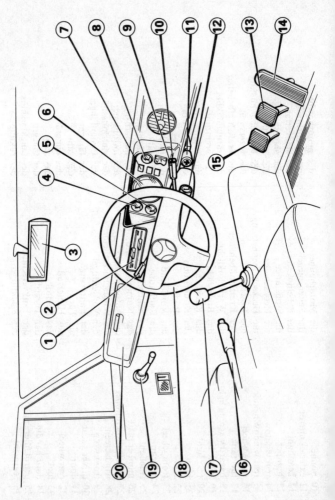

1	dipswitch	der Abblendschalter	der **ablendshalter**
2	heater	die Heizung	dēē **hītsūn̄g**
3	interior mirror	der Rückblickspiegel	der **rükblikshpēgel**
4	water temperature gauge	das Kühlwasserthermometer	das **kühlvasərtermomāytər**
5	ammeter	das Amperemeter	das amperə**māytər**
6	speedometer	das Tachometer	das takə**māytər**
7	oil pressure warning light	die Kontrollampe für Öldruck	dēē **kontrollampə führ ȫldrük**
8	fuel gauge	der Kraftstoffanzeiger	der **kraftshtofantsīgər**
9	horn	die Hupe	dēē **hōōpə**
10	direction indicator	der Fahrtrichtungsanzeiger	der **fartrihtūn̄gsantsīgər**
11	choke	die Luftklappe/der Choke	dēē **luftklapə/der chokə**
12	ignition switch	der Zündschalter	der **tsüntshaltər**
13	brake pedal	das Bremspedal	das **bremzpedāl**
14	accelerator	das Gaspedal	das **gāspedāl**
15	clutch pedal	das Kupplungspedal	das **küplūn̄gspedāl**
16	handbrake	die Handbremse	dēē **hantbremzə**
17	gear lever (selector)	der Schalthebel	der **shalthāybəl**
18	steering wheel	das Lenkrad	das **len̄krāt**
19	window winder	die Fensterkurbel	dēē **fenstərkōōrbəl**
20	glove compartment	das Handschuhfach	das **hantshōōfakh**

261

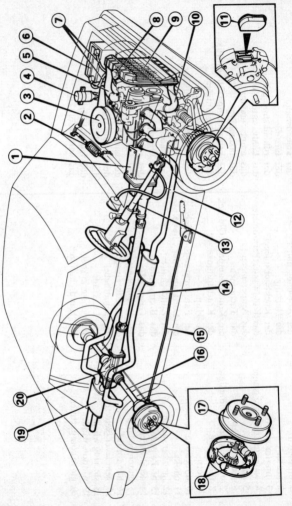

1 gearbox	das Wechselgetriebe	das **veks**əlgetrēēbə
2 fuse box	die Sicherungskasten	dēē **zi**hərüngskasten
3 air filter	der Luftfilter	der **lüft**filter
4 ignition coil	die Zündspule	dēē **tsünt**shpōōlə
5 radiator hose (top)	der obere Kühlerschlauch	der obərə **kühlər**shlowkh
6 battery	die Batterie	dēē bater**ēē**
7 leads (battery) (pl)	die Leitungen (pl)	dēē **līt**üngən
8 filler cap (radiator)	der Tankverschluß	der **tang**kfərshlüs
9 radiator	der Kühler	der **kühl**ər
10 radiator hose (bottom)	der untere Kühlerschlauch	der **ünt**ərə **kühlər**shlowkh
11 disc brake pad	der Scheibenbremsbelag	der **shīb**ənbremzbəlāg
12 speedometer cable	das Tachometerkabel	das takom**ā**ytərkābəl
13 steering column	die Lenksäule	dēē **leng**kzoylə
14 exhaust pipe	das Auspuffrohr	das **owspuf**ror
15 handbrake cable	das Handbremsseil	das **hant**bremszīl
16 rear axle	die Hinterachse	dēē **hint**ərakse
17 brake drum	die Bremstrommel	dēē **bremz**trroməl
18 brake shoe	die Bremsbacke	dēē **bremz**bakə
19 silencer	der Schalldämpfer	der **shall**dempfər
20 differential	das Differential	das difərent**sy**al

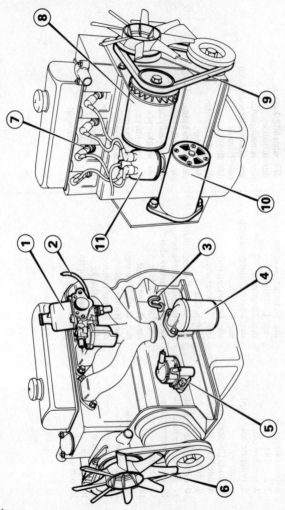

264

1 carburettor	der Vergaser	der fərgāzər
2 cable	das Kabel	das kābəl
3 oil dip stick	der Ölmeßstab	der œlmesshtāp
4 oil filter	der Ölfilter	der œlfilter
5 fuel pump	die Kraftstoffpumpe	dēē kraftshtofpŭmpə
6 fan	der Ventilator	der fentēēlātər
7 sparking plug	die Zündkerze	dēē tsŭntkertsə
8 alternator	die Lichtmaschine	dēē lihtmashēēnə
9 fan belt	der Keilriemen	der kīlrēēmən
10 starter motor	der Anlasser	der anlasər
11 distributor	der Zündverteiler	der tsŭntfərtīlər

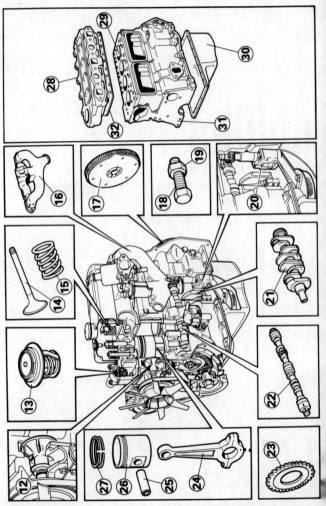

12	water pump	die Wasserpumpe	dē͞e vasərpûmpə
13	thermostat	der Thermostat	der termoshtät
14	valve	das Ventil	das ventil
15	spring (n)	die Feder	dē͞e fāydər
16	manifold, inlet and exhaust	der Auspuffkrümmer	der owspûfkrümər
17	fly wheel	das Schwungrad	das shvûngrät
18	bolt	der Bolzen	der bɔltsən
19	nut	die Mutter	dē͞e mûtər
20	oil pump	die Ölpumpe	dē͞e œlpûmpə
21	crankshaft	die Kurbelwelle	dē͞e kûrbəlvelə
22	camshaft	die Nockenwelle	dē͞e nɔkənvelə
23	sprocket	das Ketternrad	das ketərnät
24	connecting rod	die Kurbelstange	dē͞e kûrbəlshtangə
25	gudgeon pin	der Kolbenbolzen	der kɔlbənbɔltsən
26	piston	der Kolben	der kɔlbən
27	piston rings (pl)	die Kolbenringe (pl)	dē͞e kɔlbənriṉgə
28	cylinder head	der Zylinderkopf	der tsilindərkɔpf
29	cylinder	der Zylinder	der tsilindər
30	oil sump	die Ölwanne	dē͞e œlvanə
31	cylinder block	der Zylinderblock	der tsilindərblɔk
32	gasket	die Dichtung	dē͞e diḫtûṉg

The motorist abroad

Useful words and expressions

Remember: It's /the battery/	Es ist /die Batterie/	es ist /dēē baterēē/
accident	der Unfall	der ŭnfal
air pressure	der Luftdruck	der lŭftdrŭk
could you check the /tyre pressures/ please	könnten Sie den /Reifendruck/ prüfen, bitte?	**kœn**tən zēē /den **rī**fəndrŭk/ **prüh**fən **bit**ə

lb/sq in	=	kg/cm²	lb/sq in	=	kg/cm²	lb/sq in	=	kg/cm²
20	=	1.40	24	=	1.68	30	=	2.10
21	=	1.47	26	=	1.82	34	=	2.39
22	=	1.54	28	=	1.96	40	=	2.81

NB The decimal point is expressed in German by a comma, and is called 'Komma' eg 1,40 = eins komma vierzig.

antifreeze	das Frostschutzmittel	das **frost**shŭtsmitəl
a can of a.	eine Dose F.	īnə **doz**ə **frost**shŭtsmitəl
automatic (adj)	automatisch	owto**māt**ish
a. transmission	das automatische Getriebe	das owto**mat**ischə gə**trēē**bə
axle	die Achse	dēē **aks**ə
rear a.	die Hinterachse	dēē **hint**əraksə
battery	die Batterie	dēē batə**rēē**
I'd like the b. charged	ich möchte die B. aufladen lassen	ih **mœh**tə dēē batə**rēē** **owf**lādən **las**ən
I've got a flat b.	meine B. ist leer	**mīn**ə batə**rēē** ist **lāy**r
braking system/brakes	das Bremssystem	das **brems**züstāym
brake fluid	die Bremsflüssigkeit	dēē **brems**flüsihkīt
brake pads/linings (pl)	die Bremsbeläge (pl)	dēē **brems**bəlegə
breakdown	die Panne	dēē **pan**ə
b. service	der Unfalldienst	der **ŭnfall**dēēnst

268

b. vehicle	das Abschleppauto	das **ap**shlepowto
I have broken down	ich habe eine P.	ih **hā**bə īnə **pa**nə
breathalyser	die Blastüte	dēē **blā**ztühtə
cable	das Kabel	das **kā**bəl
car	das Auto	das **ow**to
by c.	mit dem A.	mit dem **ow**to
c. wash	die Autowäsche	dēē **ow**toveshə
carsick		
I get c.	mir wird schlecht vom Fahren	mēēr wirt **shleht** fom **fā**rən
change (vb)	wechseln	**vek**səln
I'd like /the tyre/ changed	ich möchte /den Reifen/ wechseln lassen	ih **mœh**tə /den **rī**fən/ **vek**səln **la**sən
change gear	den Gang wechseln	den gang **vek**səln
charge (vb)	aufladen	**owf**lādən
I'd like /the battery/ charged	ich möchte /die Batterie/ a. lassen	ih **mœh**tə /dēē batə**rēē**/ **owf**lādən **la**sən
chassis	das Chassis	das sha**sēē**
check	prüfen	**prüh**fən
could you c. the /oil and water/ please?	könnten Sie /Öl und Wasser/ p., bitte?	**kœn**tən zēē /œl ünt **va**sər/ **prüh**fən **bi**tə
could you c. the /tyre pressure/ please?	könnten Sie /den Reifendruck/ p., bitte?	**kœn**tən zēē /den **rī**fəndrük/ **prüh**fən **bi**tə
clutch	die Kupplung	dēē **kŭp**lŭng
crash (n)	der Unfall	der **ŭn**fal
crash /to have a crash	einen Unfall haben	īnən **ŭn**fal **hā**bən
cross-ply tyres (pl)	die Diagonalreifen (pl)	dēē dēēago**nāl**rīfən
deicer	das Enteisungsmittel	das ent**ī**zŭngsmitəl
derv	das Dieselöl	das **dēē**zəlœl
diesel oil	das Dieselöl	das **dēē**zəlœl
dip (vb)	abblenden	**ap**blendən
	ich blende (die Scheinwerfer) ab	ih **blen**də (dēē **shīn**verfər) ap
dip stick	der Ölmeßstab	der **œl**messhtāb

269

disc brakes (pl)	die Scheibenbremsen (pl)	dēē shībənbremzən
distributor	der Zündverteiler	der tsüntvərtīlər
drive (vb)	fahren	fārən
drive shaft	die Antriebswelle	dēē antrēēpsvelə
driver	der Fahrer	der fārər
electrical system	die elektrische Anlage	dēē elektrishə anlāgə
exhaust system	das Auspuffsystem	das owspüfzüstāym
fit (eg exhaust)	einbauen	īnbowən
fly wheel	das Schwungrad	das shvūngrāt
footpump	die Fußpumpe	dēē fōōspümpə
garage	die Autowerkstatt	dēē owtoverkshtat
gears	die Gänge	dēē gengə
first gear	der erste Gang	der āyrstə gang
second gear	der zweite Gang	der tsvītə gang
third gear	der dritte Gang	der dritə gang
fourth gear	der vierte Gang	der fēērtə gang
fifth gear	der fünfte Gang	der fünftə gang
reverse	der Rückwärtsgang	der rükvertsgang
grease (n)	die Schmiere	dēē shmēērə
grease (vb)	schmieren	shmēērən
headlamp bulb	die Scheinwerferlampe	dēē shīnverfərlampə
hire (vb)	mieten	mēētən
hood (sports car)	das Dach	das dakh
hose	der Schlauch	der shlowkh
hub	die Radnabe	dēē rātnābə
hydraulic brakes (pl)	die hydraulischen Bremsen (pl)	dēē hüdrowlishən bremzən
ignition system	die Zündanlage	dēē tsüntanlāgə
inner tube (tyre)	der Schlauch	der shlowkh
insurance certificate	die Versicherungskarte	dēē fərzihərüngskártə
international driving licence	der Internationale Führerschein	der intərnatsionālə führərshīn
jack	der Wagenheber	der vāgənhāybər
jeep	der Jeep	der djēēp
key	der Schlüssel	der shlüsəl
layby	der Rastplatz	der rastplats
leak (n)	das Loch	das lokh
leak (vb)	undicht sein	ündiht zīn
/the radiator/ is leaking	/der Kühler/ ist undicht	/der kühlər/ ist ündiht

licence (driving licence)	der Führerschein	der **führ**ərshīn
log book	das Fahrtenbuch	das **fär**tənbōōkh
lorry	der Lastwagen	der **last**vāgən
make (n) (car)	die Marke	dēē **mär**kə
mechanic (n)	der Autoschlosser	der **ow**toshlosər
mend	reparieren	reparēērən
I'd like /the tyre/ mended please	ich möchte /den Reifen/ r. lassen, bitte	ih **mēh**tə /den **rī**fən/ reparēērən lasən **bit**ə
oil (engine oil)	das Öl	das œl
could you check the /o. and water/ please?	könnten Sie /Ö. und Wasser/ prüfen, bitte?	**kœn**tən zēē /œl ŭnt **vas**ər/ **prüh**fən **bit**ə
a can of o.	eine Kanne Ö.	**ī**nə kanə œl
o. filter	der Ölfilter	der **œl**filtər
o. pump	die Ölpumpe	dēē **œl**pŭmpə
overdrive	fünfter Gang	**fünf**tər gaṅg
overheat	überhitzen	**üh**bərhitsən
overheated	überhitzt	**üh**bərhitst
part (car)	das Autoteil	das **ow**totīl
petrol	das Benzin	das bent**sēēn**
** (91/92 octane)		
*** (94/95 octane)	Normal	norm**āl**
**** (97/98 octane)	Super	**zōō**pər
/18 litres/ of /3 star/, please	/18 Liter/ /Normal/, bitte	/a**kh**tsāyn **lēē**tər/ /norm**āl**/ **bit**ə
/40 marks/ worth /of 4 star/, please	/Super/, für /40 Mark/, bitte	/**zōō**pər/ führ /**fēē**rtsih märk/ **bit**ə
fill it up please	Voll, bitte	fol **bit**ə
petrol can	die Benzinkanne	dēē bent**sēēn**kanə
petrol coupon	der Benzingutschein	der bent**sēēn**gōōtshīn
petrol station	die Tankstelle	dēē **taṅk**shtelə
puncture	ein platter Reifen	īn **plat**ər **rī**fən
I've got a p.	ich habe einen platten Reifen	ih **häb**ə **ī**nən **plat**ən **rī**fən
radial tyres (pl)	die Radialreifen	dēē radi**āl**rīfən
radio (car)	das Radio	das **rā**dio
repair (vb)	reparieren	reparēērən
reverse (n)	der Rückwärtsgang	der **rük**vertsgaṅg

reverse (vb)	rückwärts fahren	**rük**verts **fā**rən
run over	überfahren	**üh**bərfārən
seat	der Sitz	der zits
service (n)	die Inspektion	dēē inspek**tsion**
service (vb)	die Inspektion machen	dēē inspek**tsion** **mak**hən
it needs servicing	es braucht eine Inspektion	es brow**kh**t **ī**nə inspek**tsion**
shammy leather	das Chamois	das **sha**moa
shock absorber	der Stoßdämpfer	der **shtos**dempfər
rear s.a.	der hintere S.	der **hin**tərə **shtos**dempfər
spare parts (pl)	die Ersatzteile (pl)	dēē er**zats**tīlə
sparking plug	die Zündkerze	dēē **tsünt**kertsə
sports car	der Sportwagen	der **shport**vāgən
spring (n)	die Feder	dēē **fā**ydər
start (vb)	starten	**shtar**tən
it won't s.	es springt nicht an	es shpri**ng**t ni**h**t **an**
starter motor	der Anlasser	der **an**lasər
steer (car)	lenken	**le**ngkən
steering	die Lenkvorrichtung	dēē **le**ngkforihtŭ**ng**
suspension	die Aufhängung	dēē **owf**he**ng**ŭ**ng**
front s.	die Hinterachsaufhängung	dēē **hin**təraksowfhe**ng**ŭ**ng**
rear s.	die Vorderradaufhängung	dēē **for**dərrātowfhe**ng**ŭ**ng**
switch (n)	der Schalter	der **shal**tər
switch off (vb)	ausschalten	**ows**shaltən
I s. o.	ich schalte aus	ih **shal**tə ows
switch on (vb)	einschalten	**ī**nshaltən
I s. o.	ich schalte ein	ih **shal**tə īn
tow rope	das Schleppseil	das **shlep**zīl
could you give me a tow	könnten Sie mich abschleppen	**kön**tən zēē mih **ab**shlepən
trailer	der Anhänger	der **an**he**ng**ər
transmission	das Getriebe	das gə**trēē**bə
automatic t.	das automatische Getriebe	das owto**mā**tishə gə**trēē**bə
transmission shaft	die Antriebswelle	dēē an**trēē**psvelə
tubeless (tyre)	der schlauchlose Reifen	der **shlowkh**lozə **rī**fən

272

twin carburettor	der Doppelvergaser	der dɔpəlfergāzər
tyre	der Reifen	der rīfən
could you check the /tyres/ please?	könnten Sie /die Reifen/ prüfen, bitte?	**kēn**tən zēē /dēē rīfən/ **prüh**fən bitə
I've got a flat t.	ich habe einen platten Reifen	iḥ **hā**bə īnən **plat**ən rīfən
tyre pressure	der Reifendruck	der **rī**fəndrŭk
van	der Lieferwagen	der **lēē**fərvāgən
water	das Wasser	das **vas**ər
could you check the /oil and w./ please?	könnten Sie /Öl und W./ prüfen, bitte?	**kēn**tən zēē /œl ŭnt vasər/ **prüh**fən bitə
wheel	das Rad	das rāt
window	das Fenster	das **fens**tər
wing	der Flügel	der **flüh**gəl
work (vb)	funktionieren	fŭnḡktsio**nēē**rən
it doesn't w.	das funktioniert nicht	das fŭnḡktsio**nēē**rt niḥt

Mini Grammar

This section is for reference only and is not intended to be a complete grammar of German. It contains a summary of the more important grammatical forms which occur in the Study Section.

GENDER

In German there are three genders: masculine, feminine and neuter. All nouns (and pronouns) belong to one of these three genders.

The definite article

Masculine words: <u>der</u> Kaffee (<u>the</u> coffee), <u>der</u> Brief (<u>the</u> letter)
Feminine words: <u>die</u> Reservierung (<u>the</u> reservation), <u>die</u> Karte (<u>the</u> ticket)
Neuter words: <u>das</u> Bier (<u>the</u> beer), <u>das</u> Messer (<u>the</u> knife)
Each noun is given with the definite article in the Mini Dictionary.

The indefinite article

Masculine words: <u>ein</u> Kaffee (<u>a</u> coffee), <u>ein</u> Brief (<u>a</u> letter)
Feminine words: <u>eine</u> Reservierung (<u>a</u> reservation), <u>eine</u> Karte (<u>a</u> ticket)
Neuter words: <u>ein</u> Bier (<u>a</u> beer), <u>ein</u> Messer (<u>a</u> knife)

The plural

The definite article for all three genders is 'die' in the plural:
    <u>die</u> Briefe (the letters), <u>die</u> Karten (the tickets), <u>die</u> Messer (the knives)
Each noun is given with its plural form in the Mini Dictionary. See 'How to get the most out of the Mini Dictionary' p64.

Describing your nationality

In German you say 'I'm an Englishman', and *not* 'I'm English' eg 'Ich bin Engländer' (*not* 'ich bin englisch').

The feminine form to describe nationality is usually made by adding '–in' to the masculine form:
    Engländer (Englishman)   Engländer<u>in</u> (English woman)
    Italiener (Italian)   Italiener<u>in</u> (Italian woman)

But there are some exceptions, eg
    Deutscher (German)   Deutsch<u>e</u> (German woman)

See p252 for a full list of nationalities.

Which?

'Which' = 'Welcher', 'welche' or 'welches'.

Wel<u>cher</u> is used with masculine nouns:

Welcher Bahnsteig, bitte?   Which platform please?

Wel<u>che</u> is used with feminine nouns:

Welche Bushaltestelle, bitte?   Which bus stop please?

Wel<u>ches</u> is used with neuter nouns:

Welches Zimmer, bitte?   Which room please?

NB 'Dieser' (this) follows the same pattern.

Many names of jobs and professions have both a masculine and a feminine form.

The feminine is usually made by adding '–in' to the masculine form:

der Lehrer (teacher)	die Lehrer<u>in</u> (teacher)
der Polizist (policeman)	die Polizist<u>in</u> (policewoman)
der Verkäufer (salesman)	die Verkäufer<u>in</u> (saleswoman)

SUBJECTS AND OBJECTS

Subjects

Nouns can be the subjects of sentences, indicating *who* or *what* is useful, expensive etc:

<u>Der</u> Kaffee ist kalt	The coffee is cold
<u>Die</u> Karte ist teuer	The ticket is expensive
<u>Das</u> Bier ist warm	The beer is warm
<u>Ein</u> Zug kommt an	A train is coming
<u>Eine</u> Reservierung ist nötig	A reservation is necessary
<u>Ein</u> Fahrrad ist sehr nützlich	A bicycle is very useful
<u>Die</u> Karten sind teuer	The tickets are expensive

Subject pronouns may replace these nouns:

<u>ich</u>	I
<u>du</u>	you – use 'du' only with people you know very well indeed, or with children
<u>er</u>	he and it (masculine words)
<u>sie</u>	she and it (feminine words)

es it (neuter words)
wir we
ihr you – the plural of 'du', so avoid it (except with children)
sie they
Sie you – use this with everyone (singular and plural) except children
and people you know very well

Examples:

Ich bin müde	I'm tired
Hast du einen Bruder?	Have you got a brother?
Er spielt Fußball	He plays football
Er (der Kaffee) ist kalt	It (the coffee) is cold
Sie spielt Federball	She plays badminton
Sie (die Karte) ist teuer	It (the ticket) is expensive
Es (das Auto) fährt gut	It (the car) goes well
Sie (die Karten) sind teuer	They (the tickets) are expensive

Objects

Nouns can also be the direct object of sentences, indicating *what* you would like, *what* you've got etc. In German, the definite and indefinite articles change only in the masculine singular when the noun is the direct object:

Ich habe den Koffer	I've got the suitcase
Haben Sie die Karte?	Have you got the ticket?
Haben Sie das Fahrrad?	Have you got the bicycle?
Ich möchte einen Kaffee	I'd like a coffee
Ich habe eine Reservierung	I've got a reservation
Ich möchte ein Bier	I'd like a beer
Haben Sie die Schlüssel?	Have you got the keys?

Points to remember

When the word 'Herr' (Mr) is the direct object of a sentence, it changes to 'Herrn':

Kann ich Herrn Schmidt sprechen?	Can I speak to Herr Schmidt?

Obviously, where there is no article, there is no change:

Ich habe Geld	I've got some money
Ich habe Streichhölzer	I've got some matches
Haben Sie Kaffee?	Have you got any coffee?
Haben Sie Umschläge?	Have you got any envelopes?

Note that there is no equivalent of 'some' or 'any' in German. However 'some more' does exist in German.

'Noch etwas mehr' or simply 'noch' for substances like tea, coffee etc:

Noch etwas mehr Kaffee? ⎫
Noch Kaffee? ⎭ Some more coffee?

'Noch einige' or simply 'noch' for things in the plural:

Noch einige Kartoffeln? ⎫
Noch Kartoffeln? ⎭ Some more potatoes?

Direct object pronouns

Like nouns, pronouns can be the direct object of a sentence:

mich	me
dich	you – 'du' form. Be careful!
ihn	him and it (masculine words)
sie	her and it (feminine words)
es	it (neuter words)
uns	us
euch	you – plural of 'du' form. Avoid it!
sie	them
Sie	you – the polite form

Examples:

Er versteht mich	He understands me
Ich verstehe dich	I understand you
Sie kennen ihn	They know him
Er kauft ihn (den Kaffee)	He is buying it (the coffee)
Sie kennen sie nicht	They don't know her
Sie kauft sie (die Karte)	She is buying it (the ticket)
Sie kaufen es (das Haus)	They are buying it (the house)
Sie sehen uns	They can see us
Ich verstehe euch	I understand you
Wir kennen sie	We know them
Ich vergesse Sie nie!	I will never forget you!

Points to remember

Certain prepositions are followed by direct object pronouns:

für	for	ohne	without
durch	through	gegen	against
um	about		

Examples:

Das ist <u>für mich</u>   That is for me
Ich kann nicht <u>ohne ihn</u> leben!   I can't live without him!
Sie spielen <u>gegen uns</u>   They are playing against us

SUMMARY

1) Articles (the, a)

	Subject (singular)	Direct Object (singular)	Subject/Direct Object (plural)
the	der, die, das	den, die, das	die
a/an	ein, eine, ein	einen, eine, ein	—

2) Pronouns (I, you etc)

	Subject Pronouns		Direct Object Pronouns	
Singular	ich	I	mich	me
	du	you (infml)	dich	you (infml)
	er	he	ihn	him
	sie	she	sie	her
	es	it	es	it
Plural	wir	we	uns	us
	ihr	you (infml)	euch	you (infml)
	sie	they	sie	them
	Sie	you (singular and plural)	Sie	you (singular and plural)

PREPOSITIONS

Some prepositions are followed by the *indirect object* form:
<u>Mit</u> ('with', or 'by' for methods of transport) is followed by 'dem' when it is used with a masculine or neuter noun.

Mit dem Zug (m)   By train (literally 'with the
                                 train')
Mit dem Kind (n)   With the child

'Mit' is followed by 'der' when used with a feminine noun:

Mit der Karte (f)   With the ticket

It can also be used with an indirect object pronoun (see p281):

Mit mir	With me

<u>Gegenüber</u> (opposite) is followed by 'dem' when used with a masculine or neuter noun:

Gegenüber dem Bahnhof (m)	Opposite the station
Gegenüber dem Hotel (n)	Opposite the hotel

It is followed by 'der' when used with a feminine noun:

Gegenüber der Bank (f)	Opposite the bank

It can also be used with an indirect object pronoun:

Gegenüber dir	Opposite you (infml)

<u>Neben</u> (next to) is also followed by 'dem' when used with a masculine or neuter noun:

Neben dem Bahnhof (m)	Next to the station
Neben dem Hotel (n)	Next to the hotel

and by 'der' when used with a feminine noun:

Neben der Bank (f)	Next to the bank

It can also be used with an indirect object pronoun:

Neben ihm	Next to him

Two prepositions, 'nach' and 'zu' indicate the direction in which you are going or wish to go:

<u>Nach</u> (to) is used with the name of a town or village:

Nach Köln	To Cologne
Nach München	To Munich

Otherwise, use <u>zu</u>. 'Zu' changes to 'zum' or 'zur':

<u>Zum</u> (zu + dem) is used with a masculine or neuter noun:

<u>Zur</u> (zu + der) is used with a feminine noun:

Zur Bismarckstraße	To Bismarck Street
Zur Schule	To school

<u>Nach</u> can also mean 'after', and is followed by 'dem' when used with a masculine or neuter noun:

Nach dem Besuch (m)	After the visit
Nach dem Abendessen (n)	After the evening meal (after supper)

and by 'der' when used with a feminine noun:

Nach der Reise	After the journey

It can also be used with an indirect object pronoun:

Nach Ihnen   After you

<u>In</u> (in, at) changes to 'im' (in + dem) when used with a masculine or neuter noun:

Im Moment	At the moment
Im Sommer	In summer
Im Juli	In July

'In' is followed by 'der' when used with a feminine noun:

In der Schule   At school

<u>An</u> (at, on) changes to 'am' (an + dem) when used with a masculine or neuter noun:

Am Apparat	Speaking (literally 'at the instrument' ie telephone)
Am Montag	On Monday
Am siebten Juli	On July 7th

'An' is followed by 'der' when used with a feminine noun:

An der Ecke   At the corner

Prepositions and plural nouns

When the prepositions 'in' (in) and 'vor' (ago) are used with plural nouns, the letter 'n' is added to the noun (except when the noun already ends in '–n')

Vor zwei Woche<u>n</u>	Two weeks ago
In vier Woche<u>n</u>	In four weeks
In zehn Minute<u>n</u>	In ten minutes
In zwei Tage<u>n</u>	In two days

SUMMARY

		Subject	Indirect Object
the (definite article)	masc	der	dem
	fem	die	der
	neut	das	dem
a/an (indefinite article)	masc	ein	einem
	fem	eine	einer
	neut	ein	einem

	Subject Pronoun	Indirect Object Pronoun
I	ich	mir
you (infml)	du	dir
he, it	er, es	ihm
she	sie	ihr
we	wir	uns
you (infml)	ihr	euch
they	sie	ihnen
you (sing. and plural)	Sie	Ihnen

Note: the indirect object pronoun is also used when the English literally means 'to me' or 'for me':

Könnten Sie <u>mir</u> ein Taxi rufen	Could you call me a taxi
Könnten Sie <u>mir</u> sagen, wann wir ankommen	Could you tell me when we get there – literally 'Could you say to me'

Note also:

Wie geht es <u>dir</u>?	How are you?
Wie geht es <u>Ihnen</u>?	How are you?
Darf ich <u>Ihnen</u> etwas anbieten?	May I offer you something? – literally 'May I offer something to you?'

THE NEGATIVE

Nicht

'Nicht' translates 'not':

Ich verstehe <u>nicht</u>	I don't (do not) understand
Das stimmt <u>nicht</u>	That's not right

NB Nicht<u>s</u> = nothing. But note 'Das macht <u>nichts</u>' (It doesn't matter).

Kein

'Not a' is translated by 'kein', *never* by 'nicht ein'! 'Kein' behaves like 'ein':

Subject
Ich bin kein Amerikaner	I'm not an American
Ich bin keine Amerikanerin	I'm not an American (woman)

Direct object
Singular	Ich habe keinen Koffer	I haven't got a suitcase
	Ich habe keine Karte	I haven't got a ticket
Plural	Ich möchte kein Bier	I don't want a beer
	Ich habe keine Zigaretten	I haven't got any cigarettes

NB Ich spreche kein Deutsch (I don't speak German).

POSSESSIVES

MY	Subject	Object	
Singular	**mein** Koffer	**meinen** Koffer	(**der** Koffer)
	meine Karte	**meine** Karte	(**die** Karte)
	mein Auto	**mein** Auto	(**das** Auto)
Plural	**meine** Karten	**meine** Karten	(**die** Karten)

Note: 'dein' (your, familiar form) and 'sein' (his, its) follow the same pattern

HER	Subject	Object	
Singular	**ihr** Koffer	**ihren** Koffer	(**der** Koffer)
	ihre Karte	**ihre** Karte	(**die** Karte)
	ihr Auto	**ihr** Auto	(**das** Auto)
Plural	**ihre** Karten	**ihre** Karten	(**die** Karten)

OUR	Subject	Object	
Singular	**unser** Koffer	**unseren** Koffer	(**der** Koffer)
	unsere Karte	**unsere** Karte	(**die** Karte)
	unser Auto	**unser** Auto	(**das** Auto)
Plural	**unsere** Karten	**unsere** Karten	(**die** Karten)

YOUR ('ihr' form)	Subject	Object	
Singular	**euer** Koffer	**euren** Koffer	(**der** Koffer)
	eure Karte	**eure** Karte	(**die** Karte)
	euer Auto	**euer** Auto	(**das** Auto)
Plural	**eure** Karten	**eure** Karten	(**die** Karten)

YOUR ('Sie' form)	Subject	Object	
Singular	**Ihr** Koffer	**Ihren** Koffer	(**der** Koffer)
	Ihre Karte	**Ihre** Karte	(**die** Karte)
	Ihr Auto	**Ihr** Auto	(**das** Auto)
Plural	**Ihre** Karten	**Ihre** Karten	(**die** Karten)

Remember the different ways of saying 'you' and 'your':

<u>Du</u> (you)/<u>dein</u> (your) is used when talking to one person you know well.

<u>Ihr</u> (you)/<u>euer</u> (your) is used when talking to several people you know well.

<u>Sie</u> (you)/<u>Ihr</u> (your) is used when talking to either one person or several people you do not know very well. It is safest to begin by using this form.

Note: the word for 'their' (ihr) is the same as the word for 'your' (Ihr) when using the polite form, but it is written with a small letter 'i'.

SUMMARY

Subject	Possessive	
ich	mein	(I)/(my)
du	dein	(you)/(your)
er, es	sein	(he), (it)/(his, its)
sie	ihr	(she)/(her)
wir	unser	(we)/(our)
ihr	euer	(you)/(your)
sie	ihr	(they)/(their)
Sie	Ihr	(you)/(your)

VERBS

Regular verbs

In the Mini Dictionary, verbs are given in the infinitive form ('wohnen' = 'to live', 'zahlen' = 'to pay' etc). Take off '–en' and add the following endings:

		verstehen (to understand)	**wohnen** (to live)
(I)	ich – **e**	ich versteh**e**	ich wohn**e**
(you, informal)	du – **st**	du versteh**st**	du wohn**st**
(he, she, it)	er, sie, es – **t**	er/sie/es versteh**t**	er/sie/es wohn**t**
(we)	wir – **en**	wir versteh**en**	wir wohn**en**
(you, informal pl)	ihr – **t**	ihr versteh**t**	ihr wohn**t**
(they)	sie – **en**	sie versteh**en**	sie wohn**en**
(you, polite)	Sie – **en**	Sie versteh**en**	Sie wohn**en**

The following verbs from the Study Section can be used in this way:

zahlen	to pay	beginnen	to begin
schreiben	to write	schließen	to close
rauchen	to smoke	bleiben	to stay/remain
heißen	to be called	brauchen	to need
wohnen	to live		

The following verbs are regular but take '-et' with 'er', 'sie', and 'es' (eg 'er arbeitet'):

arbeiten	to work	er arbeitet
finden	to find	sie findet
enden	to end	es endet
mieten	to rent	sie mietet

Irregular verbs from the Study Section

Unfortunately, many common verbs are irregular:

sein – to be
ich bin (I am)
du bist (you are)
er, sie, es ist (he, she, it is)
wir sind (we are)
ihr seid (you are)
sie sind (they are)
Sie sind (you are)

haben – to have
ich habe (I have)
du hast (you have)
er, sie, es hat (he, she, it has)
wir haben (we have)
ihr habt (you have)
sie haben (they have)
Sie haben (you have)

wissen – to know (something)
ich weiß (I know)
du weißt (you know)
er, sie, es weiß (he, she, it knows)
wir wissen (we know)
ihr wißt (you know)
sie wissen (they know)
Sie wissen (you know)

kommen – to come
ich komme (I come)
du kommst (you come)
er, sie, es kommt (he, she, it comes)
wir kommen (we come)
ihr kommt (you come)
sie kommen (they come)
Sie kommen (you come)

fahren – to go (by a means of transport)
ich fahre (I go)
du fährst (you go)
er, sie, es fährt (he, she, it goes)
wir fahren (we go)
ihr fahrt (you go)
sie fahren (they go)
Sie fahren (you go)

gehen – to go (on foot)
ich gehe (I go)
du gehst (you go)
er, sie, es geht (he, she, it goes)
wir gehen (we go)
ihr geht (you go)
sie gehen (they go)
Sie gehen (you go)

empfehlen – to recommend
ich empfehle (I recommend)
du empfiehlst (you recommend)
er, sie, es empfiehlt (he, she, it recommends)
wir empfehlen (we recommend)
ihr empfehlt (you recommend)
sie empfehlen (they recommend)
Sie empfehlen (you recommend)

sprechen – to speak
ich spreche (I speak)
du sprichst (you speak)
er, sie, es spricht (he, she, it speaks)
wir sprechen (we speak)
ihr sprecht (you speak)
sie sprechen (they speak)
Sie sprechen (you speak)

schlafen – to sleep
ich schlafe (I sleep)
du schläfst (you sleep)
er, sie, es schläft (he, she, it sleeps)
wir schlafen (we sleep)
ihr schlaft (you sleep)
sie schlafen (they sleep)
Sie schlafen (you sleep)

sehen – to see
ich sehe (I see)
du siehst (you see)
er, sie, es sieht (he, she, it sees)
wir sehen (we see)
ihr seht (you see)
sie sehen (they see)
Sie sehen (you see)

285

Verbs used mainly with 'it' as the subject

Kosten (to cost), wiegen (to weigh), dauern (to last):

Er/sie/es <u>kostet</u> zehn Mark	It costs ten marks
Er/sie/es <u>wiegt</u> ein Kilo	It weighs one kilo
Er/sie/es <u>dauert</u> zwei Stunden	It lasts two hours

Modal verbs

'Modal verbs' ('must', 'can' etc) are often used with another verb in the same sentence. The second verb comes at the end of the sentence in its infinitive form.

mögen

ich möchte (I would like)
du möchtest (you would like)
er, sie, es möchte (he, she, it would like)
wir möchten (we would like)
ihr möchtet (you would like)
sie möchten (they would like)
Sie möchten (you would like)

ein Auto mieten (to hire a car)
in München wohnen (to live in Munich)

eg ich möchte ein Auto mieten

(I'd like to hire a car)

können

ich kann (I can)
du kannst (you can)
er, sie, es kann (he, she, it can)
wir können (we can)
ihr könnt (you can)
sie können (they can)
Sie können (you can)

mit dem Zug fahren (go by train)
etwas ausrichten (give a message)

eg sie kann mit dem Zug fahren

(she can go by train)

wollen
ich will (I want)
du willst (you want)
er, sie, es will (he, she it wants)
wir wollen (we want)
ihr wollt (you want)
sie wollen (they want)
Sie wollen (you want)

mit Reisechecks zahlen (to pay with traveller's cheques)
in Köln arbeiten (to work in Cologne)

eg wir wollen mit Reisechecks zahlen

(we want to pay with traveller's cheques)

müssen
ich muß (I must)
du mußt (you must)
er, sie, es muß (he, she, it must)
wir müssen (we must)
ihr müßt (you must)
sie müssen (they must)
Sie müssen (you must)

mit dem Auto fahren (go by car)
Herrn Schmidt sprechen (speak to Mr Schmidt)

eg Sie müssen mit dem Auto fahren

(you must go by car)

dürfen
ich darf (I may)
du darfst (you may)
er, sie, es darf (he, she, it may)
wir dürfen (we may)
ihr dürft (you may)
sie dürfen (they may)
Sie dürfen (you may)

hier parken (park here)
die Straßenkarte borgen (borrow the roadmap)

eg sie dürfen die Straßenkarte borgen

(they may borrow the roadmap)

287

Questions

To ask a question, put the subject after the verb:

Verstehen Sie?	Do you understand?
Wohnt er in München?	Does he live in Munich?

Reflexive verbs

Certain verbs always need the German equivalent of 'myself', 'yourself' etc even if they don't in English:

Ich wasche mich	I'm washing/I wash (literally 'I wash myself')
Ich rasiere mich	I'm shaving/I shave
Sie schminkt sich	She's putting on her make-up/She puts on her make-up

In the Mini Dictionary, all reflexive verbs are preceded by 'mich' eg 'mich rasieren' to shave (myself)

For other parts of the verb (with 'you', 'he' etc) the reflexive pronoun must agree with the subject.

ich wasche	**mich**
du wäschst	**dich**
er, sie, es wäscht	**sich**
wir waschen	**uns**
ihr wascht	**euch**
sie waschen	**sich**
Sie waschen	**sich**

Separable Verbs

Some verbs sometimes divide into two parts; they are known as separable verbs and work in a similar way to English verbs such as 'to turn (the light) off' or 'to draw (a chair) up'. The table shows how these verbs are used in a sentence.

288

Verb	Word Order – Sentences from the Study Section				
	1	2	3	4	
abfahren	Wann	**fährt**	der Zug	**ab**?	1.13
ankommen	Wann	**kommt**	der Bus	**an**?	1.13
aufmachen	Wann	**machen**	die Geschäfte	**auf**?	1.13
zumachen	Wann	**machen**	die Banken	**zu**?	1.13
aussehen	Es	**sieht**	so	**aus**.	6.3

Note that the prefix 'ab', 'an', etc comes at the end of the sentence.
In the Mini Dictionary, the first person singular form of all separable
verbs is given eg:

return	zurückkommen
return /on Monday/	/am Montag/ zurückkommen
	ich komme /am Montag/ zurück

The following sentences contain separable verbs. They are very
useful expressions and are worth learning by heart:

Wann sind Sie angekommen?	When did you arrive?
Ich schaue mich nur um	I'm just looking (in a shop)
Wo muß ich mich eintragen?	Where do I have to sign? (at a hotel reception)
Könnten Sie auf /meine Tasche/ aufpassen?	Could you mind my bag?
Könnten Sie auf /meinen Platz/ aufpassen?	Could you keep my seat?
Es hängt davon ab	It depends

Letters you may need to write

Letter of thanks

When writing letters in German, put the name of the town you are writing from in the top right-hand corner. The date follows on the same line:
  eg Colchester, den 10. August.
Germans write their full address on the back of the envelope so it can easily be returned if it is not delivered. The abbreviation 'Abs.' which you might see on the back of a letter stands for 'Absender' (sender).

                                                    Your address
                                                    /September 4th 19—/

Dear Mr/Mrs/Mr and Mrs/...

  (I've/We've) just returned home after (my/our) wonderful (holiday/stay) in (Germany) and (I am/we are) writing to thank you again for being so kind to me/us.
  I/We spent a marvellous (day/afternoon/evening) with you and it gave (me/us) a real glimpse of life in (Germany). (I/We do hope) you will be able to come and see (me/us) if/when you come to England.
  Warmest regards to (your family/children/ mother/father/parents).

        Yours (sincerely),

Town, /den 4. September 19—/

Lieber Herr!/Liebe Frau!/Liebe Herr und Frau!/...

(Ich bin/Wir sind) gerade von (meinem/unserem)
wunderschönen (Urlaub/Aufenthalt) in
(Deutschland) zurückgekommen und (möchte/
möchten) Ihnen nochmals herzlich für Ihre
Gastfreundschaft danken.

Der (Tag/Nachmittag/Abend) bei Ihnen war
wunderschön und gab (mir/uns) einen wirklichen
Einblick ins (deutsche) Leben. (Ich hoffe/Wir
hoffen), daß es Ihnen möglich sein wird, (mich/uns)
zu besuchen, wenn Sie nach England kommen.

Herzliche Grüße an (Ihre ganze Familie/Ihre
Kinder/Ihre Mutter/Ihren Vater/Ihre Eltern).

Ihr(e)

NB Use 'Ihr' for a man and 'Ihre' for a woman or if more than one person is signing.

Your address
/February 2nd 19—/

Address of hotel

Dear Sir,

I would like to book (a room/(two) rooms) with
you for the nights of (July 27th) to (July 31st)
inclusive. I would like (a single room/a double room/
a twin-bedded room/(two) single rooms/(two)
double rooms/(two) twin-bedded rooms) (with/
without) (bath/shower).

I would be grateful if you could let me know if you
have (a room/rooms) available for this period and
what your terms are for (bed and breakfast/half-
board/full board).

I look forward to hearing from you in the near
future.

Yours faithfully,

Town, /den 2. Februar 19—/

Hotel ...

Sehr geehrte Herren!

Ich möchte gern (ein Zimmer/(zwei) Zimmer) bei
Ihnen reservieren, und zwar für die Zeit vom (27.
Juli) bis zum (31. Juli) einschließlich. Ich möchte
(ein Einzelzimmer/ein Doppelzimmer/ein
Zweibettzimmer/(zwei) Einzelzimmer/(zwei)
Doppelzimmer/(zwei) Zweibettzimmer) (mit/ohne)
(Bad/Dusche).
Ich wäre Ihnen dankbar, wenn Sie mir mitteilen
könnten, ob Sie zu dieser Zeit (ein Zimmer/Zimmer)
frei haben und was die Preise für (Übernachtung und
Frühstück/Halbpension/Vollpension) sind.
Im voraus herzlichen Dank für Ihre Mühe!

Hochachtungsvoll

Informal letter

Your address
/3rd May 19—/

Dear /Helga/,
Dear /Walter/,

Just a short note to thank you for putting me up. I spent (four) really fantastic days with you and your friends. I hope to see you all very soon in (Manchester). My flat is very small but if you bring your sleeping bags there won't be any problem in fitting you all in.

Thanks again — I'll write soon!

Love,

PS Lots of love to /Hans/.

Town, /den 3. Mai 19–/

Liebe /Helga/!
Lieber /Walter/!

   Ich schreibe, um mich für den netten Aufenthalt
bei Dir zu bedanken. Die (vier) Tage bei Dir und
Deinen Freunden waren wirklich toll. Ich hoffe, daß
Ihr alle bald nach (Manchester) kommt. Meine
Wohnung ist sehr klein, aber wenn Ihr Eure
Schlafsäcke mitbringt, kann ich Euch sicher alle
unterbringen.
   Nochmals vielen Dank – ein längerer Brief folgt
bald.

          Viele Grüße
          Dein(e)

P.S. Grüße auch an /Hans/.

NB Note that in German the various informal forms of 'you' and 'your'
should have capitals when used in letters. Also note how you round
off by saying 'Dein(e)' before your name. It is not at all intimate – in
fact to friends it would sound distant if you left it out! You should
use 'Dein' for a man and 'Deine' for a woman.

Equivalents in

West German, Austrian, Swiss and East German money

West German currency

Marks = DM   Pfennigs = Pf   DM1 = 100Pf
DM 2,72 = zwei Mark zweiundsiebzig Pfennig

COINS (Münzen)

DM –,1	ein Pfennig
DM –,5	fünf Pfennig
DM –,10	zehn Pfennig
DM –,50	fünfzig Pfennig
DM 1,–	eine Mark
DM 2,–	zwei Mark
DM 5,–	fünf Mark

NOTES (Banknoten)

DM 5,–	fünf Mark
DM 10,–	zehn Mark
DM 20,–	zwanzig Mark
DM 50,–	fünfzig Mark
DM 100,–	hundert Mark
DM 500,–	fünfhundert Mark

In a bank you will be asked how you would like the money:

in /tens/   in /Zehnmarkscheinen/
in /twenties/   in /Zwanzigmarkscheinen/

Although East German Currency obviously has a different value from West German currency, the denominations of coins and notes are the same. If you want to differentiate between the East and West German Mark, say 'Ostmark' for the East German and 'Deutschmark' for the West German currency.

Austrian currency
100 Groschen = 1 Schilling

COINS

2 Groschen
5 Groschen
10 Groschen
50 Groschen
1 Schilling
5 Schillinge
10 Schillinge

NOTES

20 Schillinge
50 Schillinge
100 Schillinge
500 Schillinge
1000 Schillinge

Swiss currency

100 centimes = 1 franc

In German you say 'Rappen' for centimes and 'Franken' for francs

COINS	NOTES
5 Rappen	10 Franken
10 Rappen	20 Franken
20 Rappen	50 Franken
½ Franke	100 Franken
1 Franke	1000 Franken
2 Franken	
5 Franken	

Distances

1 mile = 1.6 kilometres   1.6 Kilometer = 1 Meile

Miles	10	20	30	40	50	60	70	80	90	100	Meilen
Kilometres	16	32	48	64	80	97	113	128	145	160	Kilometer

Lengths and sizes

Some approximate equivalents:

BRITISH	METRIC
1 inch	= 2.5 Zentimeter (centimetres)
6 inches	= 15 Zentimeter
1 foot	= 30 Zentimeter
2 feet	= 60 Zentimeter
1 yard	= 91 Zentimeter
1 yard 3 inches =	1 Meter (metre)

General clothes sizes (including chest/hip measurements)

GB	USA	Germany	Europe	ins	cms
8	6	34	36	30/32	76/81
10	8	36	38	32/34	81/86
12	10	38	40	34/36	86/91
14	12	40	42	36/38	91/97
16	14	42	44	38/40	97/102
18	16	44	46	40/42	102/107
20	18	46	48	42/44	107/112
22	20	48	50	44/46	112/117
24	22	50	52	46/48	117/122
26	24	52	54	48/50	122/127

Waist measurements

(ins) GB/USA	22	24	26	28	30	32	34	36	38	40	42	44	46	48	50
(cms) Europe	56	61	66	71	76	81	86	91	97	102	107	112	117	122	127

Collar measurements

(ins) GB/USA	14	$14\frac{1}{2}$	15	$15\frac{1}{2}$	16	$16\frac{1}{2}$	17	$17\frac{1}{2}$
(cms) Europe	36	37	38	39	40	41	42	43

Shoes

GB	3	$3\frac{1}{2}$	4	$4\frac{1}{2}$	5	$5\frac{1}{2}$	6	$6\frac{1}{2}$	7	$7\frac{1}{2}$	$8\frac{1}{2}$	9	10	11	12
USA	$4\frac{1}{2}$	5	$5\frac{1}{2}$	6	$6\frac{1}{2}$	7	$7\frac{1}{2}$	8	$8\frac{1}{2}$	9	$9\frac{1}{2}$	10	$10\frac{1}{2}$	$11\frac{1}{2}$	$12\frac{1}{2}$	$13\frac{1}{2}$
Europe	36		37		38		39		40		41		42	43	44	45

Hats

GB	$6\frac{5}{8}$	$6\frac{3}{4}$	$6\frac{7}{8}$	7	$7\frac{1}{8}$	$7\frac{1}{4}$	$7\frac{3}{8}$	$7\frac{1}{2}$	$7\frac{5}{8}$
USA	$6\frac{3}{4}$	$6\frac{7}{8}$	7	$7\frac{1}{8}$	$7\frac{1}{4}$	$7\frac{3}{8}$	$7\frac{1}{2}$	$7\frac{5}{8}$	$7\frac{3}{4}$
Europe	54	55	56	57	58	59	60	61	62

Glove sizes are the same in every country.

Weights

Some approximate equivalents:
Gramm (g) (grams) and Kilogramm (kg) (kilograms):
1000 Gramm (1000 g) = 1 Kilogramm (1 Kilo/kg)

1 oz	=	25 Gramm (g)
4 ozs	=	100/125 Gramm
8 ozs	=	225 Gramm
1 pound (16 ozs)	=	450 Gramm
1 pound 2 ozs	=	500 Gramm ($\frac{1}{2}$ Kilogramm)
2 pounds 4 ozs	=	1 Kilogramm (1 Kilo/kg)
1 stone	=	6 Kilogramm

Body weight
Body weight in Europe is measured in kilograms (Kilogramm).

Some approximate equivalents:

POUNDS	STONES	KILOGRAMS
28	2	$12\frac{1}{2}$
42	3	19
56	4	25
70	5	32
84	6	38
98	7	45

298

112	8	51
126	9	$57\frac{1}{2}$
140	10	63
154	11	70
168	12	76
182	13	83
196	14	90

Liquid measure

Petrol and oil are measured in litres (Liter), so are most other liquids, including milk. Wine is sometimes sold in litre bottles, but more frequently in bottles containing $\frac{3}{4}$ litre.

Some approximate equivalents:

1 pint = 0.57 Liter (litres)   1 gallon = 4.55 litres

GB measures	Liter (litres)	GB measures	Liter (litres)
1 pint	= 0.5		
(20 fluid ounces)		4.4 gallons	= 20
(fl. ozs.)		5.5 gallons	= 25
1.7 pints	= 1	6.6 gallons	= 30
1.1 gallons	= 5	7.7 gallons	= 35
2.2 gallons	= 10	8.8 gallons	= 40
3.3 gallons	= 15	9.9 gallons	= 45

Temperature

	FAHRENHEIT (F)	GRAD CELSIUS (C)
Boiling point	212°	100°
	104°	40°
Body temperature	98.4°	36.9°
	86°	30°
	68°	20°
	59°	15°
	50°	10°
Freezing point	32°	0°
	23°	−5°
	0°	−18°

(Convert Fahrenheit to Celsius by subtracting 32 and multiplying by 5/9. Convert Celsius to Fahrenheit by multiplying by 9/5 and adding 32.)

Useful information for travellers

Useful addresses

German Tourist Information Office, Conduit Street, London, W1 (734 2600) 10–5 Mon – Fri.

East Germany (Berolina), 19 Dover Street, London, W1 (629 1664) 9–1, 2–5 Mon – Fri.

Austrian National Tourist Information Centre, 30 George Street, London W1R 9FA (629 0461) 9–5.30 Mon – Fri, 9–12 Sat.

Swiss Tourist Information Office, 1 New Coventry Street, London W1V 3HG (734 1921) 9–5.30 Mon – Fri, 9–12 Sat.

Social behaviour

Shake hands both on meeting and saying goodbye even with people you know quite well. German people may bow their heads when introduced to a foreigner, however you are not expected to do the same.

Only use Christian names with people you know very well. Even if you've worked with someone for several years you may still address them as 'Herr/Frau/Fräulein' (Mr/Mrs/Miss). Be careful though – many women over the age of 30–35 expect to be called Frau whether they are married or not.

Gift bringing – take a small gift such as a bunch of flowers or a bottle of wine.
NB. *Always* take off the wrapping paper before you give your bunch of flowers.

Don't jaywalk – you can be fined!

Accommodation

Accommodation ranges from:
Large/international hotels.
Smaller, cheaper hotels and licensed restaurants (Gasthaus) with a few rooms.
Rooms – look for signs saying 'Fremdenzimmer' or 'Zimmer frei' at boarding houses and private houses in popular tourist resorts.

A list of hotels which have vacant rooms is often displayed at main railway stations. You may have trouble in finding accommodation in cities, eg Hamburg, Frankfurt and Munich because of trade fairs, so book in advance by writing to the 'Fremdenverkehrsbüro' (Tourist Office) of the town, asking for a list of hotels and prices.

Getting around

By taxi Taxis can be found at railway stations and taxi ranks. You can hail a taxi in the street, too, if the sign on its roof says 'Frei'. Round up the fare to the nearest mark for the tip.

By bus or tram Usually, you pay the driver/conductor on entering the bus or tram. State your destination and you will be told how much to pay. Trams often have several coaches. The rear coach may be reserved for passengers who have bought a booklet of tickets in advance and will have an automatic machine (Entwerter) for cancelling your ticket. The booklets of tickets can be bought from kiosks or automatic machines at principal bus and tram stops.

By underground Buy the ticket for your destination from the booking office or an automatic machine. Maps by the machines show the various fare stages.

By train Usually 1st and 2nd class. Some 'Inter City' trains and international trains (TEE) have 1st class only. Sometimes you have to pay a supplementary charge on express trains – inquire when booking your ticket.

Changing money

Banks are usually open from 9 – 4. In some banks, once the bank clerk has completed all the formalities he will give you a form to take to the cashier at a special counter to get your money. You can also change money at a 'Sparkasse', (Savings bank).

Bureaux de Change can be found at most airports and main railway stations. Look out for the sign 'Wechsel' or 'Geldwechsel'.

Useful information for travellers

Shopping

Shops are open from 9 – 6 but are closed on public holidays. Shops close at midday on Saturday, except for the first weekend of the month.

Post Offices are open from 8 'a.m. – 6 p.m. but may close at midday for up to two hours. In city centres, they are more likely to be open all day.

Food and drink

Eating out Large towns have a variety of restaurants and snack bars. A 'Gasthaus' or 'Gasthof' offers a limited choice of hot and cold dishes at a reasonable price. Restaurants can also be found at most stations and in department stores like 'Kaufhof', 'Bilka', 'Quelle', 'Karstadt' etc. It's worth trying the fried sausages from the stalls in the street!

Drinking hours There are no restrictions. At any 'Gasthaus' or 'Gasthof' you can drink wine, beer, spirits or coffee.

Tipping

In restaurants the bill usually includes value added tax and a service charge. This 'all-inclusive' price is known as 'Endpreis'. If you wish to give an extra tip round up the price to the nearest mark.

Entertainments

To find out what's going on – entertainment guides (and street plans) from hotel reception desks and newspaper stalls give comprehensive lists of restaurants and night clubs. You can also ask for a 'Veranstaltungs-kalender' (literally 'a calendar of events').

Cinemas There are no continuous performances. Tickets can be bought in advance.
NB No smoking!

Museums and art galleries usually close on Mondays.
There is a small entrance charge.

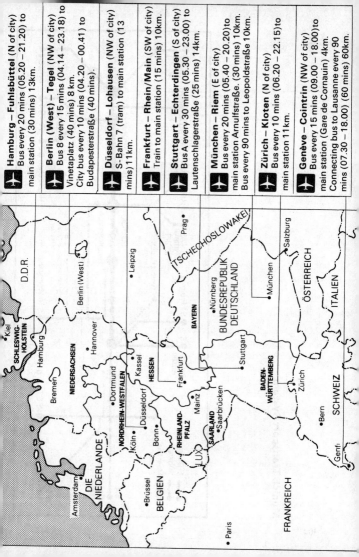

Hamburg – Fuhlsbüttel (N of city)
Bus every 20 mins (05.20 – 21.20) to main station (30 mins) 13km.

Berlin (West) – Tegel (NW of city)
Bus 8 every 15 mins (04.14 – 23.18) to Vinetaplatz (40 mins) 8 km.
City bus every 10 mins (04.20 – 00.41) to Budapesterstraße (40 mins).

Düsseldorf – Lohausen (NW of city)
S-Bahn 7 (tram) to main station (13 mins) 11 km.

Frankfurt – Rhein/Main (SW of city)
Train to main station (15 mins) 10km.

Stuttgart – Echterdingen (S of city)
Bus A every 30 mins (05.30 – 23.00) to Lautenschlagerstraße (25 mins) 14km.

München – Riem (E of city)
Bus every 20 mins (05.40 – 20.20) to main station Arnulfstraße. (30 mins) 10km.
Bus every 90 mins to Leopoldstraße 10km.

Zürich – Kloten (N of city)
Bus every 10 mins (06.20 – 22.15) to main station 11km.

Genève – Cointrin (NW of city)
Bus every 15 mins (09.00 – 18.00) to main station (Gare de Cornauin) 4km.
Connecting bus to Lausanne every 90 mins (07.30 – 18.00) (60 mins) 60km.

Munich Transport System

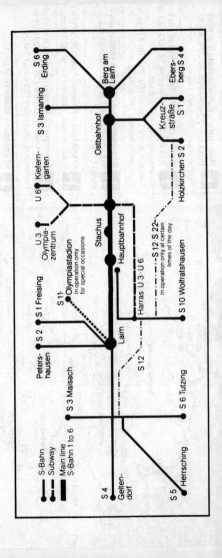

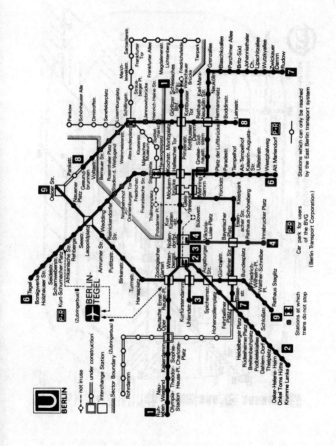

BERLIN

U

- ○-○- not in use
- ○- under construction
- □ interchange Station
- ///// Sector Boundary

Stations which can only be reached
by the East Berlin transport system

P·R Car park for users
of the BVG
(Berlin Transport Corporation)

Stations at which
trains do not stop

BERLIN-
TEGEL

(Zubringerbus)
(Zubringerbus)

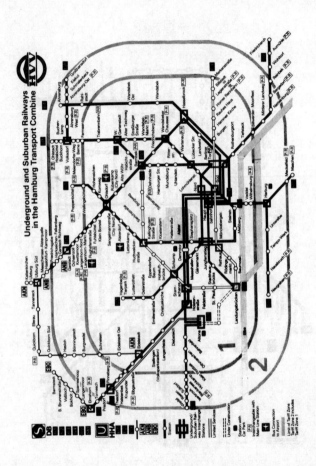

Underground and Suburban Railways in the Hamburg Transport Combine